IMAGES
of America

MINERAL POINT

WISCONSIN

IMAGES
of America

MINERAL POINT
WISCONSIN

Herbert and Barbara Apelian Beall

ARCADIA
PUBLISHING

ISBN 978-0-7385-0773-6

Published by Arcadia Publishing
Charleston, South Carolina

Printed in the United States of America

Library of Congress Catalog Card Number: 00-106519

For all general information contact Arcadia Publishing at:
Telephone 843-853-2070
Fax 843-853-0044
E-mail sales@arcadiapublishing.com
For customer service and orders:
Toll-Free 1-888-313-2665

Visit us on the Internet at www.arcadiapublishing.com

Contents

Preface

This book celebrates the history of Mineral Point, Wisconsin, and is dedicated to the many people—past and present—who contributed to making this town thrive and, in difficult times, helped it to survive.

In particular, the authors would like to celebrate the contributions of Edgar Hellum who, along with Robert Neal, began rebuilding the crumbling Cornish miners' cottages along Shake Rag in Mineral Point in the 1930s. Where others saw piles of rubble, they appreciated the past connections to the town's early history and envisioned reconstructed cottages and gardens. In 1970, they assured the continuation of their legacy for the people of Mineral Point and of Wisconsin by arranging for Pendarvis to become one of the six Wisconsin State Historic Sites. Edgar Hellum was also recognized for his contributions at Cornwall, England, where he was the second American to be honored as a Cornish Bard.

We would also like to thank numerous organizations and individuals who have made this book possible—especially the Mineral Point Historical Society and its president, Dean Connors, for allowing us to use their collection of historic photographs; the Mineral Point Room—Curator, Janice Terrill; the Mineral Point Library—Director, Barbara Polizzi; Pendarvis, Wisconsin State Historic Site—Historic Site Director, Allen L. Schroeder and Curator of Interpretation and Collections, Tamara H. Funk; the State Historical Society of Wisconsin for permitting us to use several of their photographs of Pendarvis; and Joyce P. Schaffer for sharing her own collection of photographs with us for research and publication. We also wish to thank the Chamber/ Main Street Program of Mineral Point—Director Jon Weiss, David Kjelland for sharing his expertise on the railroads, Jim and Sharon Stroschein for their research on the James Spensley estate and information on the Gundry House and family, Phil Mrozinski of the M Studio, Serena Nelson—especially for her knowledge of the Henry family, and Lucille May and Helen Flanagan for information on St. Paul's and St. Mary's churches. We encourage our readers to donate additional photographs of the area to the Mineral Point Historical Society.

In conclusion, we remember Edgar Hellum who celebrated life for 94 years, and in March 2000, joined many others who were already "on their way," as Edgar liked to say. We hope that this book is yet another small contribution to the ongoing history of Mineral Point. We invite you to visit our town and to become part of the living history as well.

Barbara Apelian Beall and Herbert Beall
June 2000, Mineral Point, Wisconsin.

A Brief History of Mineral Point

In the 1820s, non-native miners from the fledgling country of the United States arrived in the area of Mineral Point to prospect for lead, which came to be known as "gray gold." The town's history is inextricably linked to the presence of rich deposits of lead and zinc ores. The presence of these ores was due to the unique geological and topographical features the town shares with the region, called the "driftless area." This region covers most of southwestern Wisconsin, northwestern Illinois, and northeastern Iowa. It was left untouched by the glaciers of the last Ice Age approximately ten thousand years ago, leaving these rich deposits of lead and zinc.

The first prospectors were Native Americans, especially women, who mined the lead close to the surface of the hilly slopes, likely using it for body decoration and for making small objects. It was this lead that drew the next wave of prospectors here in the 1820s, many from Missouri, Illinois, and Kentucky, with the promise of this valuable mineral used primarily for lead shot. They mined the lead at their "diggings" from the surface and lived in simple holes dug into the earthen hillsides. These holes were called badger holes, thus giving Wisconsin its name—the Badger State.

Beginning in the 1830s, Cornish miners immigrated, determined to establish a permanent settlement. They introduced Cornish mining techniques, including the ability to dig deep shaft mines. The Cornish heritage is still evident in Mineral Point in the names of the residents, the foods served in area restaurants, and in the neat, yellow limestone and sandstone cottages which these miners built for their families.

The discovery of gold at Sutter's Mill in California in 1849 beckoned many local miners further west with the promise of greater prosperity. In the 1850s, zinc mining and processing began and eventually supplanted the mining of lead as the primary industrial base of the town. Concurrent with the lead and zinc mining was the construction of two railroad lines, the Mineral Point Railroad in 1857, and the Mineral Point and Northern Railroad in 1904, thus establishing Mineral Point as a shipping and supply center. The waning of the zinc industry after World War I was followed by the influx of artists and artisans and a renewal in historical preservation which is still active today.

At the beginning of the third millennium, Mineral Point has transformed itself once again—the once rutted, dirt streets populated by rough-and-ready miners is now lined with elegant artists' studios, antique shops, and restaurants. Many of the early stone miners' cottages restored in the 1930s by Robert Neal and Edgar Hellum now constitute Pendarvis, one of Wisconsin's State Historic Sites, and the Mineral Point Historical Society is in the process of recreating the former grandeur of the Gundry House built by a local Cornish merchant in the 1860s.

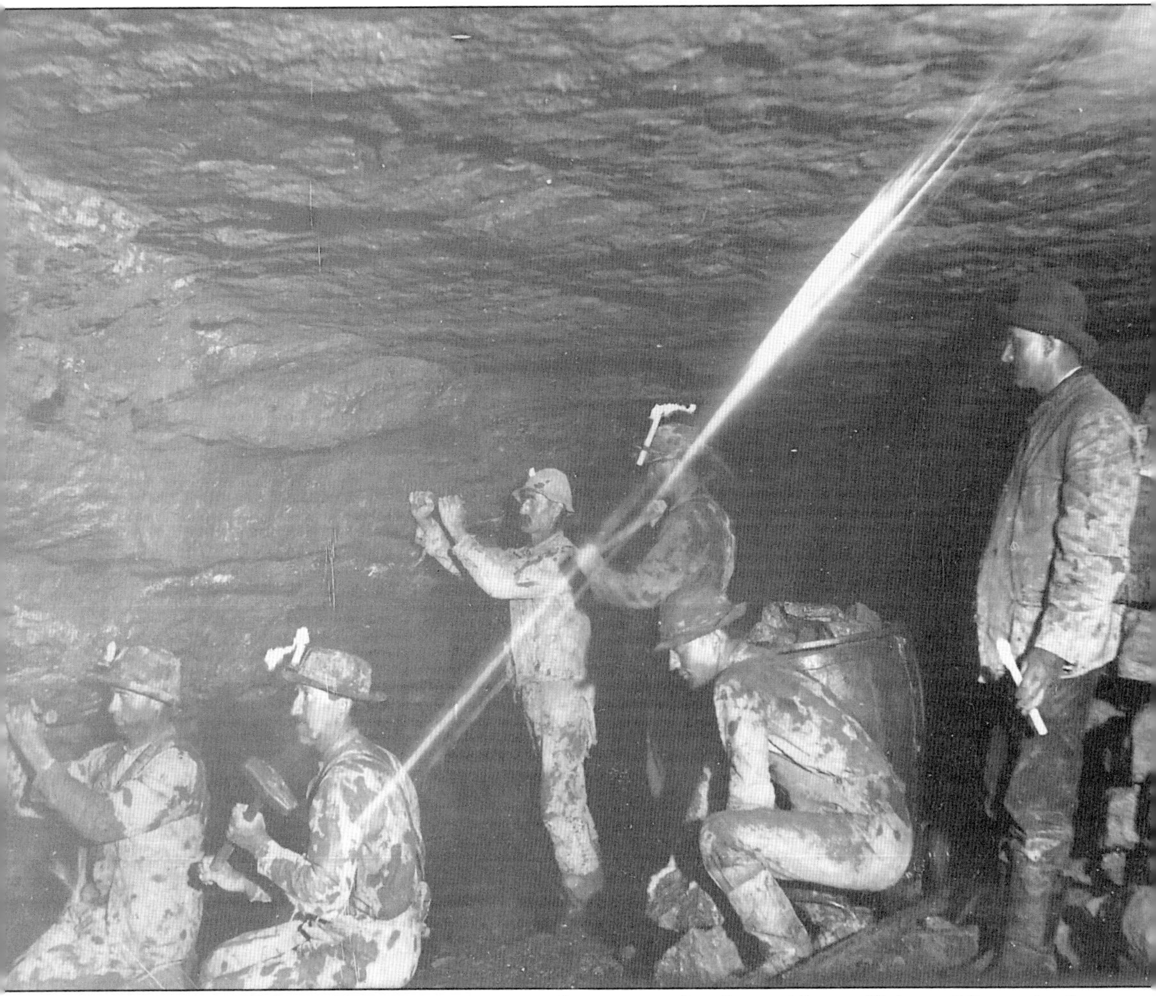

Lead mining, followed by zinc mining, was the principal industrial base of Mineral Point in the nineteenth and early twentieth centuries. By the 1870s, the output of zinc was almost equal to the lead mined. Here, a group of Mineral Point miners are at work in a deep shaft, most likely mining zinc. On the left half of the photo, two pairs of men are seen preparing holes for placing explosives. In the background is a container full of ore ready to be hauled up to the surface.

One

Industry in Mineral Point

Lead and Zinc Mining and the Railroads

Lead ore, which was also called mineral, was such an important commodity that it even gave its name to the town—Mineral Point. It was important enough for people to fight for, to die for, and to travel across an ocean to an unfamiliar land.

Primarily mined for use as lead shot, the ore drew Native Americans, prospectors from the still-young country of the United States, and eventually the Cornish from Cornwall, England. However, it was no longer in such great demand after the Civil War.

Beginning in the 1850s, zinc provided another source for prosperity that soon supplanted the lead mining. Piles of waste material from the earlier lead mining contained a high concentration of zinc, which became important as a coating for galvanizing iron to prevent corrosion and a basic component of paint. Mining was a major impetus for the establishment of two railroad lines, and Mineral Point also became a shipping and supply center for the region. Zinc mining boomed during World War I, collapsing shortly after the declaration of peace in 1917, greatly impacting the viability of the railroads as well.

Fortunately, the later zinc refinery and smelting plant are well documented in photographs. Ironically, there is little physical evidence left of the once vast complex of buildings in the southeastern section of the town and only the beginnings of documentation of later waves of immigrants.

24 MINERAL POINT CITY DIRECTORY.

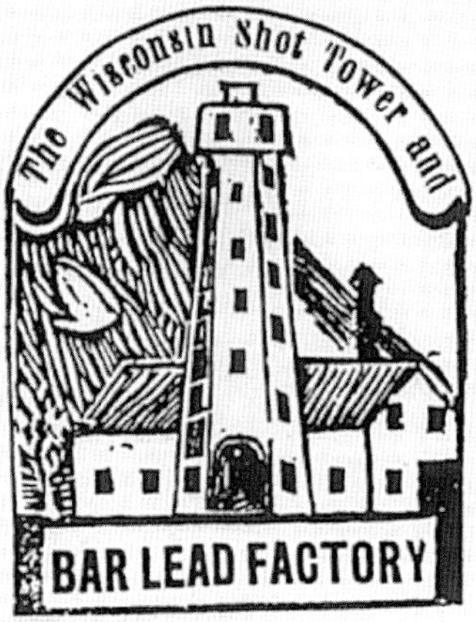

THIS TOWER is situated at Helena, Iowa County, Wisconsin, on the Wisconsin river, twenty-five miles north of Mineral Point, is now in successful operation, and a large stock of Lead, and Shot of all sizes, will be kept constantly on hand, for sale at the lowest rates for cash.

My Shot is put up in strong boxes, six sacks in each box, and can be securely transported to any distance. As the Milwaukee and Mississippi Rail Road runs near the Tower, I am able to fill all orders which may be transmitted to me, at short notice.

☞ Communications may be addressed to me either at Helena, or to Mineral Point, Wis., my place of residence.

HENRY P. GEORGE,
Proprietor.

Agencies:

A. H. GARDNER & Co., Milwaukee, Wis. | D. EATON & Co., Chicago, Ills.
H. BALDWIN, Prairie du Chien, " | J. B. SLICHTER & Co., St. Paul, Min.

This is an advertisement from the 1859 Directory of the City of Mineral Point for the making of lead shot, which represented the primary use of lead through the end of the Civil War.

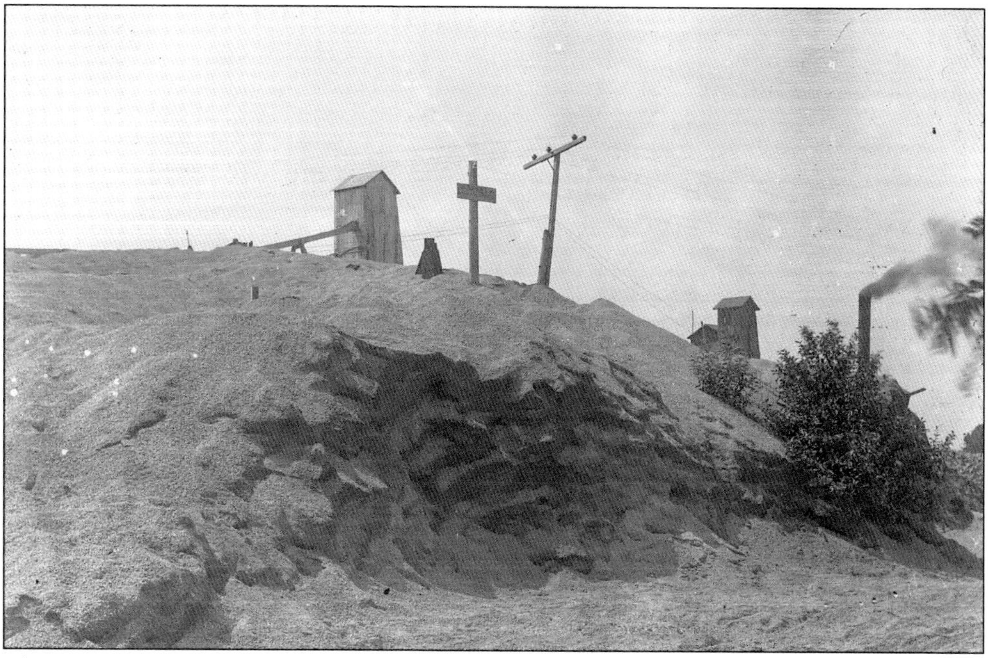

The superstructures above two Mineral Point mine shafts are pictured here. Each of these houses the machinery for raising and lowering men and machinery and hauling the ore out of the mine. The smokestack of a smelter is visible in the background, and the cross-like beams on the hill carry a warning sign of DANGER. Zinc mining in the region continued until about 1929, and was at its peak during World War I from 1914–17.

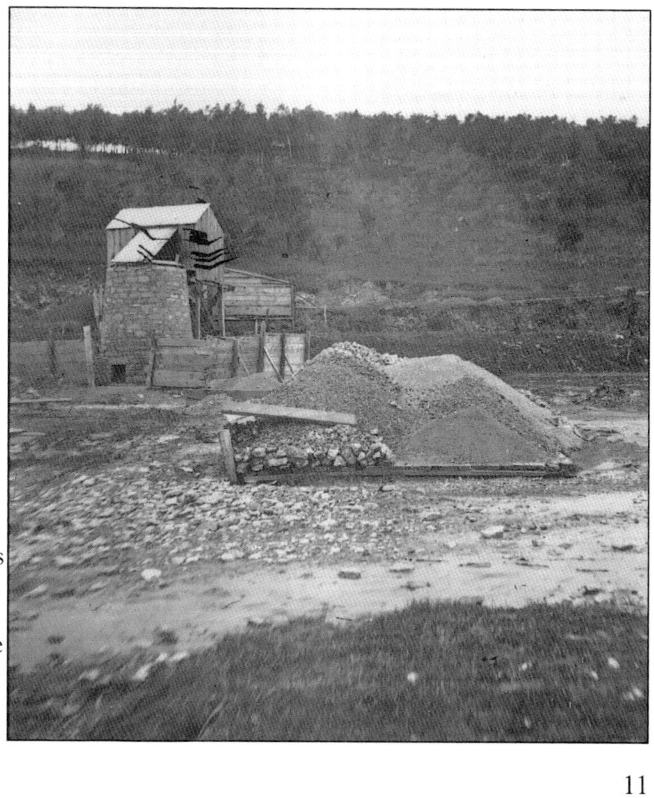

An early smelter or furnace is pictured at right. Lead can be freed from its ore simply by heating. The zinc ore is roasted with carbon to form the zinc metal. The first zinc smelter was established in Mineral Point in 1859, and they dotted the countryside. In later years, these furnaces were replaced by an enormous zinc plant, which we will see later.

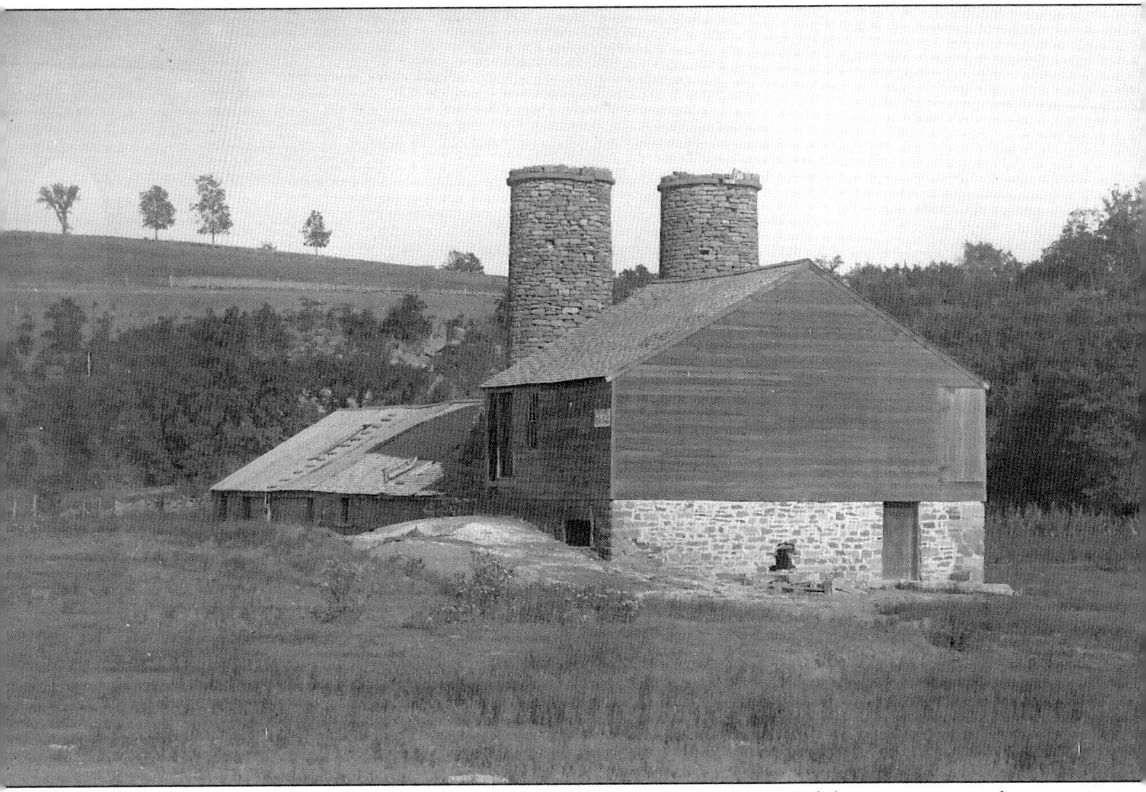

Known as Spensley's furnace, it was likely one of the earliest and longest operated private furnaces. The original furnace was built by Charles Franklin Legate in 1837, and taken over by James Spensley who came to Mineral Point in 1856 from Yorkshire. In 1914, Ruben Ellsworth, whose profession was listed as a smelter, owned the building. The foundations remain on County Road QQ near some of the extant buildings of the Spensley estate. Note the use of local stone in the two towers and the use of the drywalling technique—laying the stone without mortar.

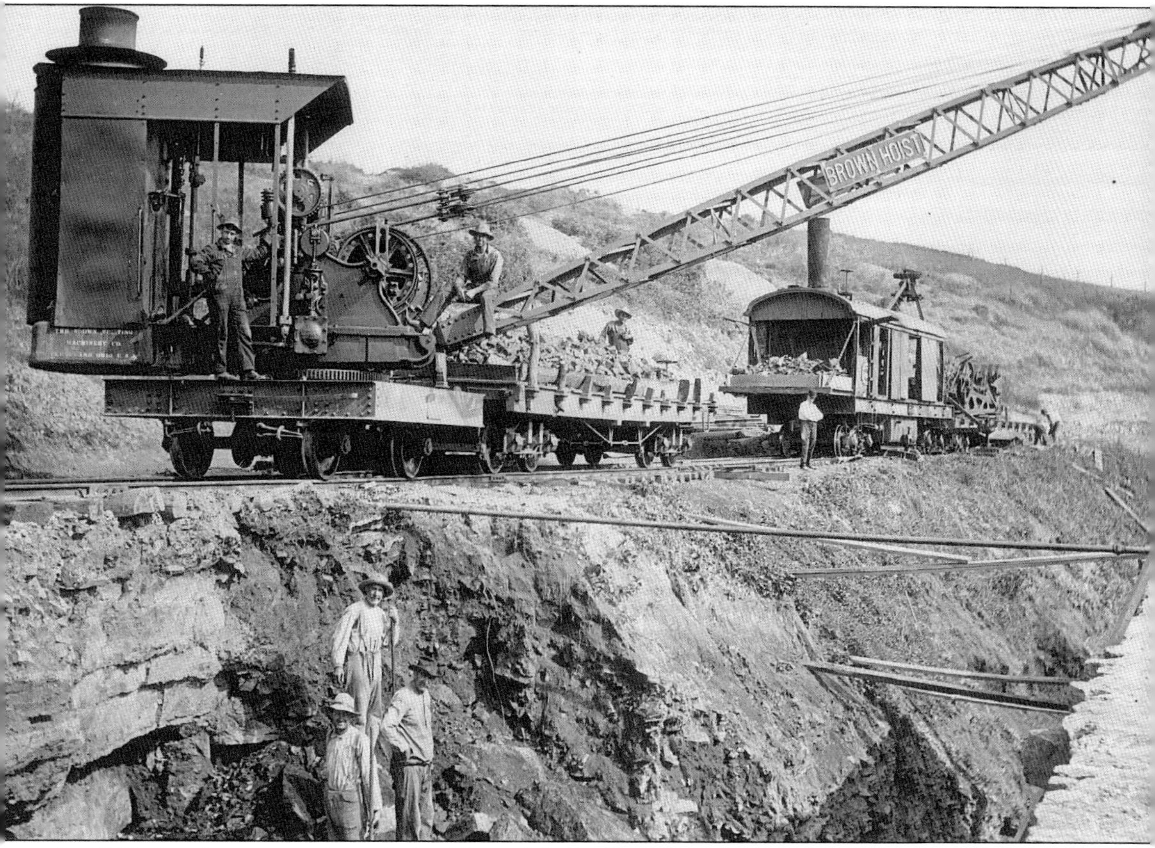

In 1882, local investors formed the Mineral Point Zinc Company with a reported capital of $35,000, and began construction of a large zinc works in southeastern section of Mineral Point. Here we see a digging operation related to the expanding of the works.

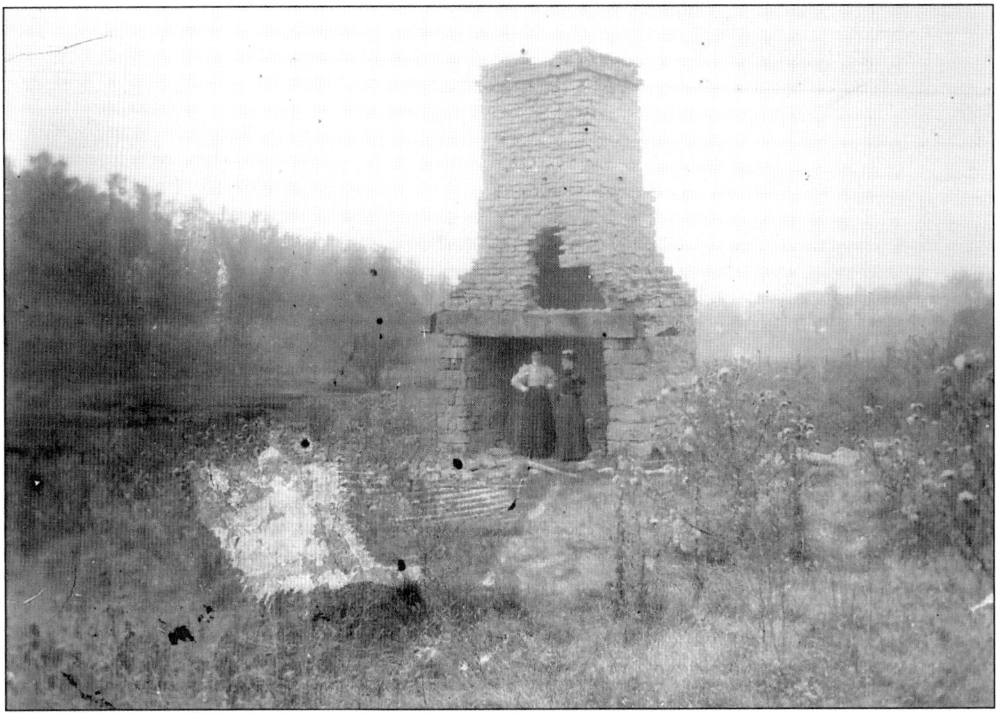

Another old furnace in nearby Dodgeville is pictured here. The first governor of the Territory of Wisconsin, Henry Dodge, who gave his name to that town, originally came to this area from Missouri to mine lead. He was sworn into office on July 4, 1836, in Mineral Point, which was then the principal town in the territory. This furnace could have been used for smelting either tin or lead. It had clearly been out of use for a long time when this photo was taken.

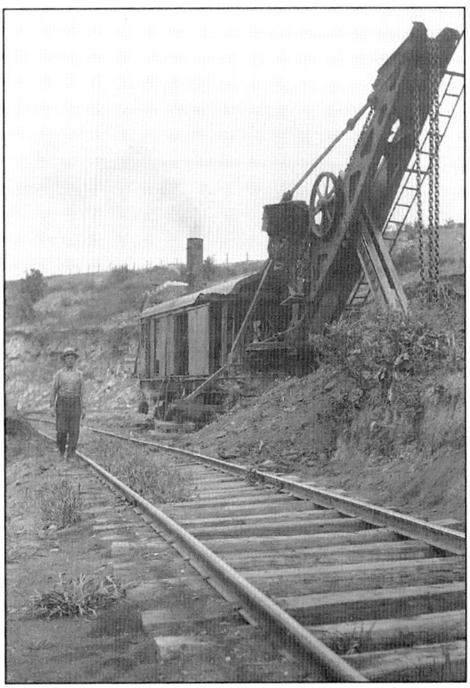

Further digging for zinc works construction is seen here. In 1883, the zinc works were taken over by three brothers—David B. Jones, William A. Jones, and Thomas D. Jones—who were from a Welsh family which had settled in Iowa County in 1851. Their capital was estimated to be $400,000. With effective management, they increased the size of the Mineral Point Zinc Works, and by 1891 it covered 2 acres and had more than one hundred employees.

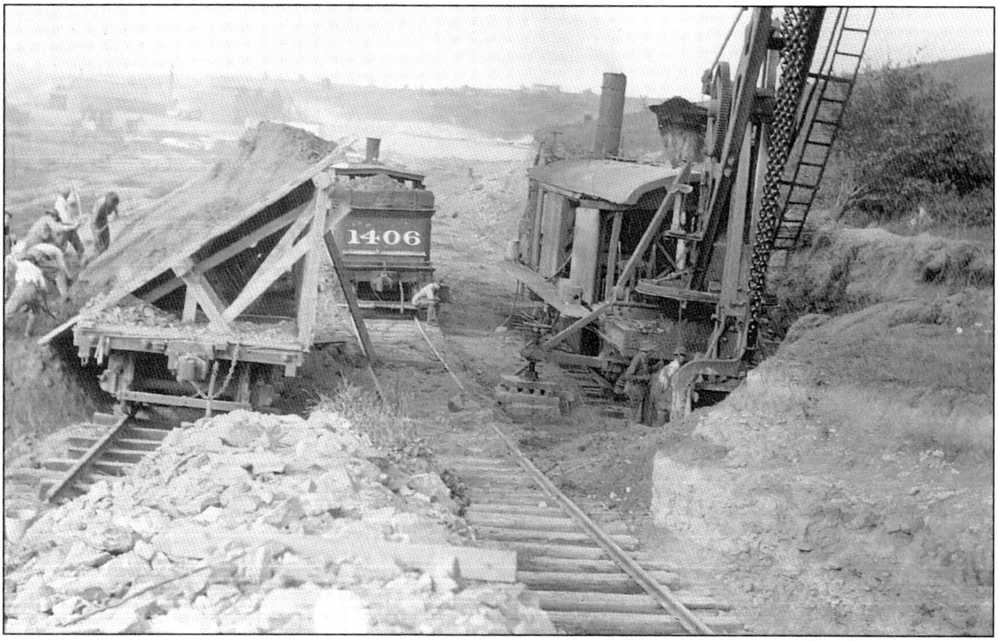

Here employees are working on railroad tracks at the zinc works, so important for linking Mineral Point to other major rail centers.

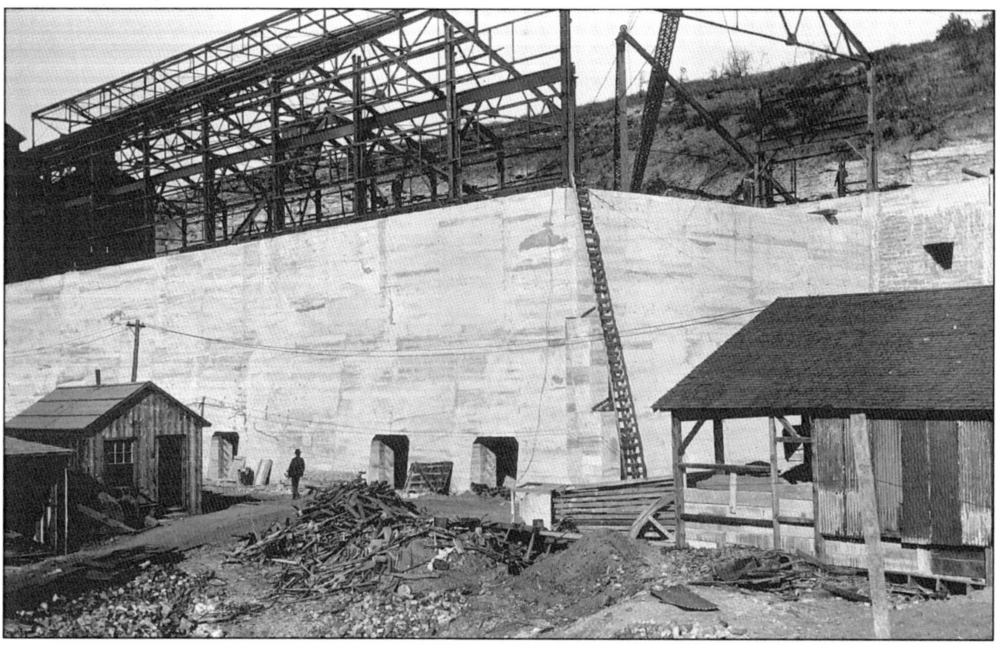

Significant enlargement of the Mineral Point Zinc Works is pictured here, and this continued over several decades. By 1891, this company was said to be the largest zinc works in the United States.

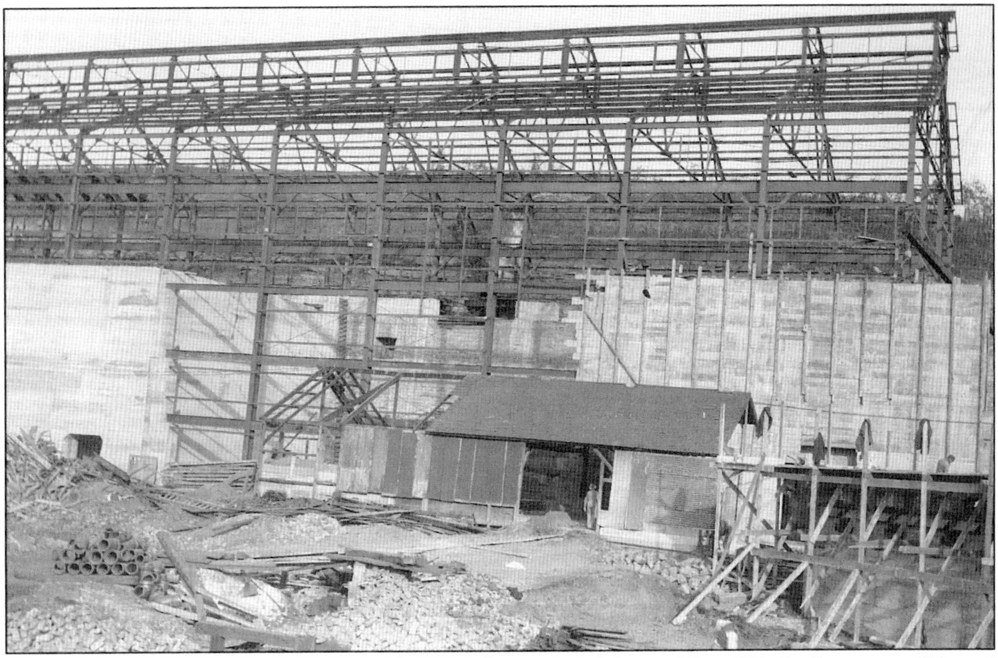

After the recovery from the Panic of 1893, the Mineral Point Zinc Works became affiliated with New Jersey Zinc Company in 1897. This called for expansion of the zinc oxide plant and the addition of a sulphuric acid plant.

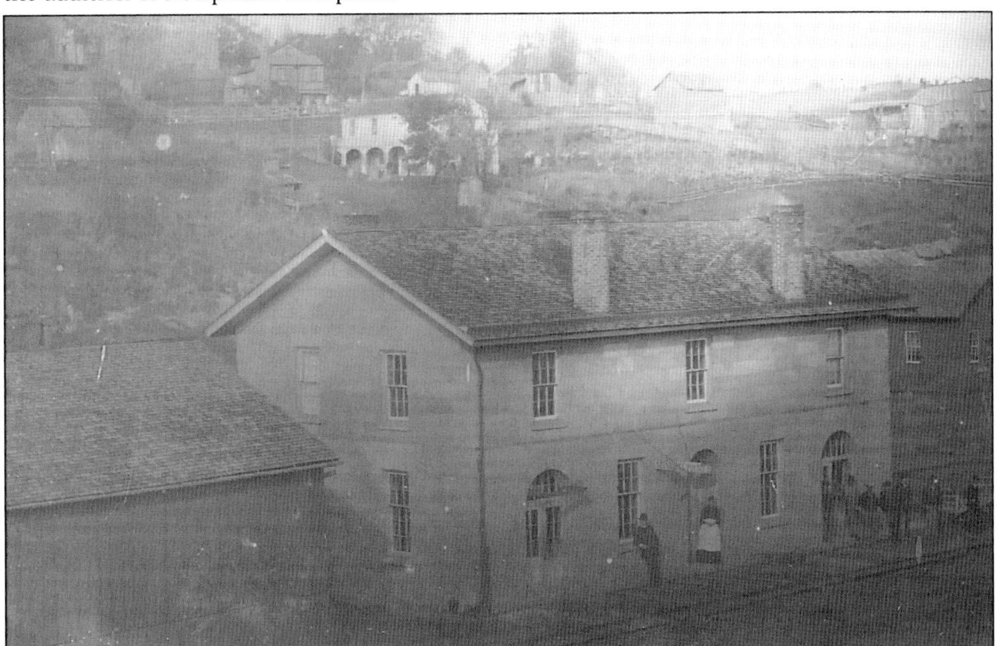

The Mineral Point Railroad was chartered in 1852 to build 32 miles of track to Warren, Illinois, in order to connect with the projected Chicago and Galena Railroad and the Illinois Central. Construction began in 1853 and was completed in 1857. The original depot shown here still stands, although the tracks are gone. It is considered to be the oldest stone depot still standing in Wisconsin.

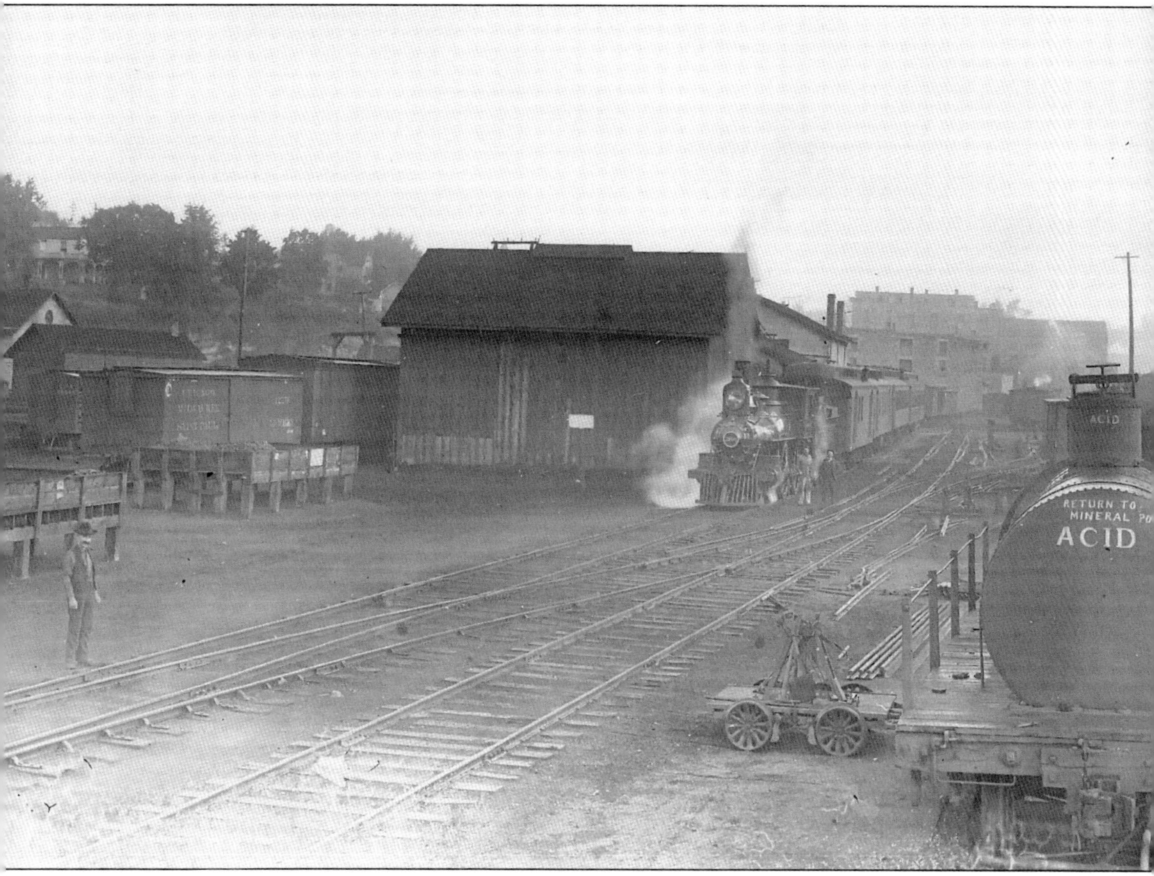

This photograph of the railroad in Mineral Point depicts a passenger train standing at the depot in the background and a tank car for sulfuric acid in the right foreground. Sulfuric acid is a by-product of the production of zinc or zinc oxide from zinc sulfide ore, which is called "black jack" by the miners because of its color.

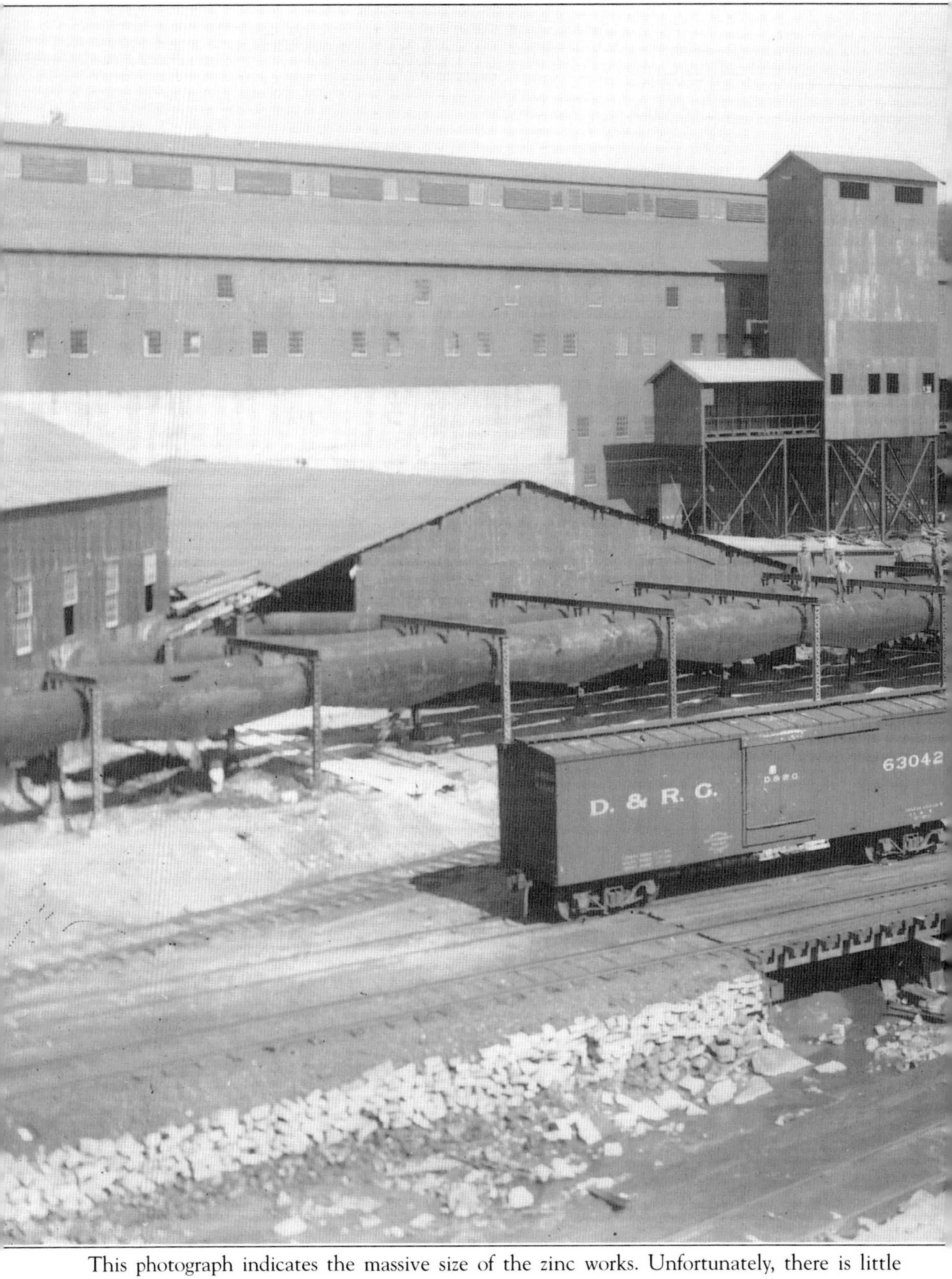

This photograph indicates the massive size of the zinc works. Unfortunately, there is little

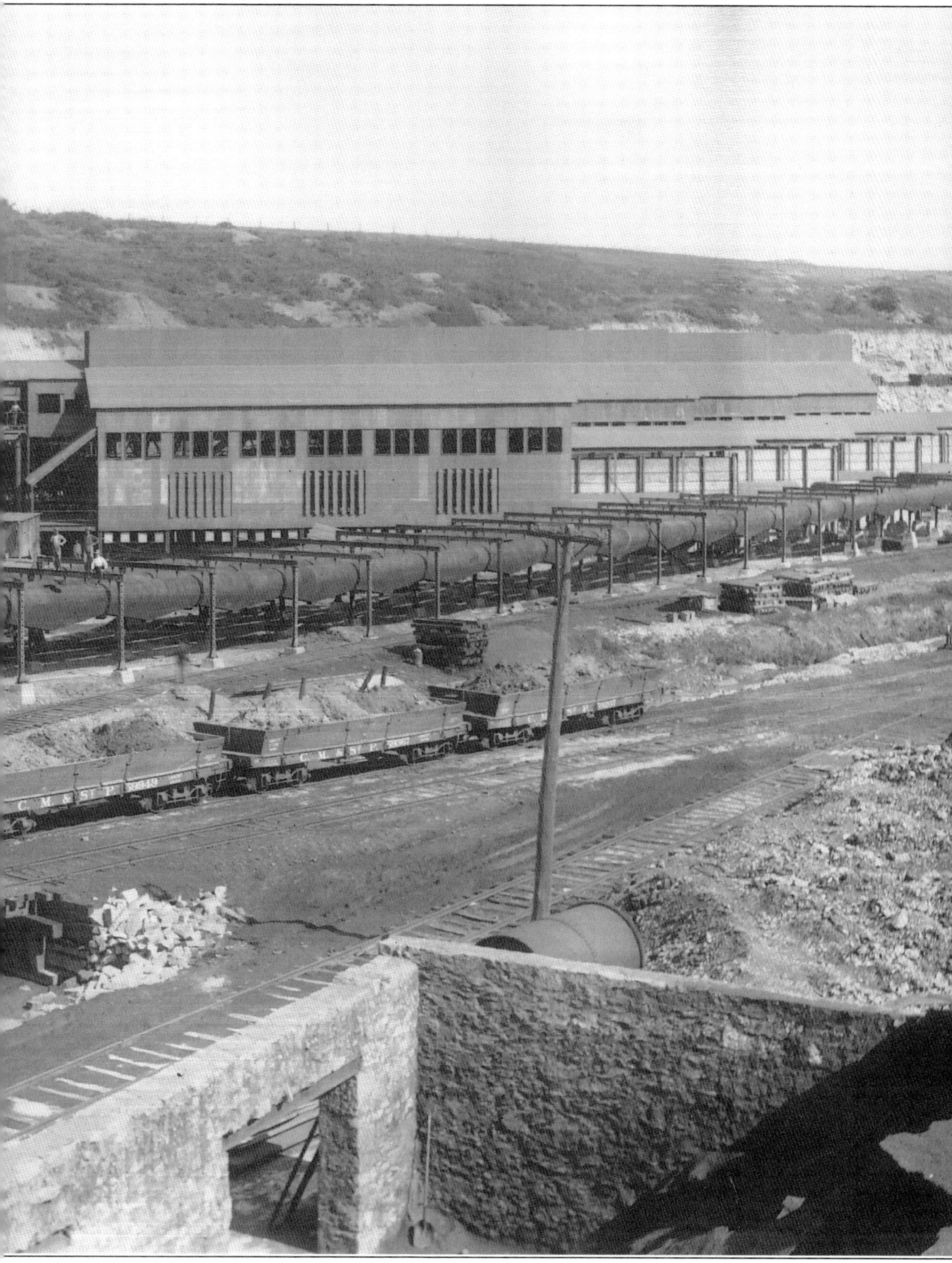
physical evidence of these buildings left today with only remnants of foundations surviving.

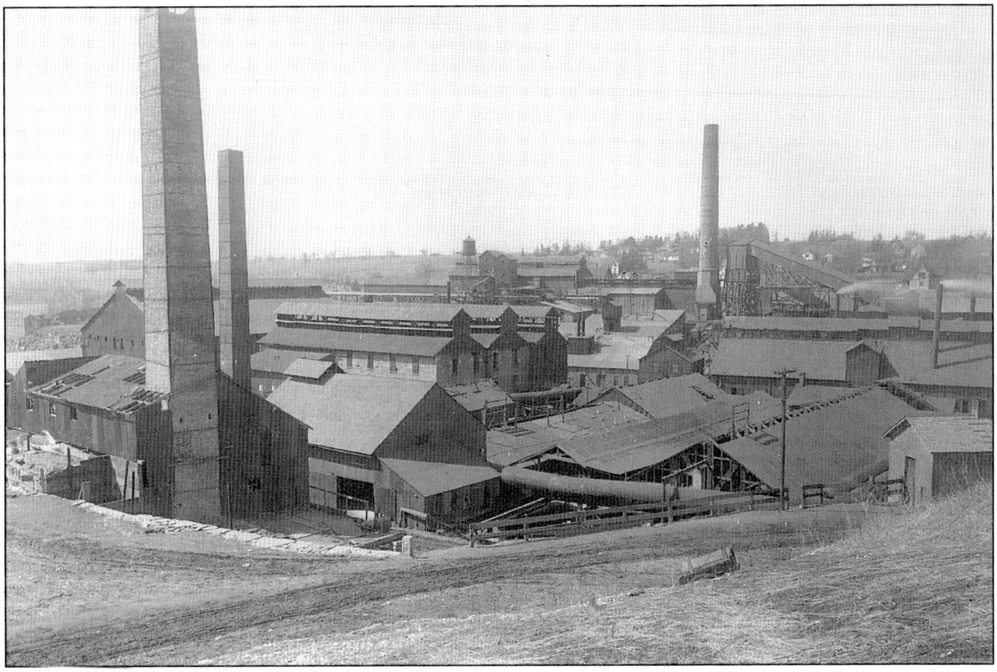

The zinc works were situated in the valley of Brewery Creek. This photograph was taken from a vantage point on the valley slope. The construction of smelters at the zinc works itself put many of the small, local smelters out of business.

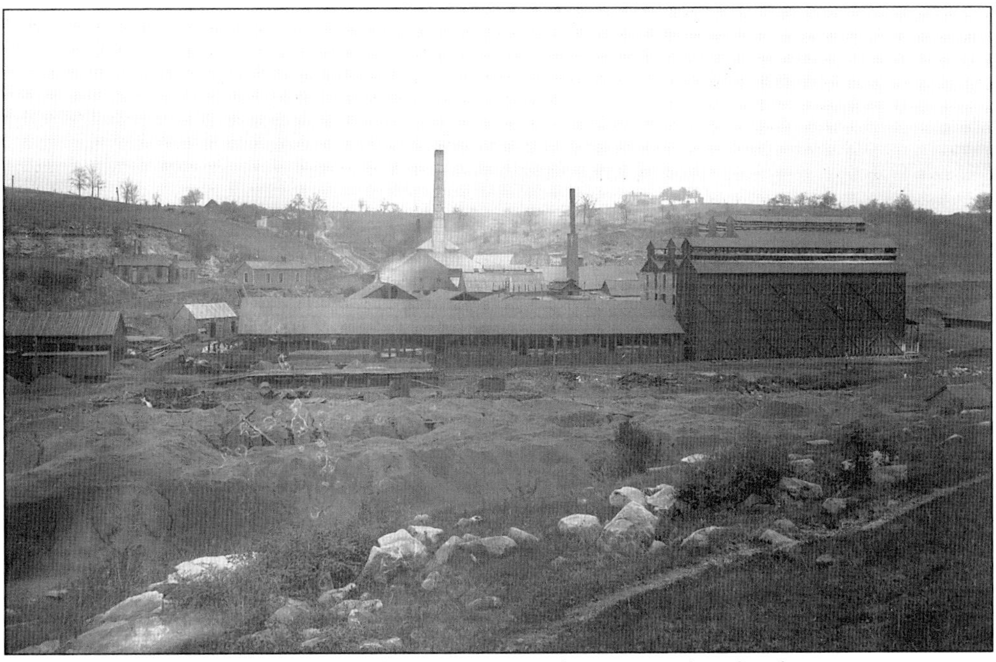

This photograph shows the zinc works at an intermediate stage of its development.

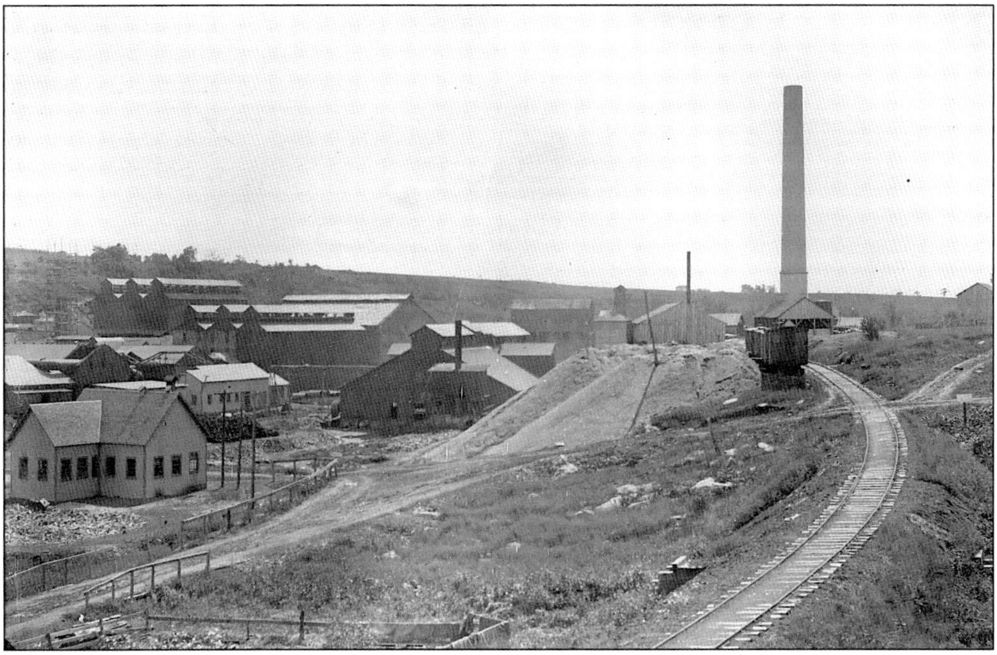

This is another picture of the zinc works prior to completion at its greatest size.

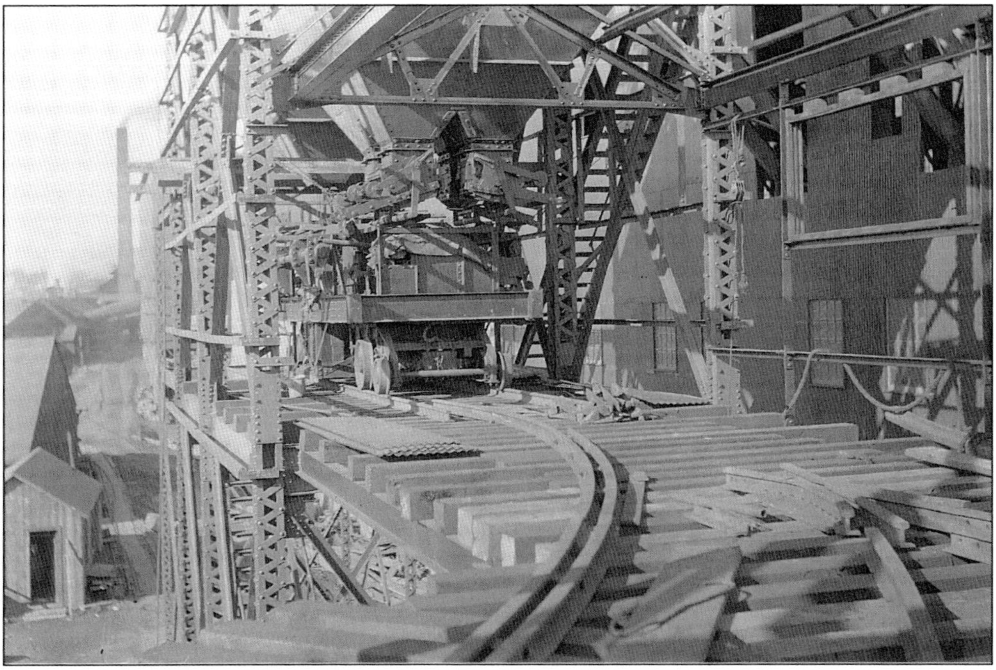

Later in the development of the zinc works, zinc ore was transported to Mineral Point for processing from the upper Mississippi valley and as far away as New Mexico. Pictured here are facilities for the transfer of ore to railway cars.

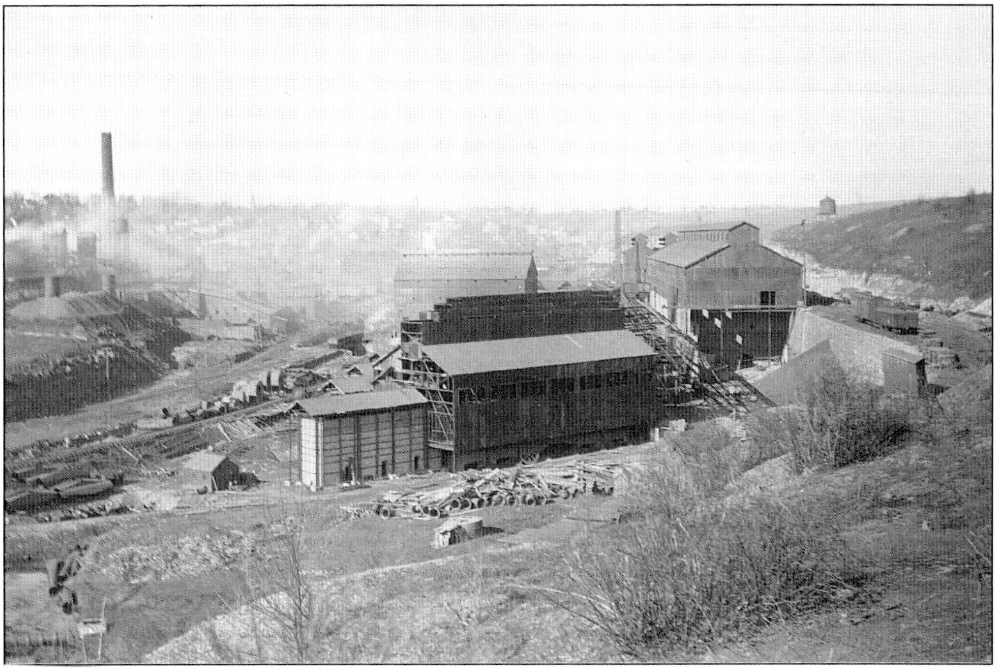

This view of the zinc works shows the City of Mineral Point, obscured by the plant's emissions, in the background. These emissions would have included sulfuric and sulfurous acids and particulates harmful to the lungs.

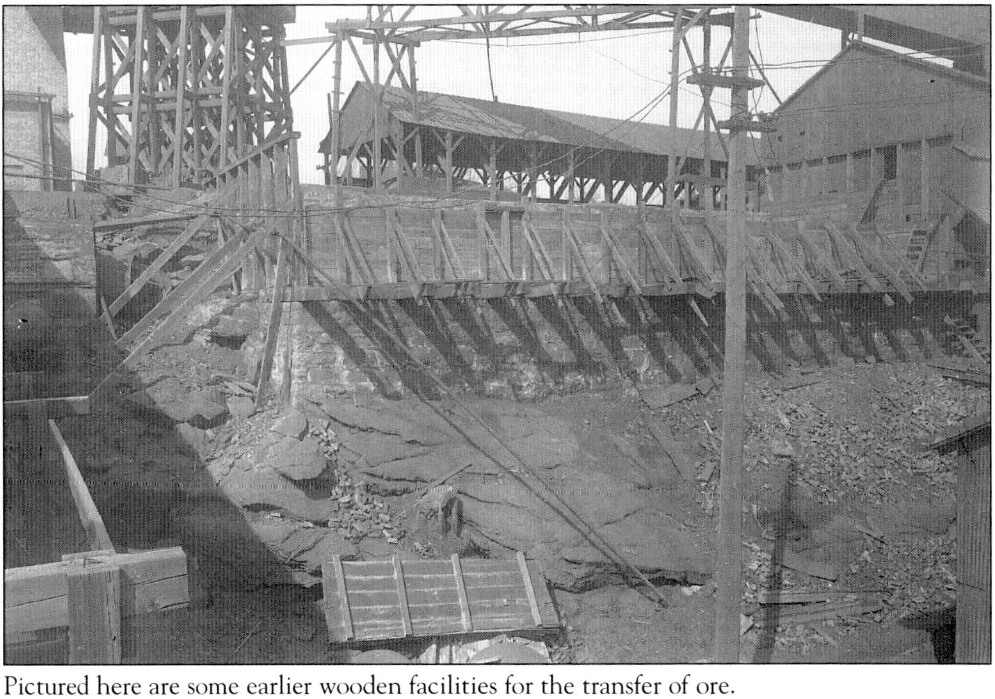

Pictured here are some earlier wooden facilities for the transfer of ore.

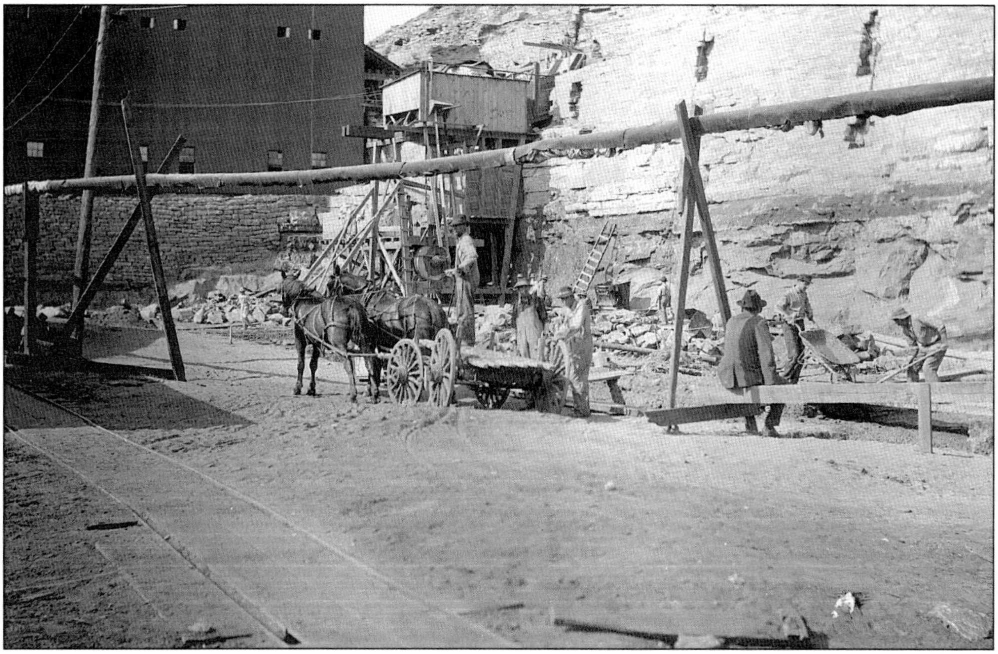

The combination of a modern industrial plant and an age-old method of transportation, the horse and wagon, are shown here.

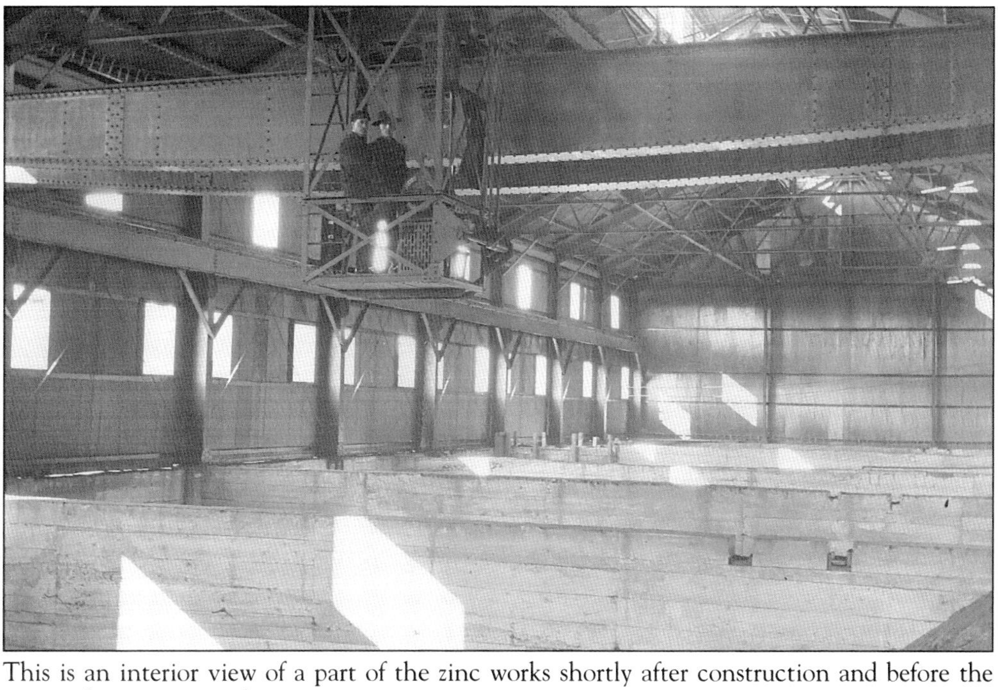

This is an interior view of a part of the zinc works shortly after construction and before the grime of usage was evident.

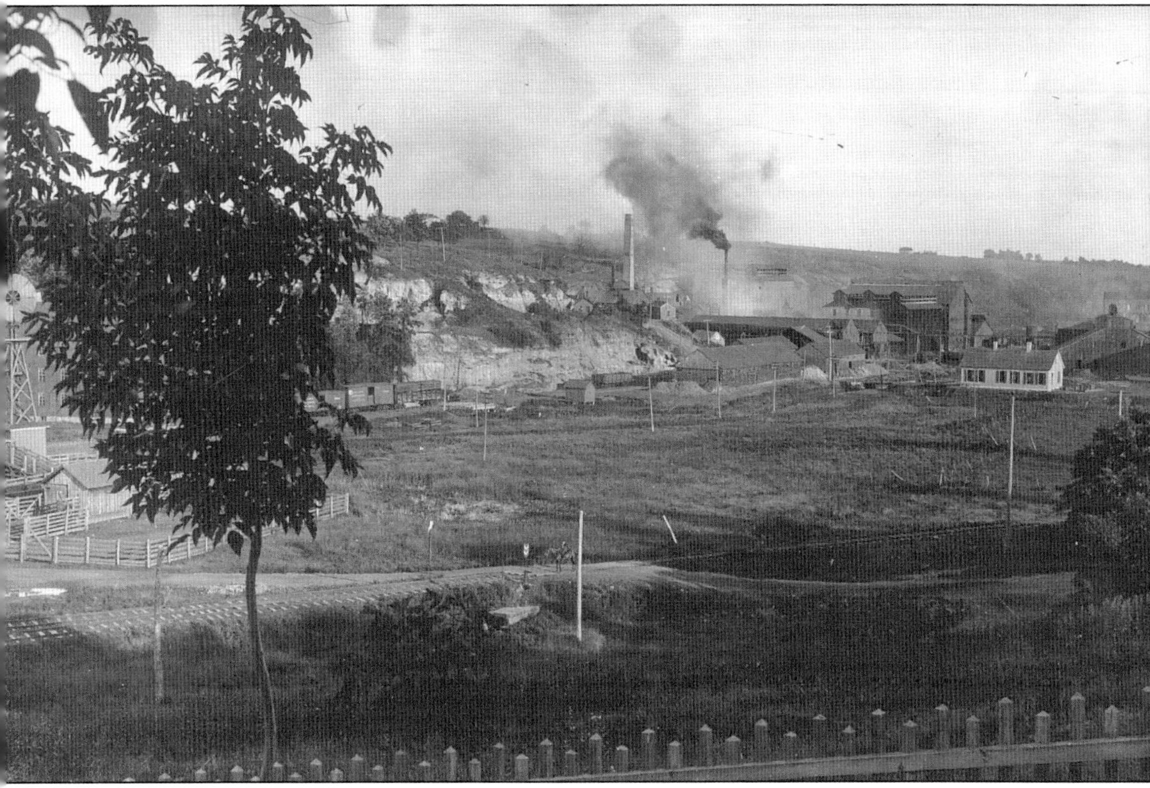

In this view of the zinc works, part of the stockyards are visible in the left foreground. New stockyards were built in Mineral Point in 1883, emphasizing the importance of the town as an agricultural as well as an industrial center. In fact, the stockyards outlasted the zinc production by many years.

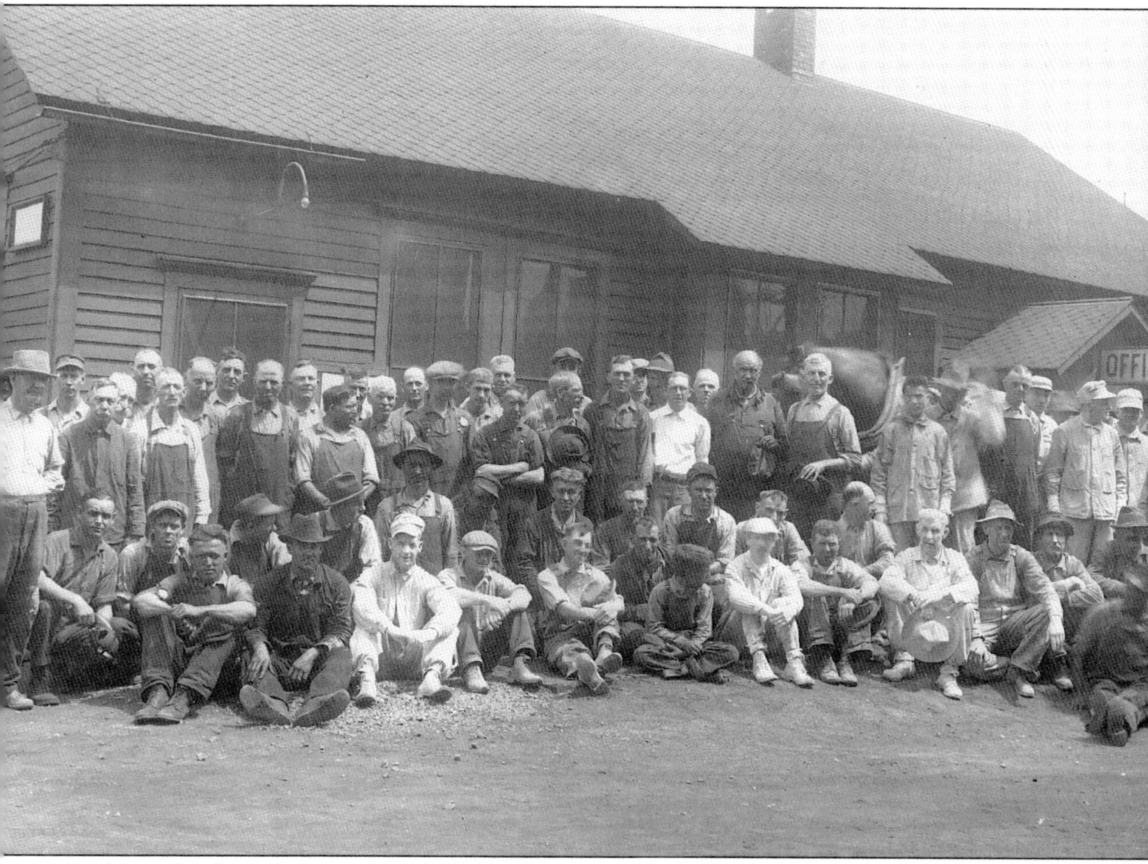

At the peak of production around 1917, the zinc works had three hundred employees and produced 59,742 tons of metallic zinc. Some of the employees are pictured here in front of the office. Wages per day for miners in 1916 were considered high and depended on the level of skill and danger. They were: $2.50 for crusher feeders, $3 for shovelers, $3.50 for hoistmen, and $5 for underground drillmen.

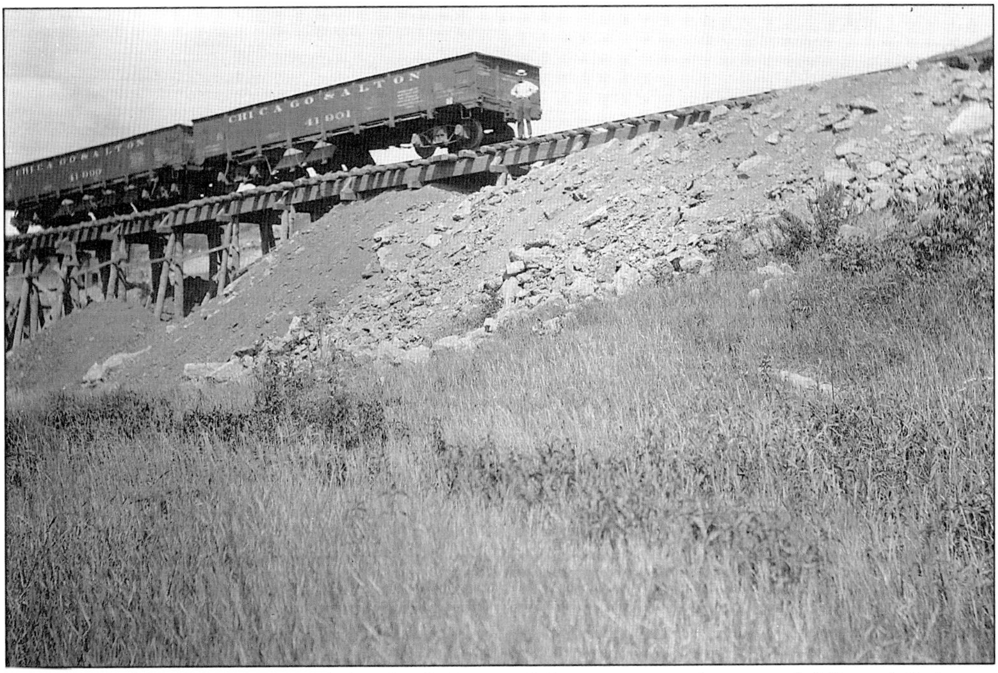

The railroad lines were crucial for the linking of the mining industry and Mineral Point to many areas of the United States. Here we see two gondola cars of the Chicago and Alton Railroad (later Gulf Mobile and Ohio) which hauled ore to St. Louis, Missouri.

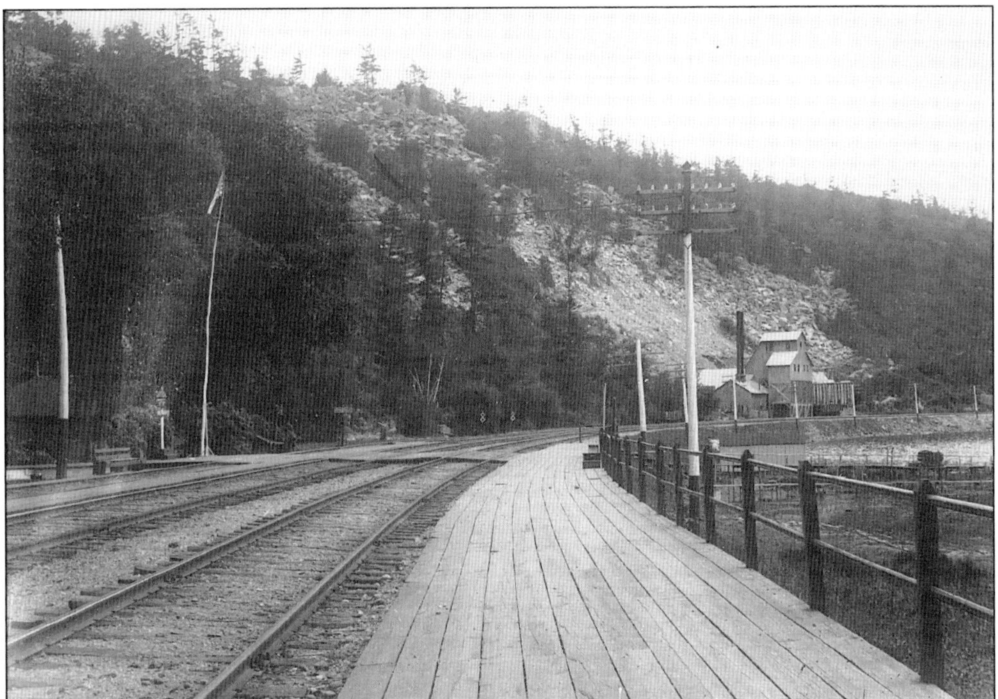

This is a railroad scene depicting a huge pile of mine tailings in the background. The tailings were the rock residue after the zinc was extracted from the ore.

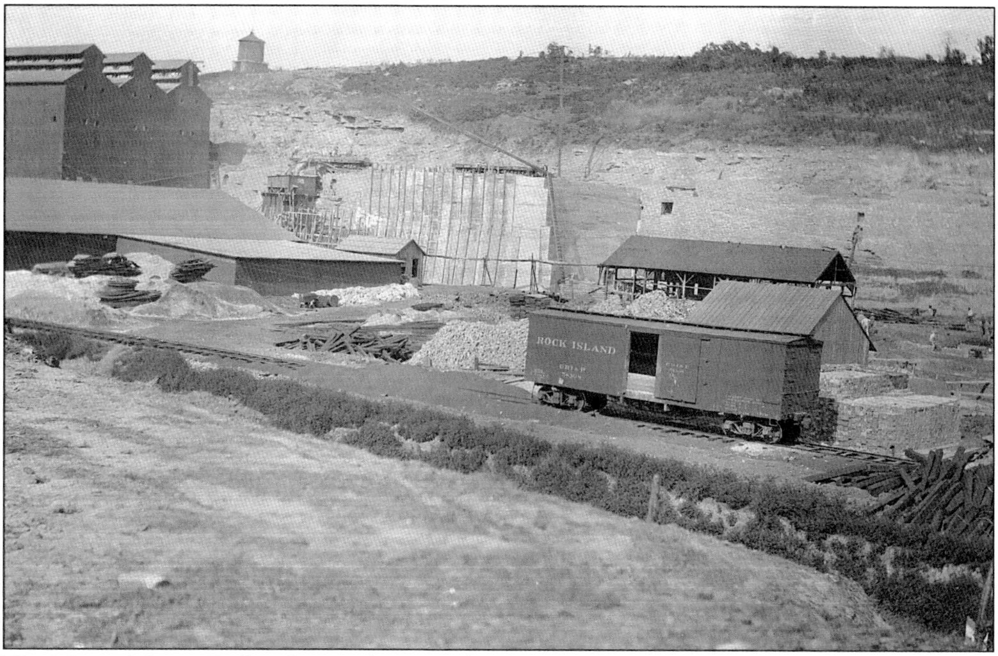

The Mineral Point Railroad was taken over by the Milwaukee Road in 1880. Service increased at that point, and in 1881, nine trains were arriving and departing the Mineral Point depot daily. This railroad scene at the zinc works shows a boxcar of the now defunct Rock Island Line.

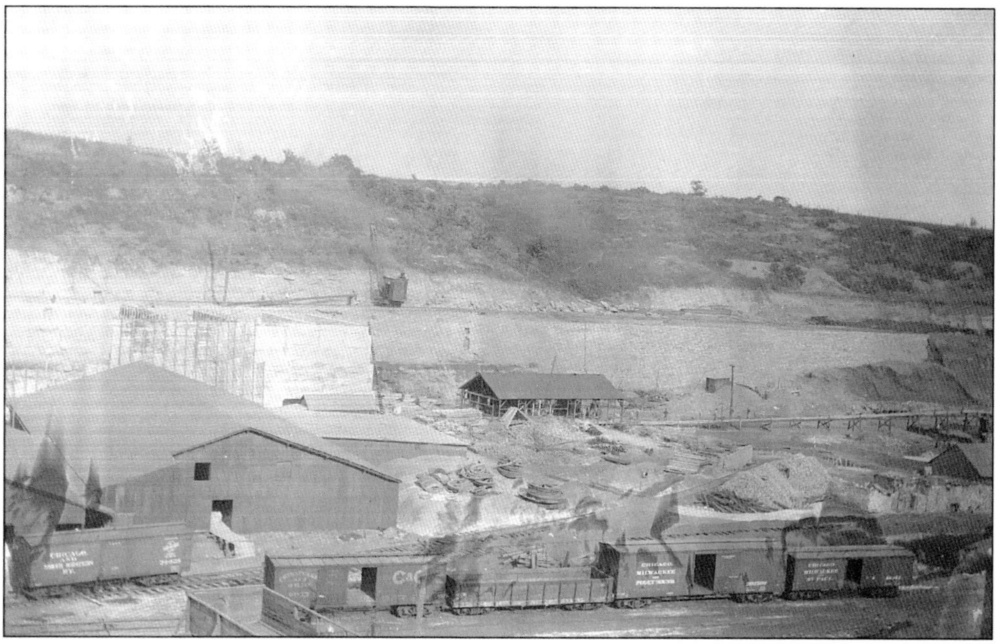

The boxcars in this photograph come from several railroads—the Chicago and Northwestern, the Chesapeake and Ohio, and the Chicago Milwaukee and St. Paul, which is better known as the Milwaukee Road.

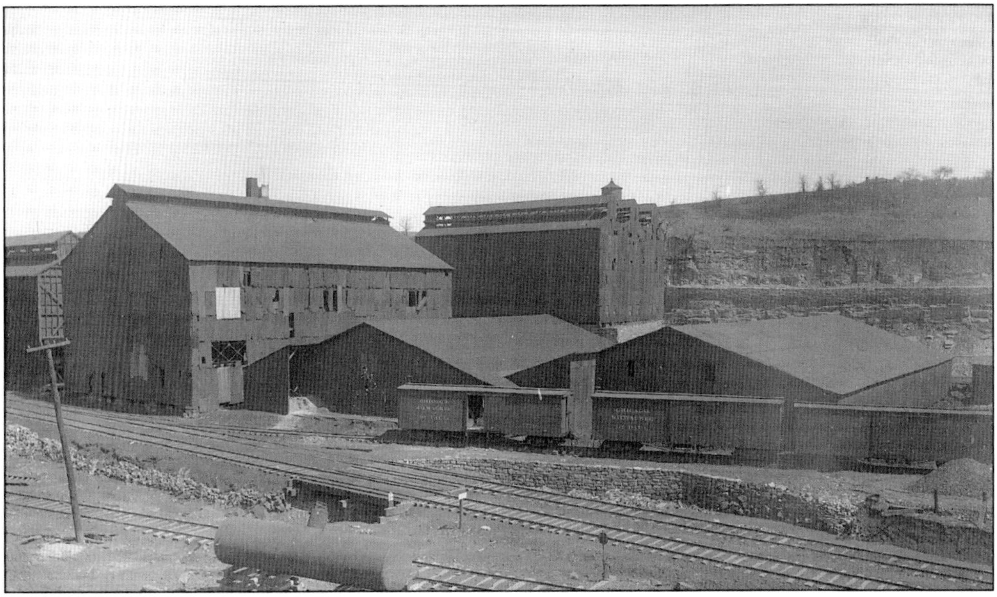

Two of the boxcars in this scene belong to the Milwaukee Road Railroad, but the one on the right belongs to the Central Railroad of New Jersey and may have contained a shipment from the parent New Jersey Zinc Company.

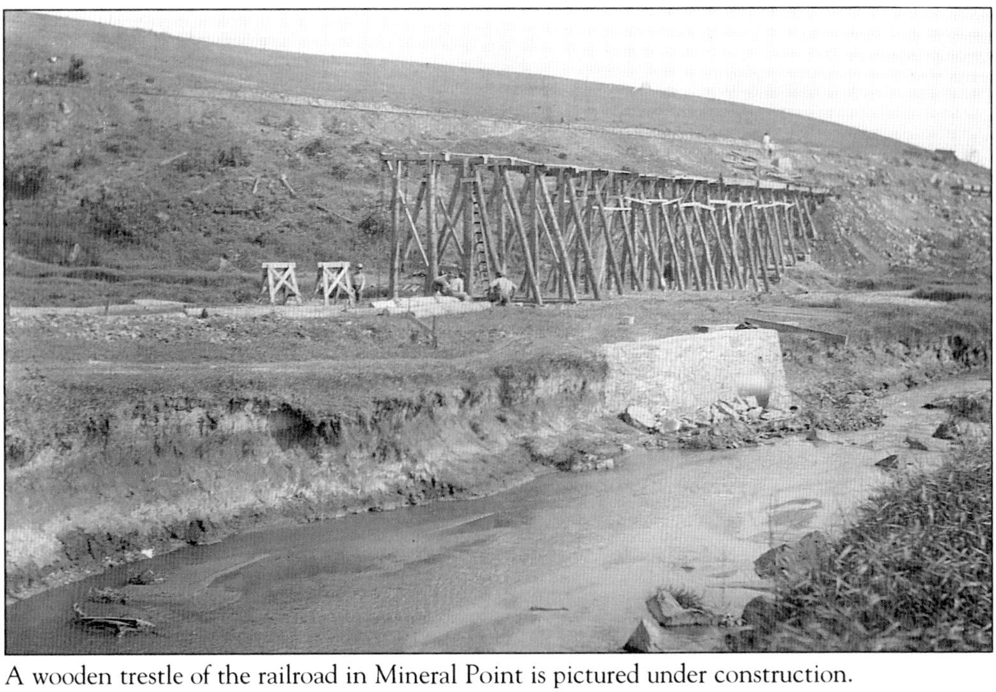

A wooden trestle of the railroad in Mineral Point is pictured under construction.

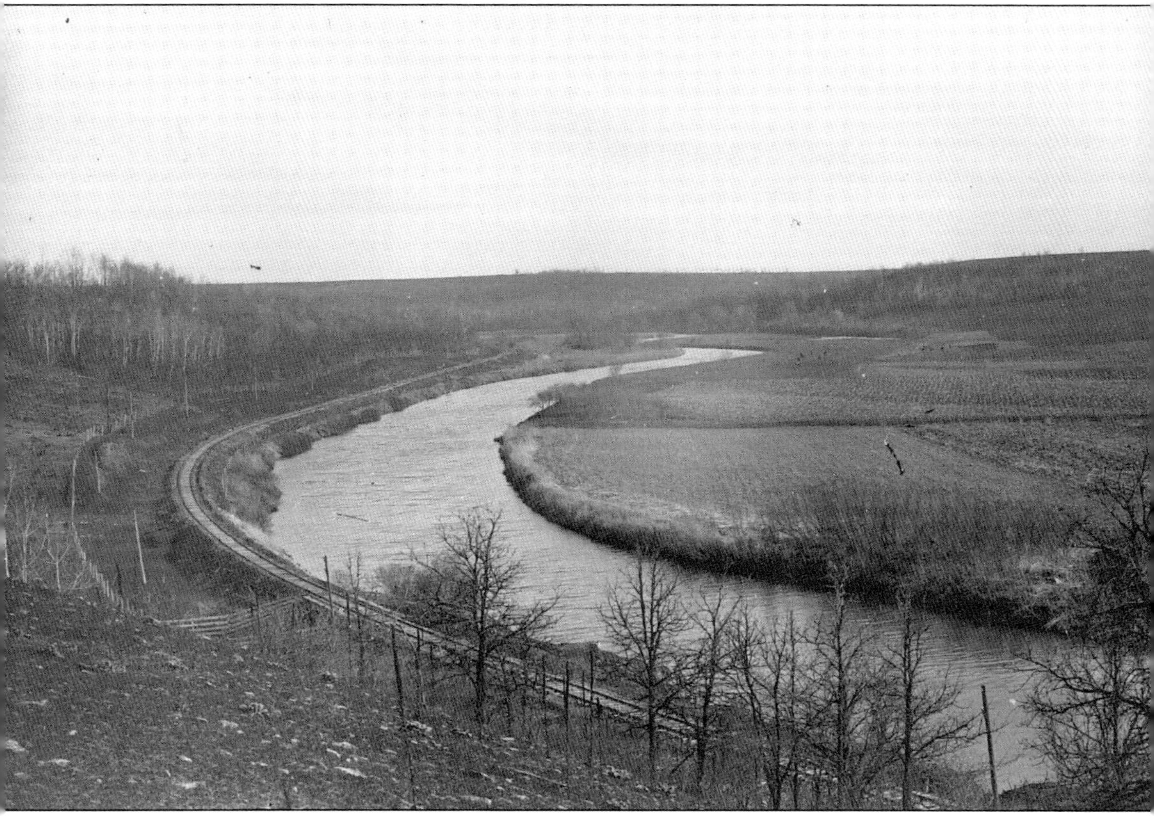

In 1904, another railroad was built to tap the zinc mines in Linden and Highland and was called the Mineral Point and Northern (MP&N). Here the rails of the MP&N are pictured in a graceful curve along the Pecatonica River. This line was constructed very lightly and was subject to flooding due to its close proximity to the river. Likely evidence of a partial washout of the line is visible at the point where the tracks are joined by the wooden rail fence.

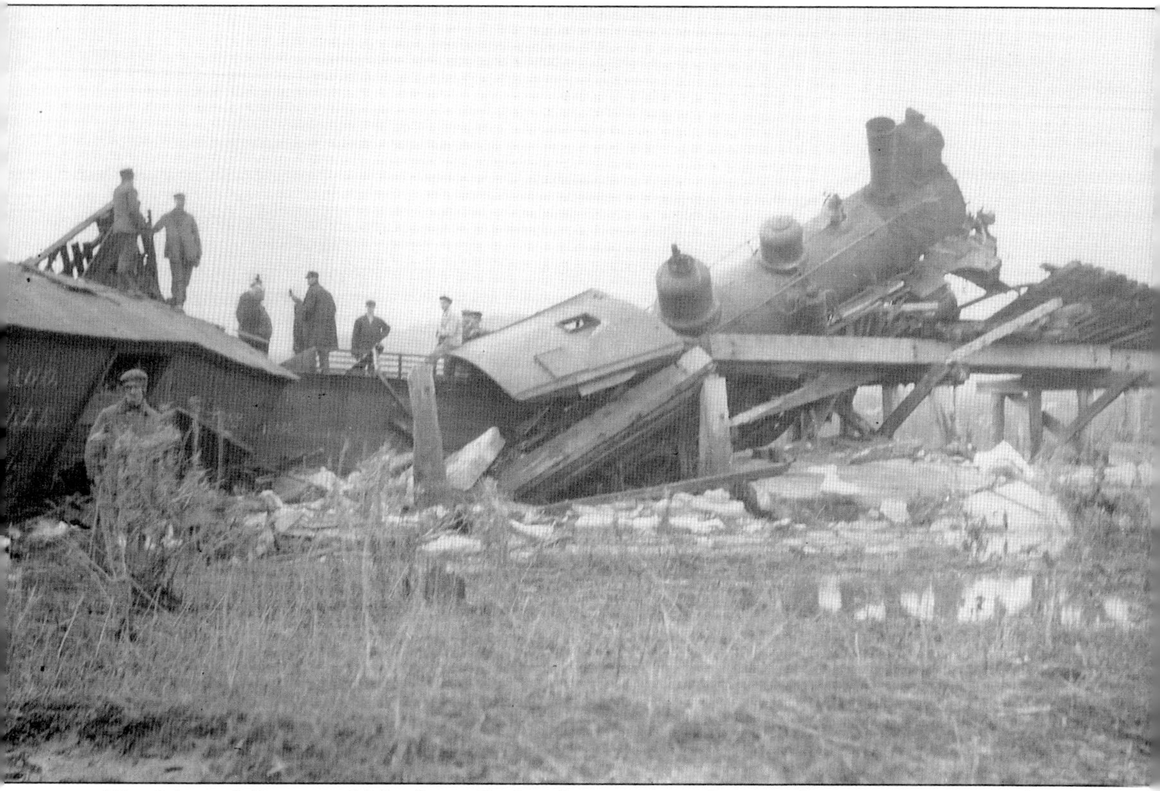

The Mineral Point and Northern Railroad was acquired soon after its construction by the Mineral Point Zinc Company. However, it was closed by the zinc company in 1930. A celebrated wreck on February 14, 1911, resulting from the light construction, further weakened by flooding from the Pecatonica River, is shown here where the weight of a locomotive has broken down the flimsy trestle supporting the tracks.

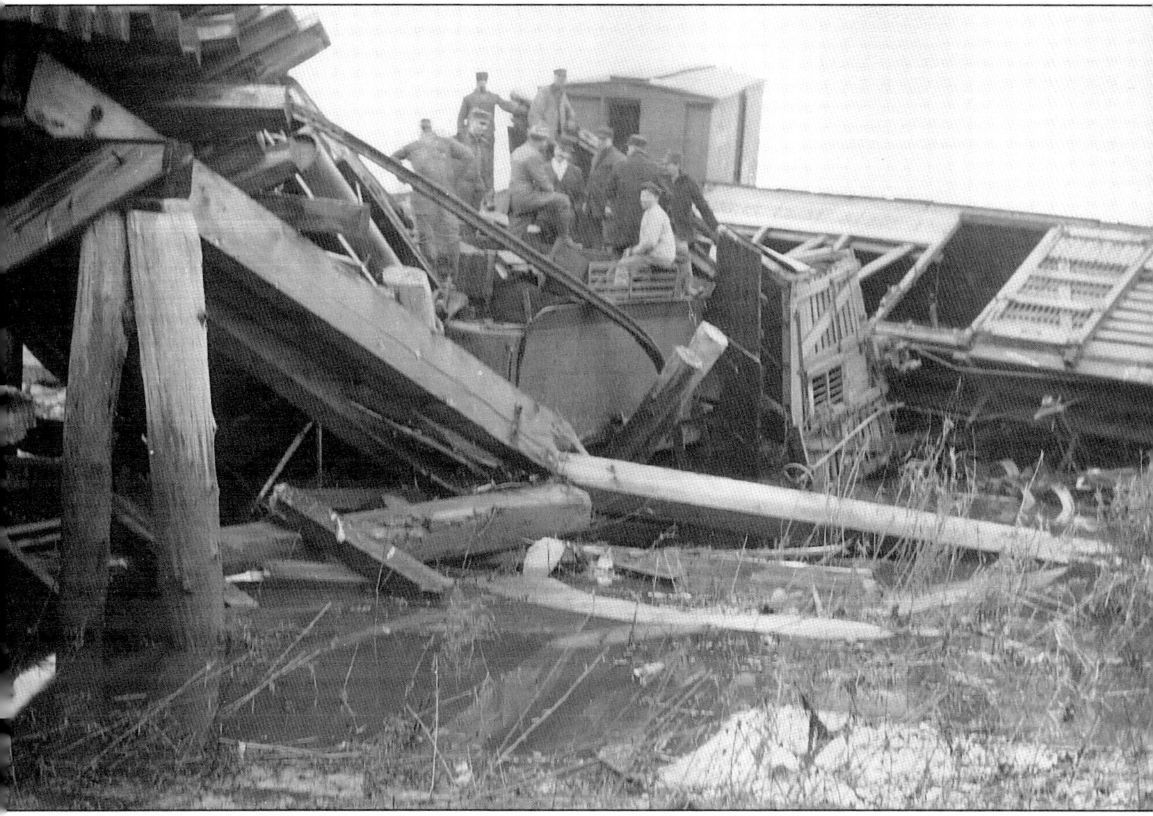

In this wreck, Henry Wald, the fireman of the train whose job was to stoke the fire in the boiler which fueled the engine, was thrown from the train into the Pecatonica River, where he was pinned down by debris and died.

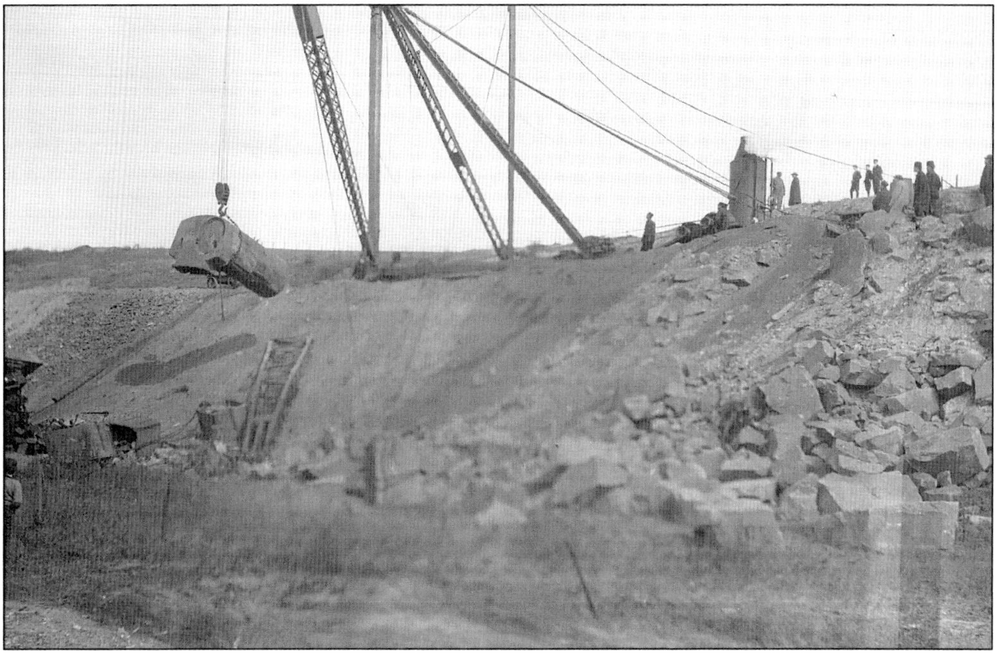

Here a crane is being employed to clean up the debris resulting from the train wreck.

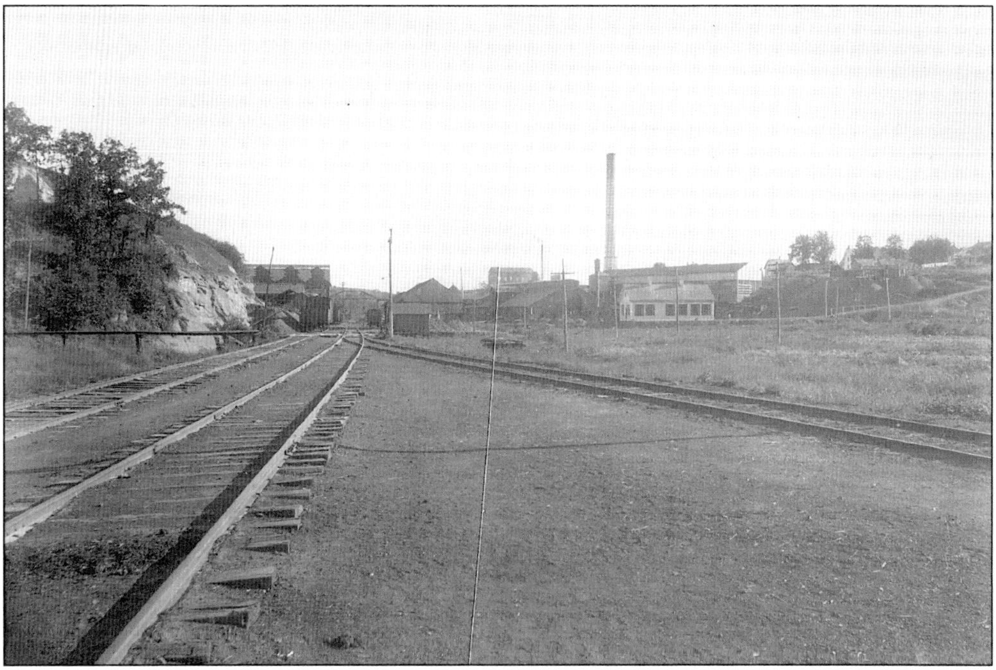

Passenger service to Mineral Point was curtailed in 1940, and the new owners, the Milwaukee Road Railroad, abandoned the line in 1980. Efforts by an independent organization to operate the line continued for about ten years. The tracks were eventually removed, and the roadbed was converted into a recreational trail. This photograph from former days was taken from the depot and shows the tracks fanning out to form the switchyard with the zinc works in the background.

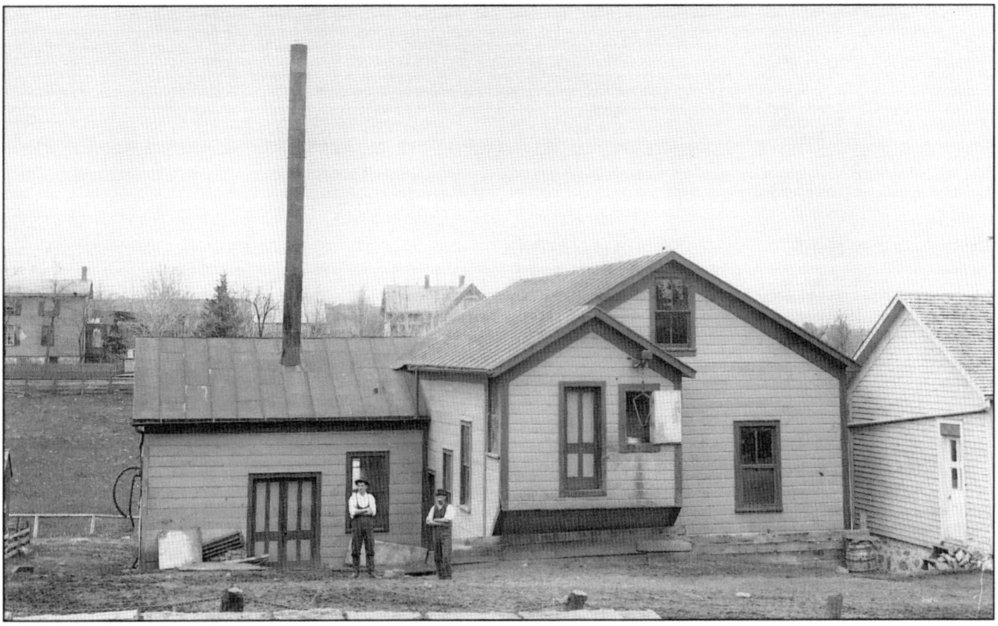

Mineral Point contained a number of other industries such as French's cheese factory, shown here representing an industry related to local agriculture. The town also had a woolen mill, producing blankets, flannels, and other woolen goods; and Lanyon's foundry, which produced a well-known ore crusher.

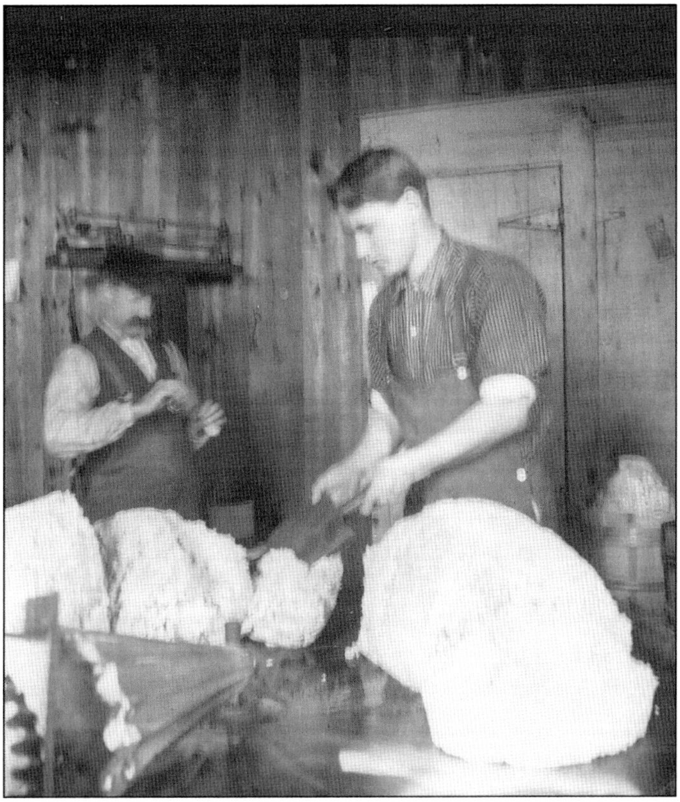

Shown here are two men in the process of making cheese from cheese curd. In the early twentieth century, three cheese factories were in operation in Mineral Point—the Swiss Cheese Company, the Purity Dairy, and the Mineral Point Cheese Company. Only the latter cheese factory at 320 Commerce Street is still standing and continues to be used for making cheese and curd under the name of Hook's Cheese Company.

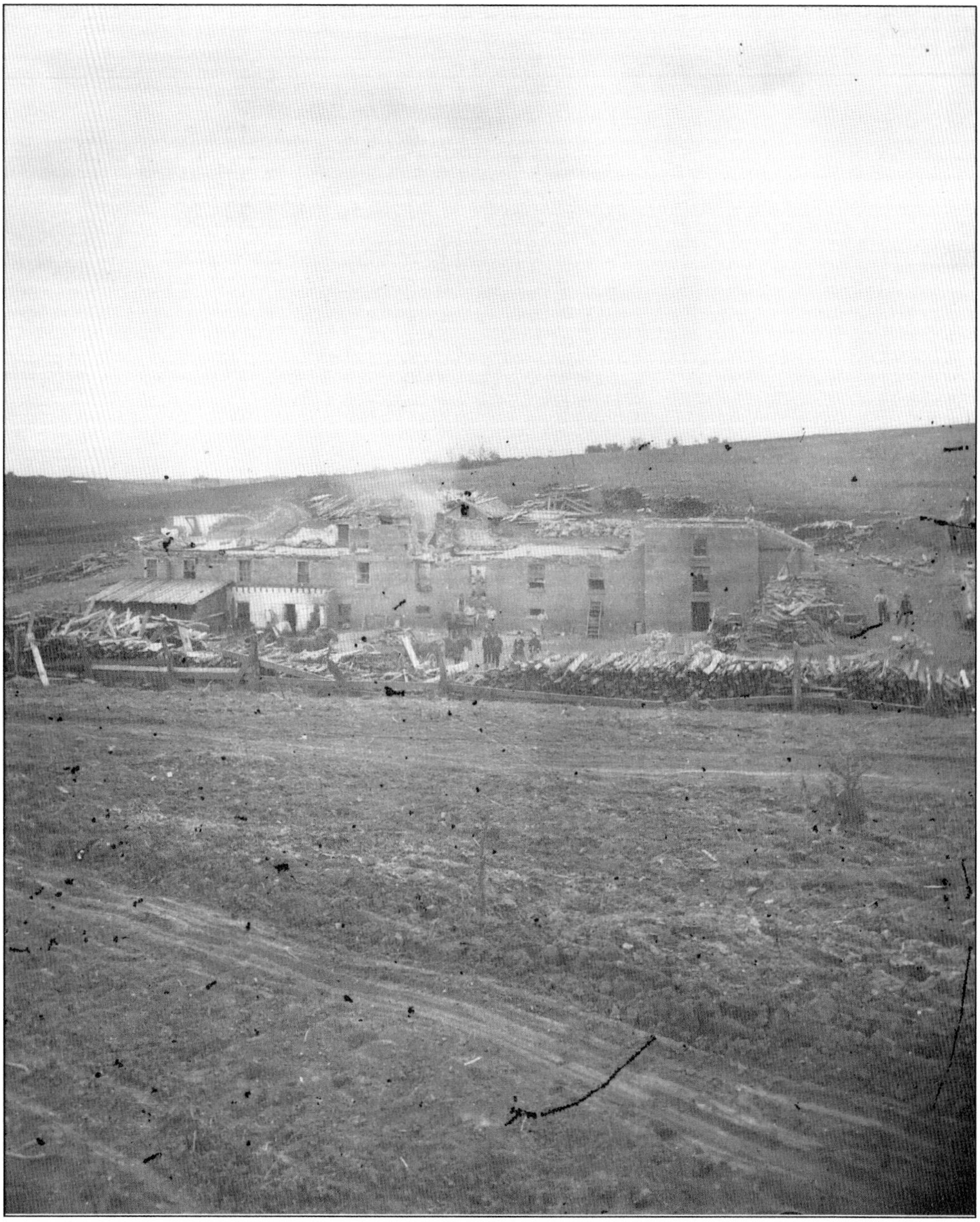

The oldest brewery in the state of Wisconsin was short-lived, established in 1835 on High Street in Mineral Point. This photo depicts another brewery established in 1852 on Shake Rag Street in Mineral Point. It was known by many names, including the Mineral Point Brewery, the Wisconsin Brewery, and the Gillman Brewery, which is pictured here after its destruction by a tornado in 1878. Immediately rebuilt, it was appropriately renamed the Tornado Brewery with an increased capacity of 6,000 barrels per year. Eventually called the Mineral Spring Brewery, it closed in 1961 and is presently a pottery studio and residence.

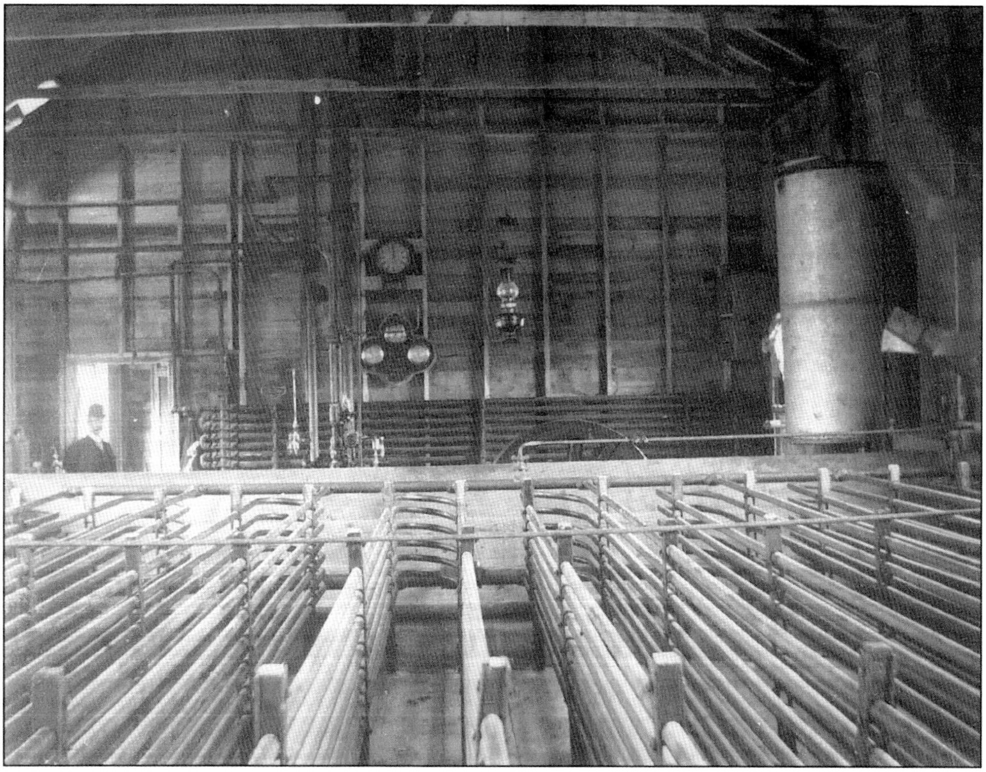

The interior of the Mineral Point ice plant is shown here.

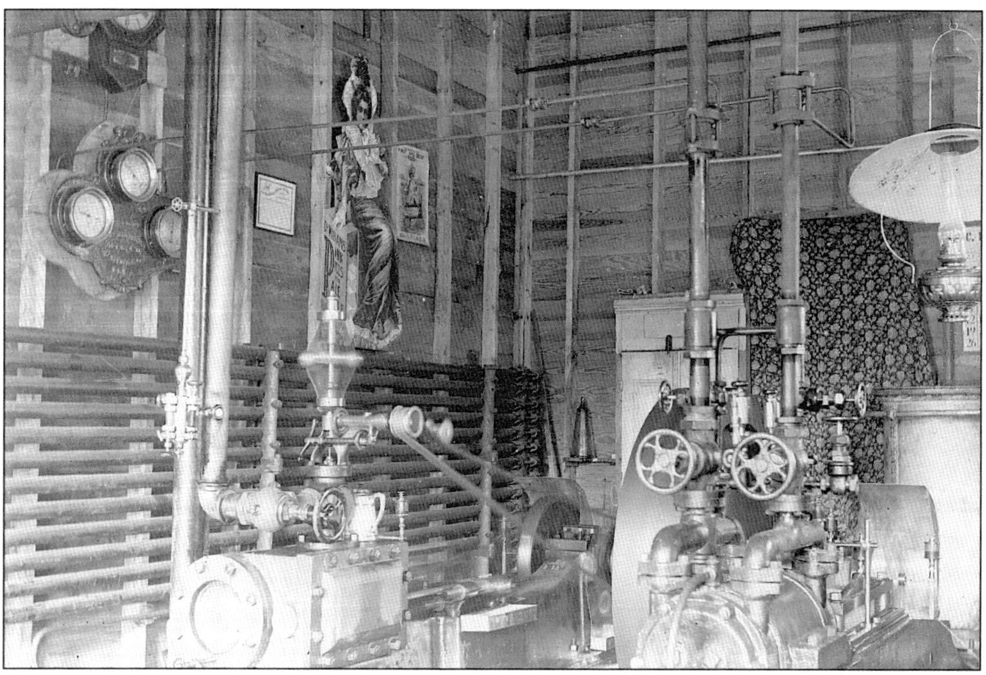

This is the compressor for the Mineral Point ice plant. Notice the illumination by a kerosene lamp.

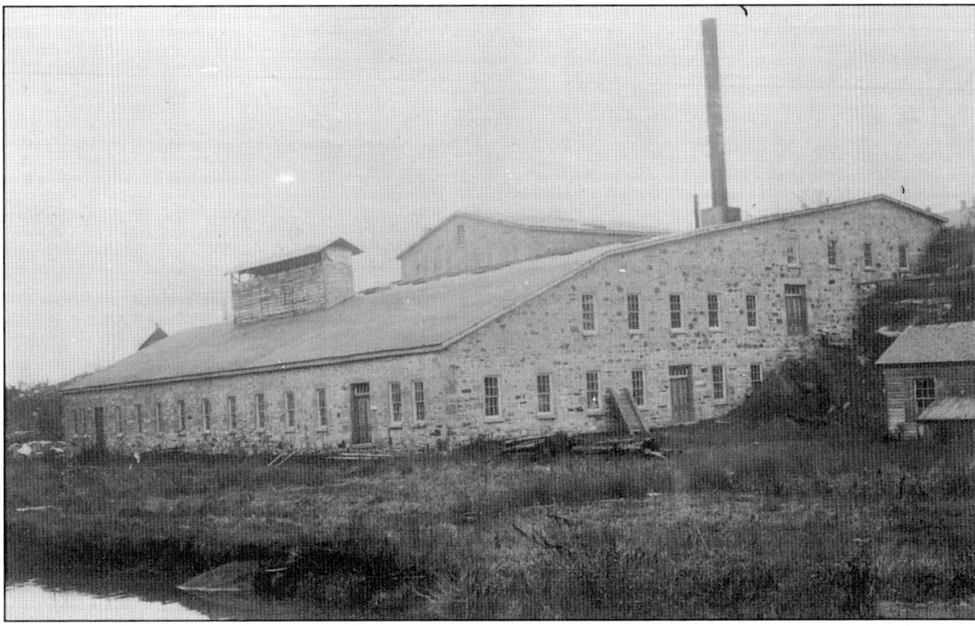

In 1906, Phil Allen Jr., president of several commercial ventures in Mineral Point, became president of the Badger Rubber Works pictured here. The rubber works occupied the building of the defunct Mineral Point Woolen Mill. Its smokestack still stands at the edge of a pond located near Old Darlington Road and the rock formation called Mineral Point.

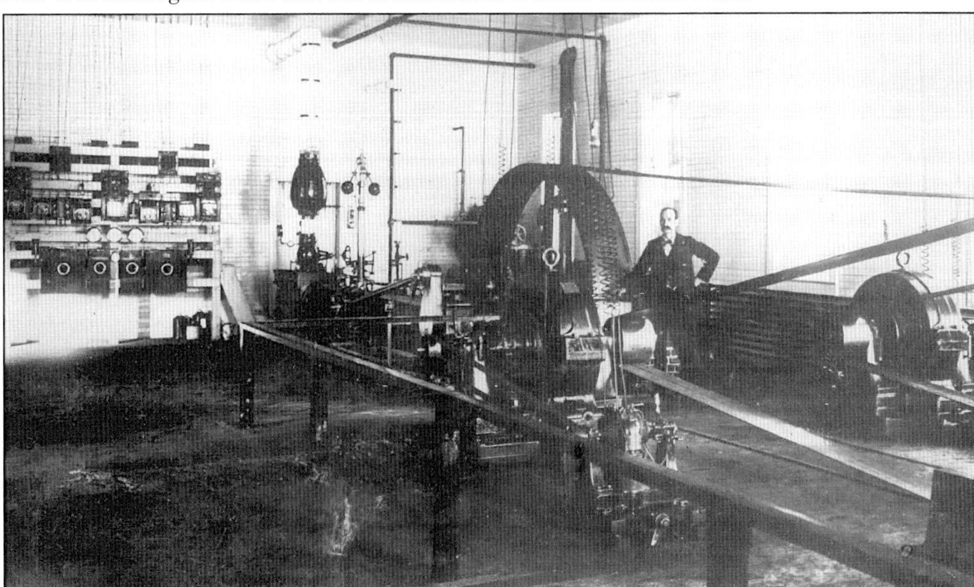

The interior of an electric power plant in Mineral Point is pictured here. Not surprisingly, the first electric power was employed at the Mineral Point Zinc Company for use in processing zinc. This service was then expanded to provide street lighting to the city. In 1907, Frank C. Ludden bought the company from William A. Jones and his brothers, David B. Jones and Thomas D. Jones, and renamed it the Mineral Point Public Service Company. By 1909, the company was expanding service beyond the city limits to neighboring towns. In 1924, it was purchased by the Wisconsin Power and Light Company, which is now part of Alliant Energy.

Two

Residences of Mineral Point

Badger Holes, Miners' Cottages, and Grand Mansions

The residences of Mineral Point span a wide variety of styles of architecture and tell us much about the people who constructed and lived in them. The early dwellings were crude shelters made by hollowing out the hillside or constructing a crude shack of prairie grass and sod. The "badger" holes, or suckers, can still be seen on Merry Christmas Hill, part of the Wisconsin State Historical Site of Pendarvis. Some early log houses were built, only to be torn down for the construction of Fort Jackson and its blockhouse during the so-called Blackhawk War of 1832.

When permanent settlers arrived in the 1830s, timber was in short supply, being used for firing the lead smelters. However, the Cornish miners were also experienced stonecutters. The local limestone and sandstone they used to build their homes, churches, and commercial buildings tell much of the architectural history of Mineral Point and give the town its distinctive character. The limestone and sandstone were cheap and readily available, and continue to be used in many of the town's buildings even to this day.

In times of prosperity, grander homes were constructed of stone, brick, and, once railroad transport was available, of wood frame. Many of the surviving larger homes were constructed by prominent townspeople. The homes in Mineral Point represent a potpourri of architectural styles, since many do not neatly fit into one particular style. Rather, they often combine elements of one or more styles or are vernacular structures reflecting the regional tastes, available materials, and local workmanship.

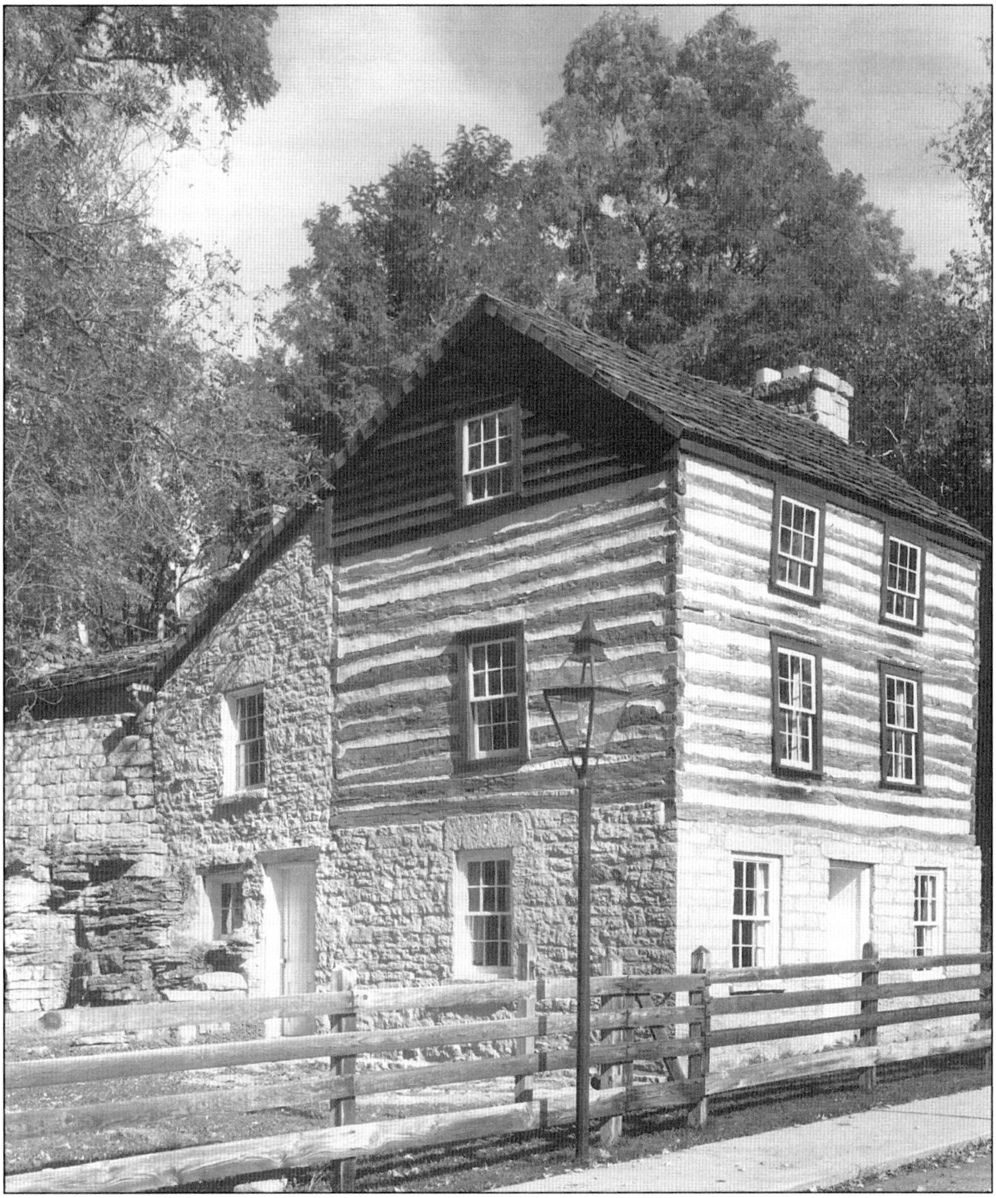

Pictured here is Polperro. (Permission granted by the Pendarvis, State Historic Site—State Historical Society of Wisconsin.) While badger holes dug into the hillsides served well enough as temporary shelters for transient miners, later miners arriving with their families to settle built more substantial dwellings. Experienced hard rock miners, the Cornish built their homes from locally available limestone and sandstone. This stone and log house was built during 1842–43 by George Kislingbury, an English miner. Many were constructed on Shake Rag Street directly across from the hills where the lead was mined. The street was named Shake Rag because the miners' wives used to go out and shake a rag as a signal that it was time to come home from the mine. By the 1930s, these cottages began to be purchased and restored by Robert Neal and Edgar Hellum. In 1970, these reconstructed cottages became the State Historic Society of Wisconsin, and which provides—with trained interpreters—a living history of the Cornish during the lead mining era.

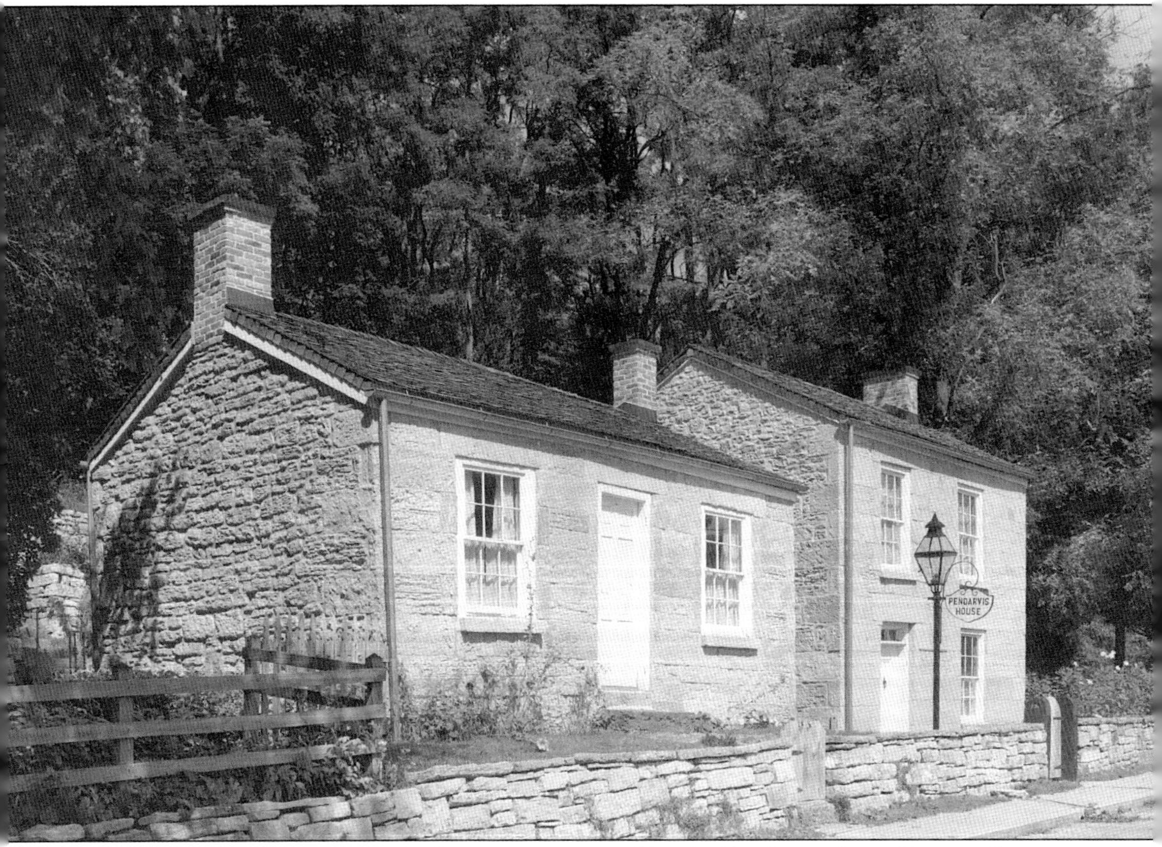

Pendarvis House is pictured above. (Permission granted by the Pendarvis, State Historic Site—State Historical Society of Wisconsin.) This one-story cottage was built of locally quarried limestone for Henry Williams by Cornish stonemasons around 1845. Typically, the stone on the front of the building is smoothed or "dressed," while on the other three sides, it is left rough and irregular. Notice the simple side-gabled roof, and the symmetry of the front façade with its centrally-placed entrance.

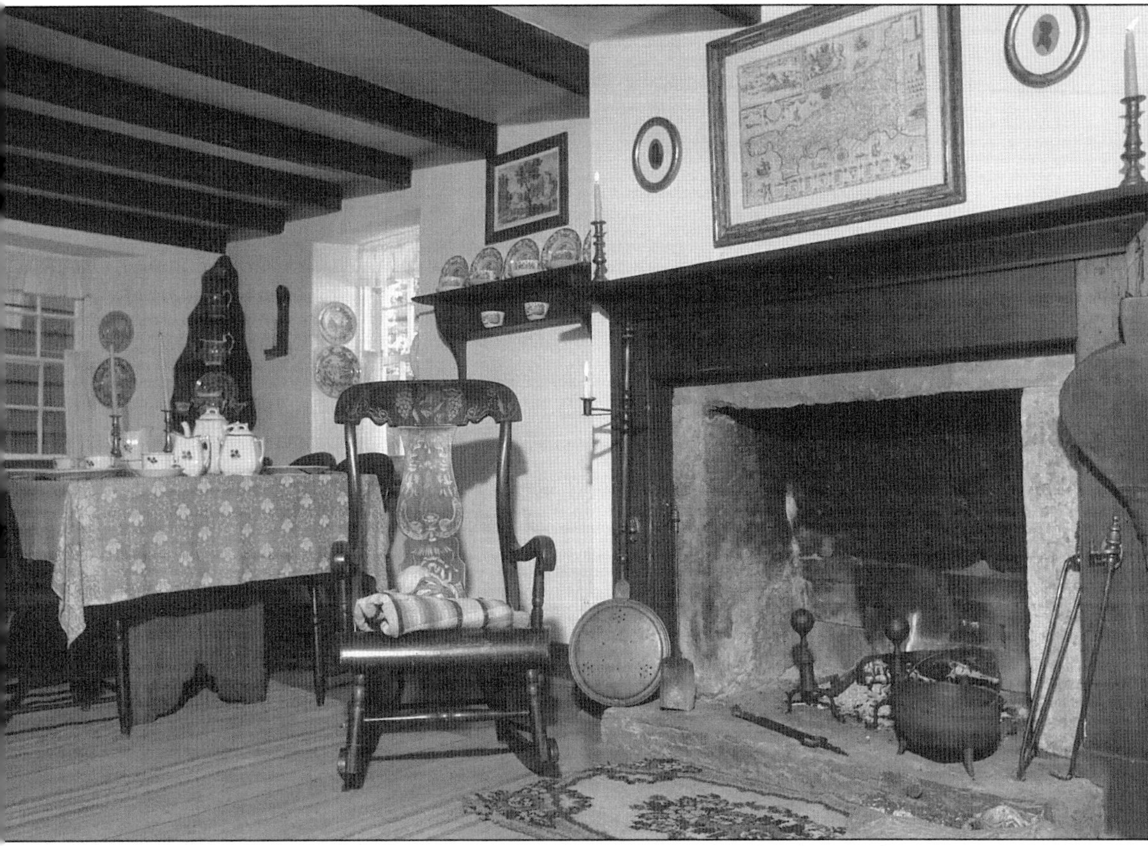

Pictured here is the interior of Trelawny. (Permission granted by the Pendarvis, State Historic Site—State Historical Society of Wisconsin.) This is the interior parlor of Trelawny, another reconstructed Cornish cottage. Notice the low, beamed ceilings, the stone fireplace with the map of Cornwall, England, above it, and the deeply-set window in the left-hand corner indicating that the walls were approximately 18 inches in thickness.

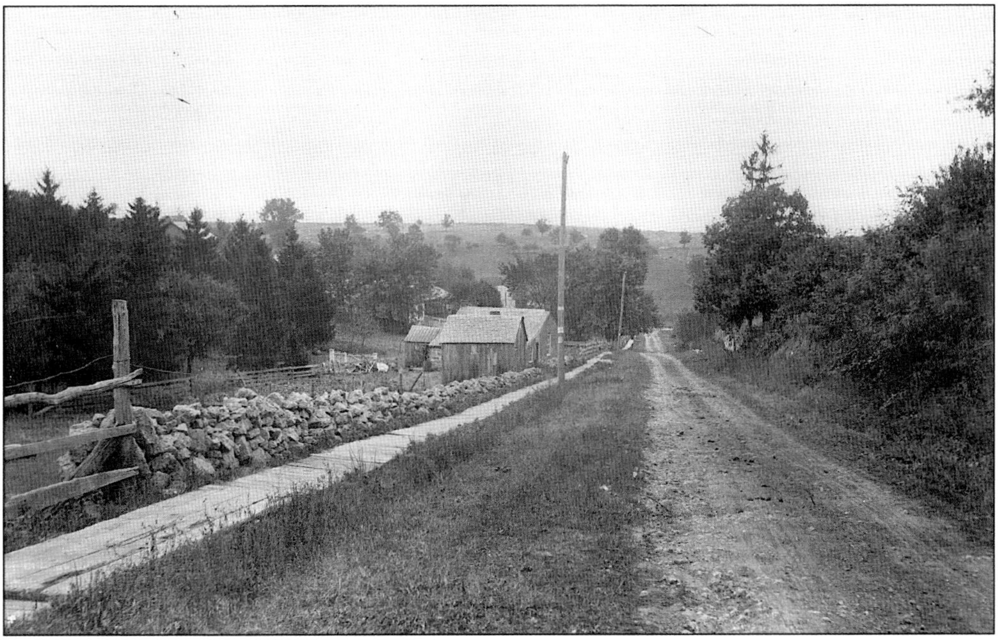

This view looking down Spruce Street shows a simple frame cottage, a couple of sheds, and a wooden sidewalk next to a stone wall continuing the entire length of the street. Pendarvis—Wisconsin State Historical Site—is located at the bottom of the street at the intersection with Shake Rag Street. In the background is Merry Christmas Hill, the site of early lead and zinc mines and the badger holes.

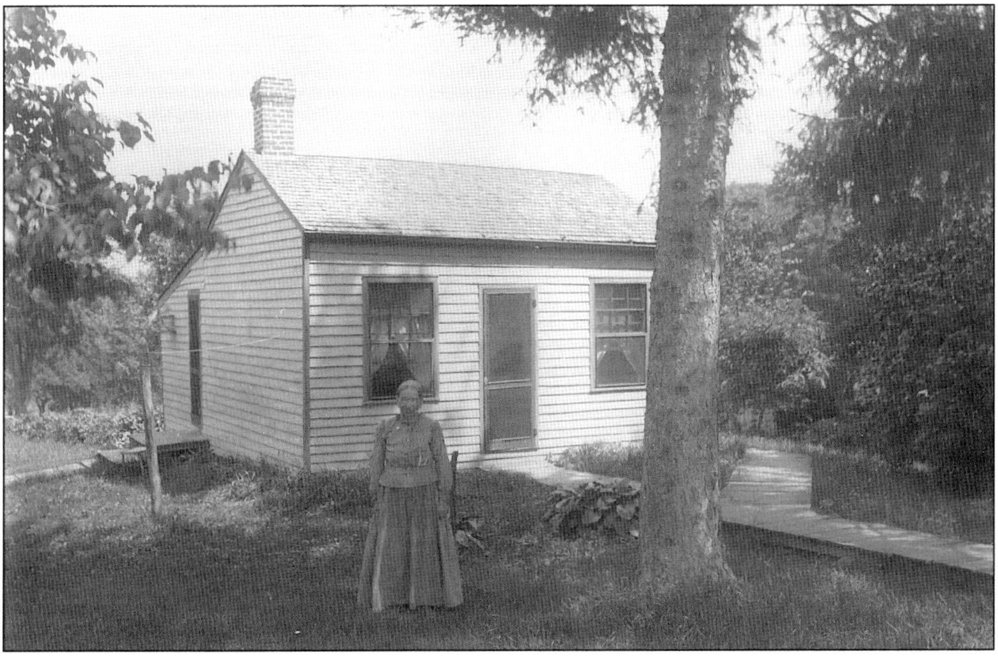

An early small, wooden-frame cottage in Mineral Point is pictured with an unidentified woman standing in front. The hosta growing beside the wooden walkway to the house are still favorite plants for landscaping in the town.

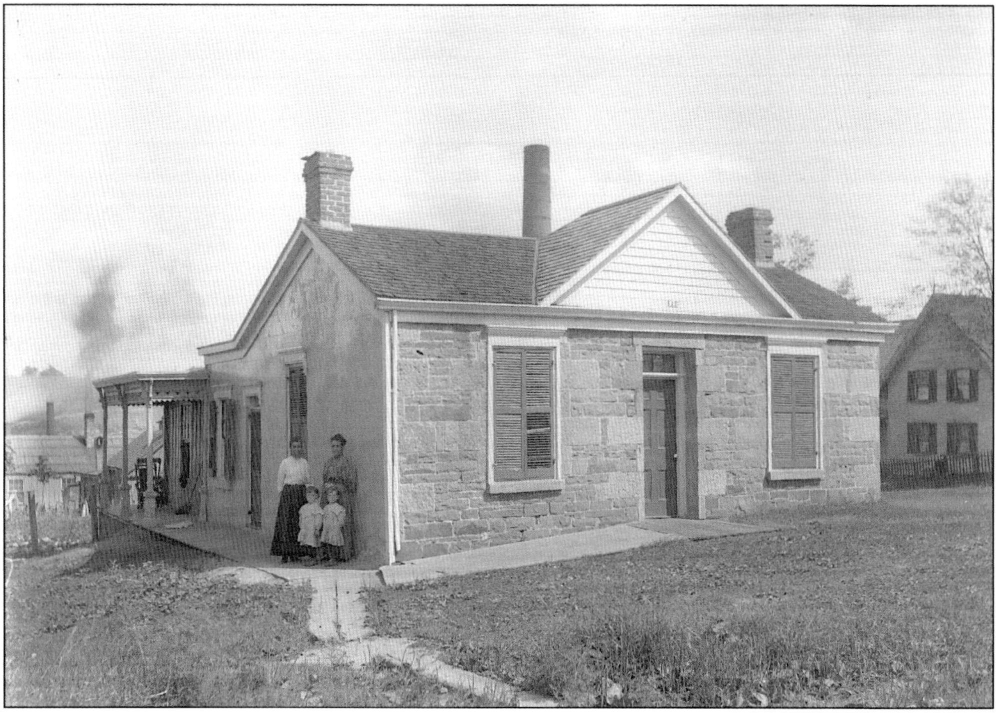

This more extensive, one-story limestone cottage demonstrates great attention to detail in the patterning when laying the stones of the front façade. Notice that there are three large stones symmetrically placed to each side of the doorway, two at each side of the windows, and again three at each side of the wall. At the rear is a porch with wooden decoration, and in the distance, the stacks and smoke of the zinc works.

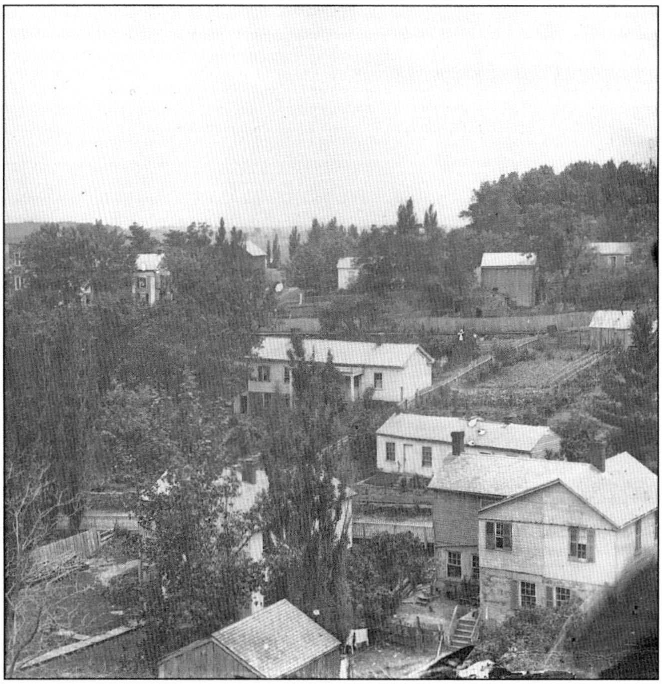

A view of the houses along Fountain Street is shown here. A number of trees, mostly fast-growing poplars, have been planted near the houses. Across the valley, however, essentially no trees are to be seen. In his logbook for May 21, 1837, the highly critical, visiting English geologist, George W. Featherstonhaugh (pronounced Fan-shaw), wrote that "not a leaf was to be seen on the few stunted trees here and there." At that time, all of the available wood had been harvested for firing the lead smelters, and the sulfurous fumes produced by this smelting had stunted whatever trees remained.

Two Mineral Point houses with gardens for ornamentals and vegetables are pictured here. On May 28, 1837, the never complimentary Featherstonhaugh recorded that "we had not tasted a morsel of fresh meat, or fish, or vegetables, since we had been here. There was not a garden in the place, and the population seemed quietly to have resigned itself to an everlasting and unvarying diet of coffee, rice, treacle and bread, and salt butter, morning, noon, and night, without any other variety than that of occasionally getting a different cup and saucer." Clearly this picture demonstrates that things had changed dramatically since Featherstonehaugh's visit.

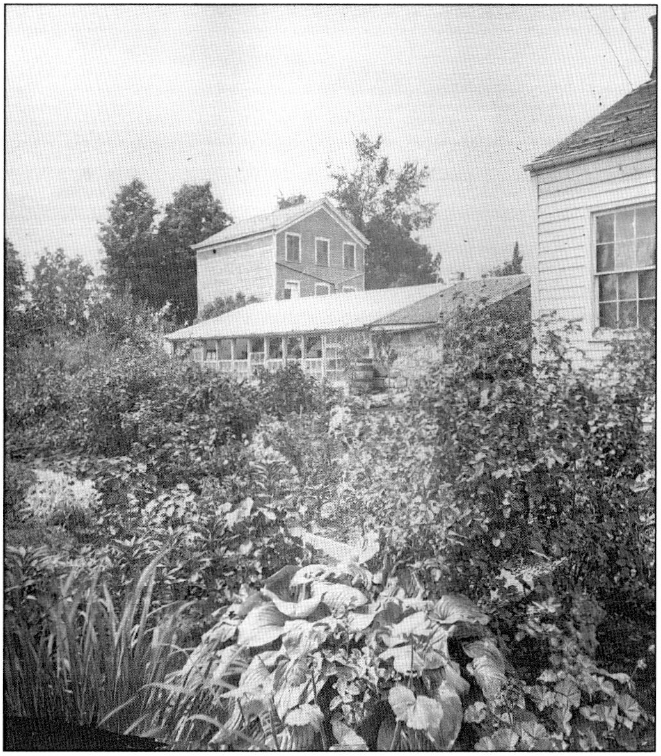

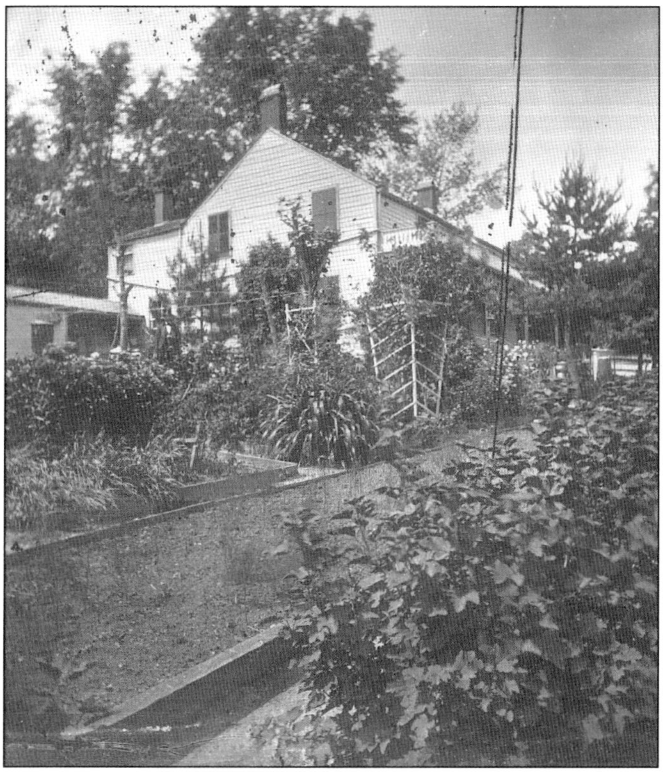

This is another Mineral Point house with its garden. The improvements since Featherstonhaugh's visit can be attributed to the arrival of miners such as the Cornish, who came with their families to establish themselves here permanently.

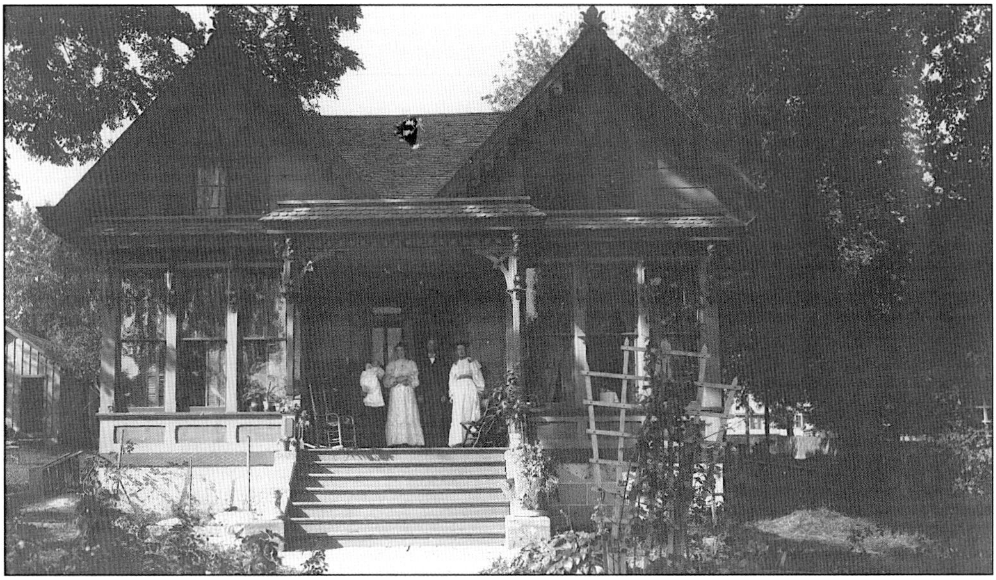

The William Lanyon house at 415 Madison Street is pictured. This house still stands, but all of the Gothic Revival decorative features, including the barge boards under the gable eaves, the pointed arch windows on the second story, and the brackets and dentals accenting the porch and eaves of the roof below the second-story windows have been removed, victims to the enthusiasm for modernization of the 1950s and 1960s.

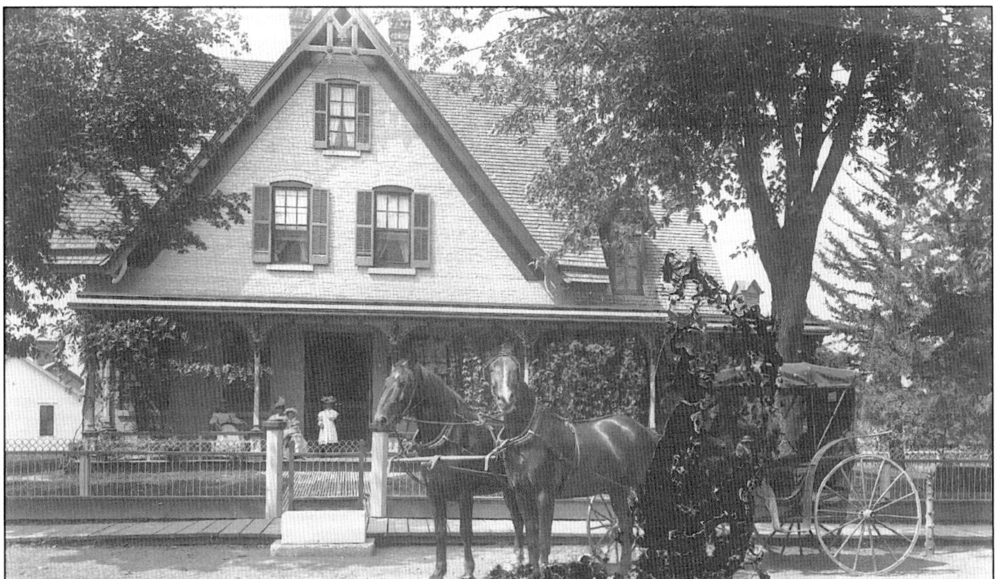

The original William A. Jones' house at 215 Ridge Street is pictured here. This house was torn down to build Jones's massive Colonial Revival-style house (1906–07), which now occupies the site. William was one of the three Jones brothers who bought up the interests in the Mineral Point Zinc Works in 1883. Graduating from Platteville Normal School (now University of Wisconsin—Platteville) in 1872, he served as principal of the Mineral Point High School, superintendent of schools for Iowa County, and in 1897, was appointed U.S. Commissioner of Indian Affairs by President McKinley and held that post for eight years.

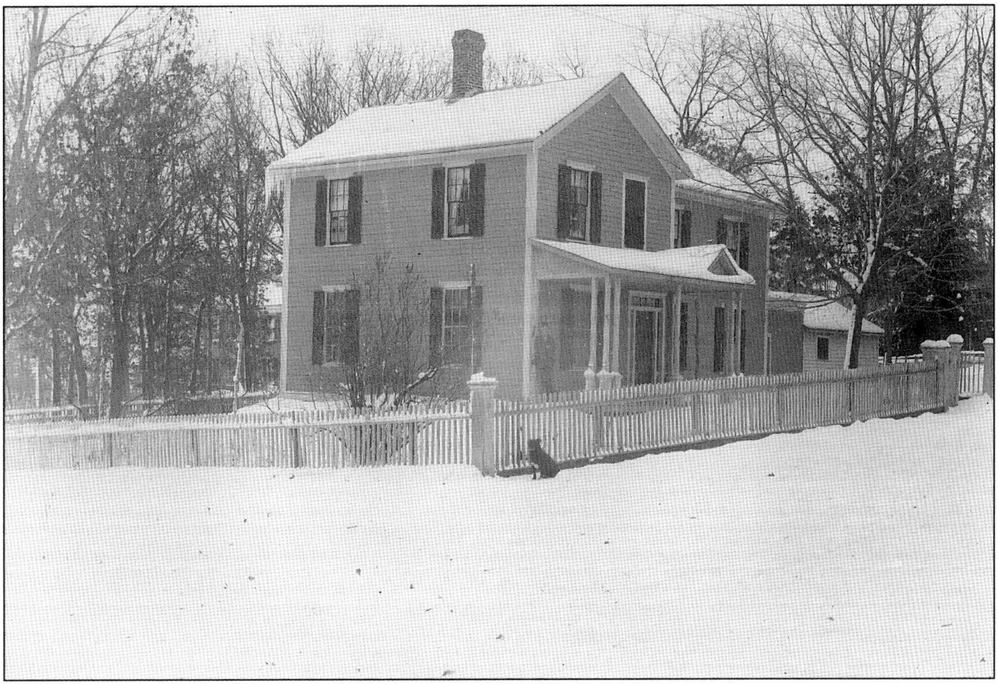

The Gale house at 404 South Iowa Street is depicted in a winter scene. The street has been left unplowed for the convenience of the passage of horse-drawn sleighs.

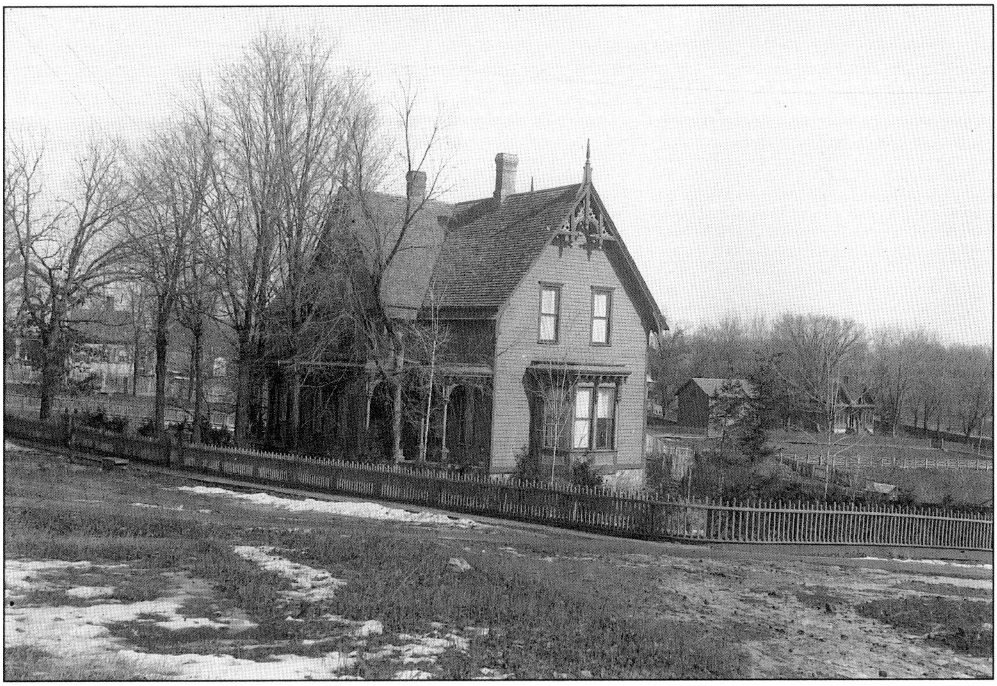

A Gothic Revival-style house on Park Street across from what is now known as Water Tower Park is pictured here. The steep roof and barge boards under the eaves characterize the style of this house, which, unfortunately, has since been torn down.

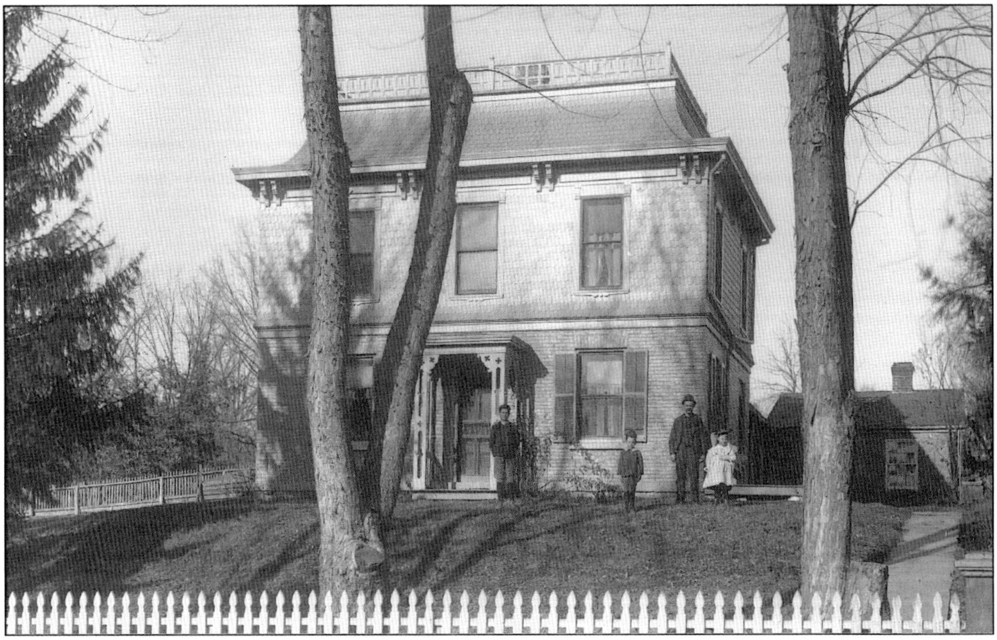

This handsome Second Empire-style house still stands at 329 Fifth Street. The mansard roof is the most conspicuous feature of the house, which has an unusual combination of fish-scale wooden shingles on the upper story and brick construction on the lower.

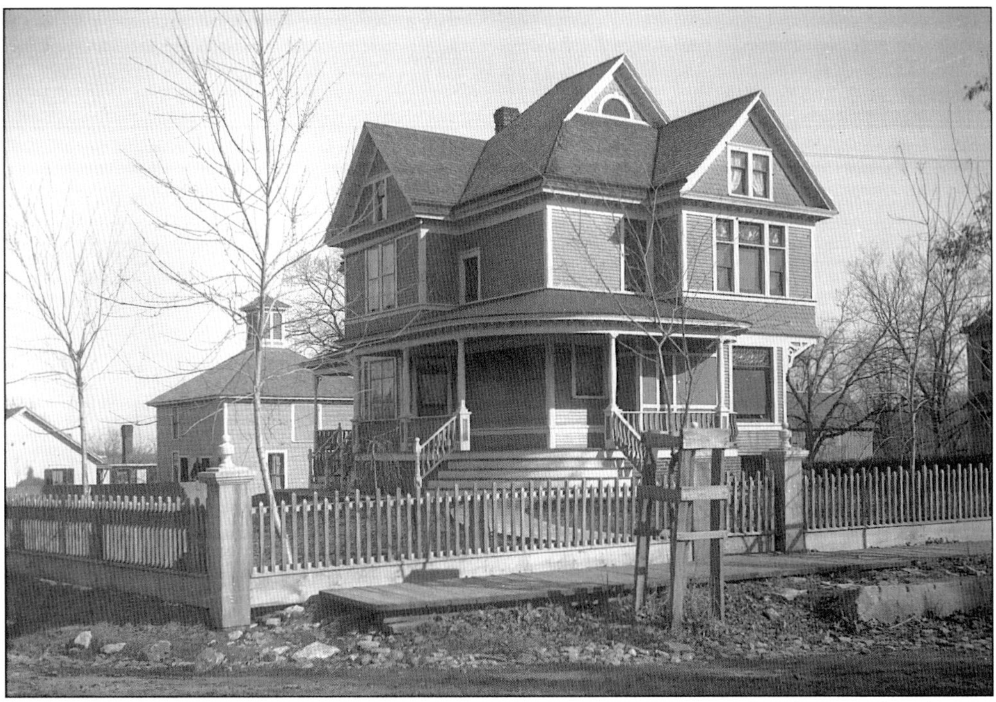

A Mineral Point Queen Anne-style house still stands at the corner of Ridge Road and Doty Street with its carriage house in the background. At the time of publication, the porch was being restored to again look the way it does in this photo. Note that trees have recently been planted between the wooden sidewalk and the dirt street.

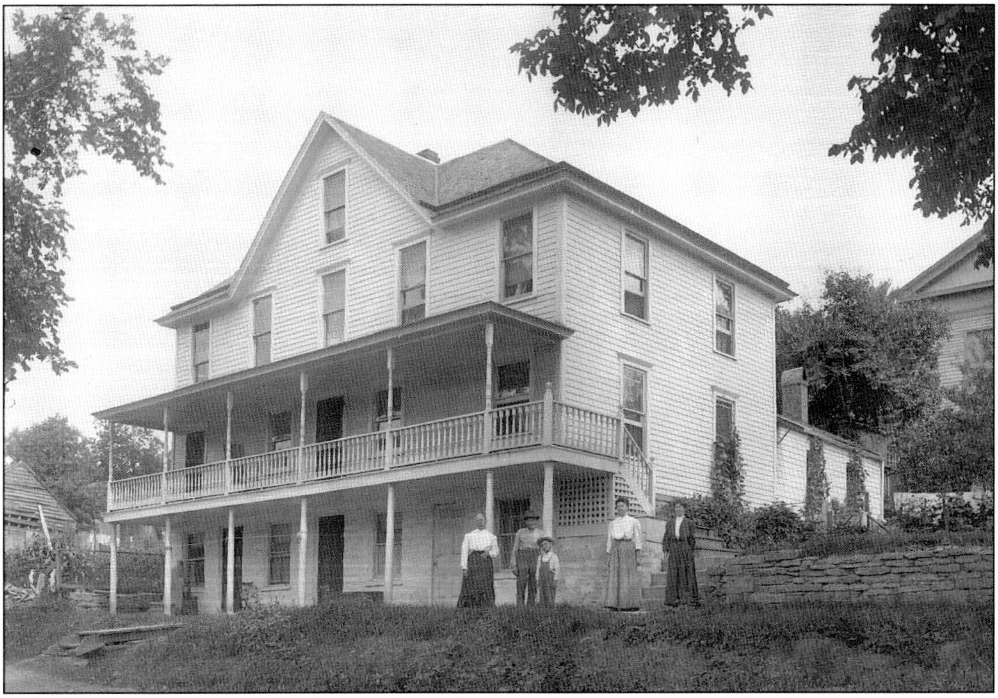

This house still stands with its expansive veranda on Fountain Street.

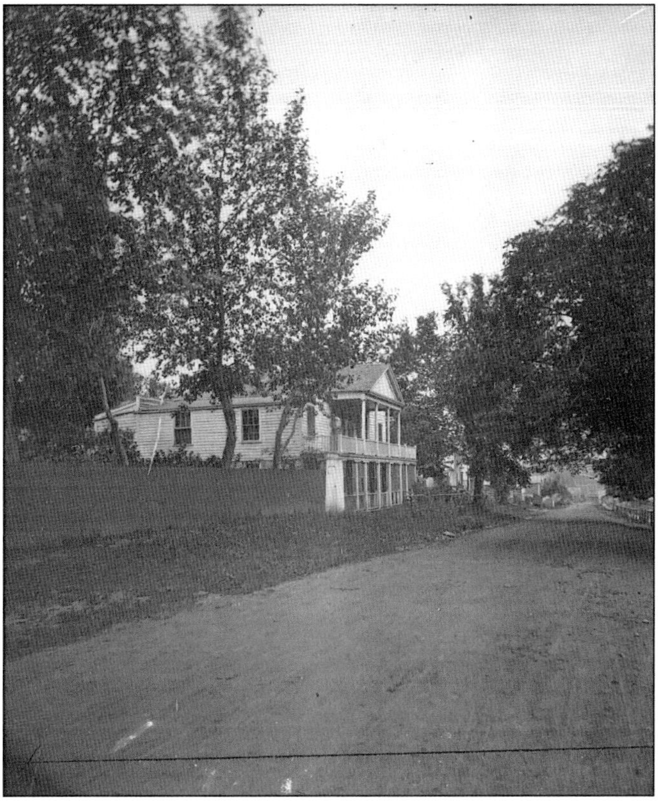

A side view of the house in the previous figure is shown looking down Fountain Street. To the extreme right in this photograph is Jerusalem Park, the site of Jerusalem spring. The spring and the park were named to celebrate the weekly procession led by Elder William Roberts, a preacher-miner, and the singing of the hymn, "Jerusalem, My Happy Home," which is thought to have begun as early as 1828.

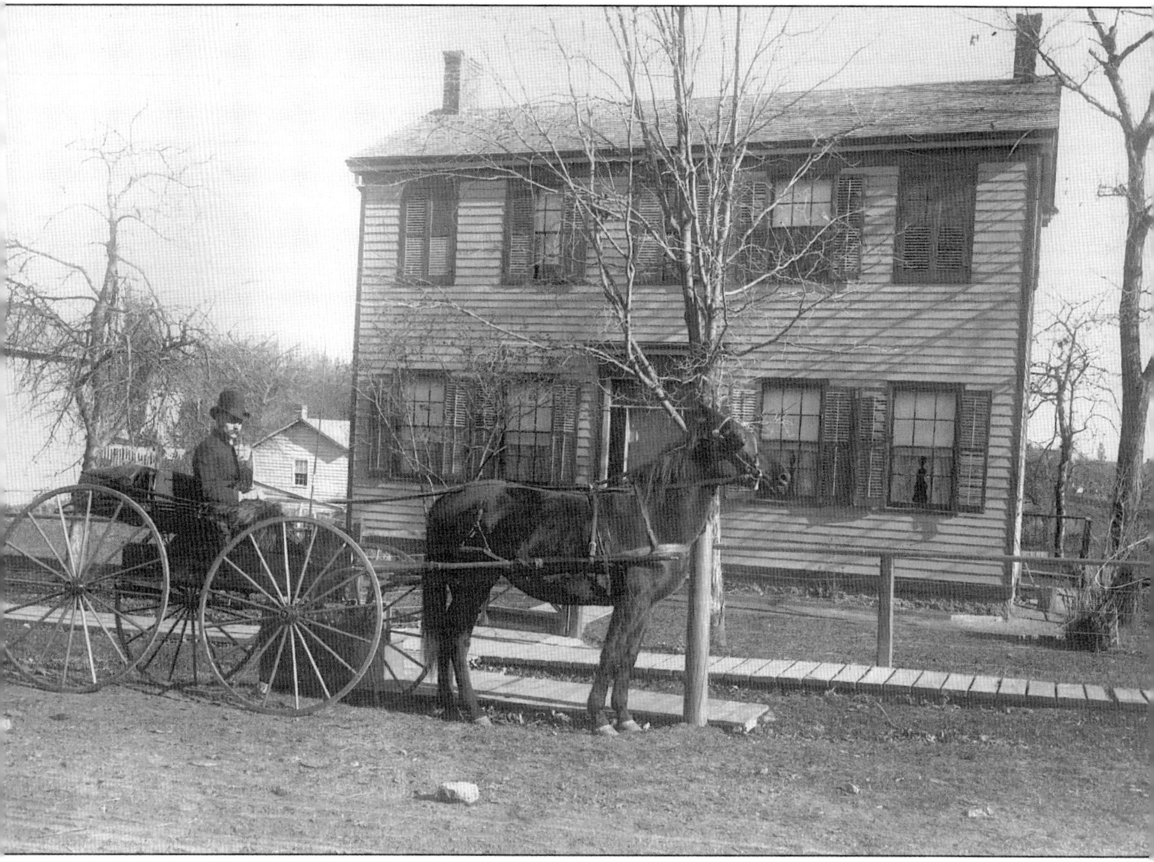

The derby and carriage identify this person as a man of some means. The front walk of the house has been extended with a hitching post to provide a means of entering or alighting from the carriage without stepping into the muddy street.

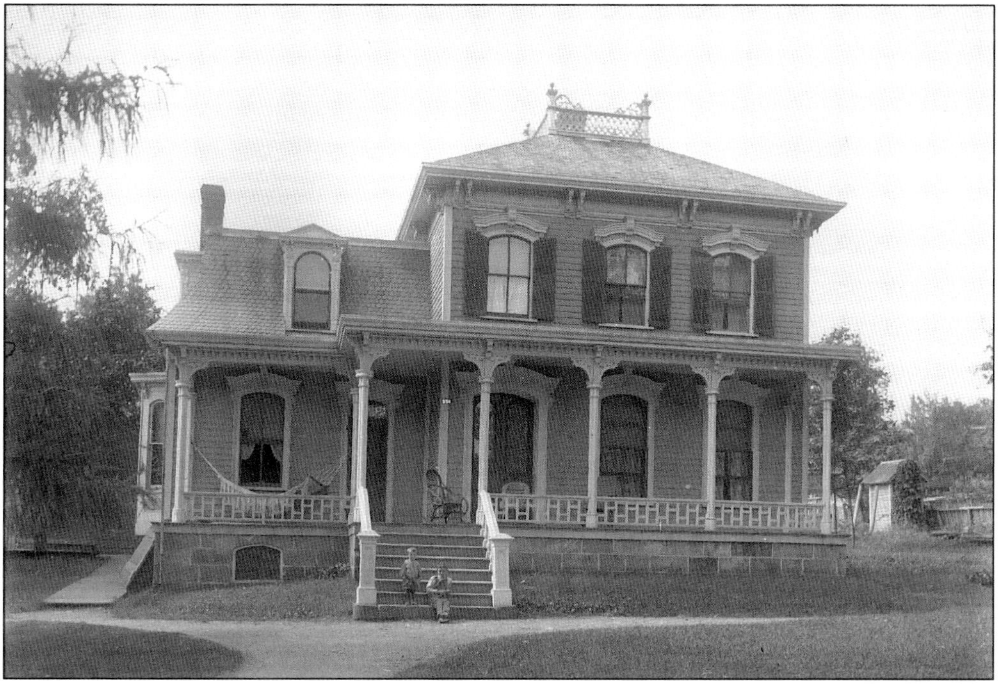

The James Brewer House at 526 Fountain Street is a marriage of two nineteenth-century architectural styles. The taller Italianate section at the right was built in the 1850s, and the smaller Second Empire addition dates to 1866. Brewer was born in Cornwall and came to southwestern Wisconsin in 1850 to be a farmer. Following the promise of gold, he went to California in 1852, returned to farm in Mineral Point in 1855, and became a merchant in 1865.

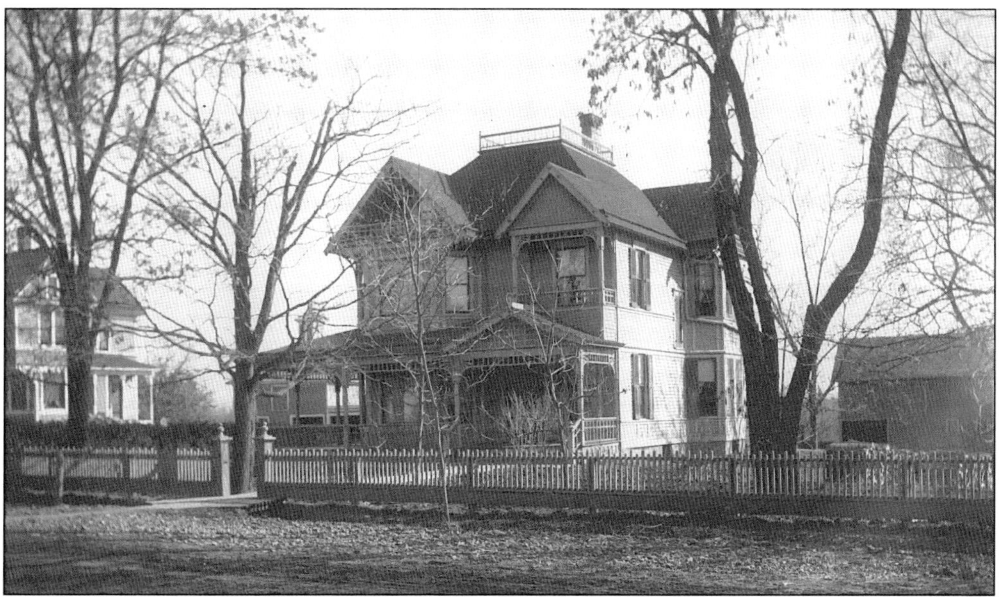

This house located at 310 Ridge Street is now Gorgen Funeral Home. Ridge Street currently serves as U.S. Highway 151, carrying heavy truck and car traffic as compared to the tranquil scene here. However, a planned bypass road will return Ridge Street to a vestige of its former serenity.

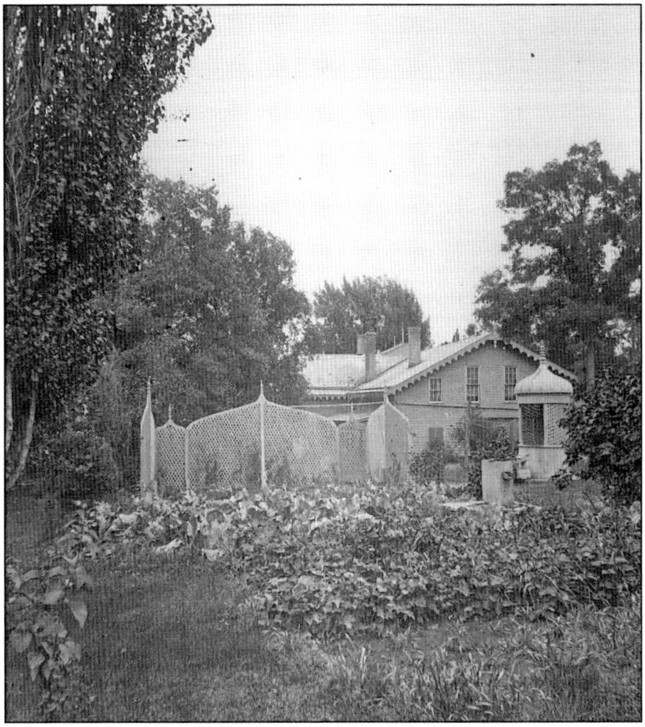

Once the home of William T. Henry, a prosperous banker, the lovely place with its attractive garden and gazebo on South Iowa Street is no longer standing.

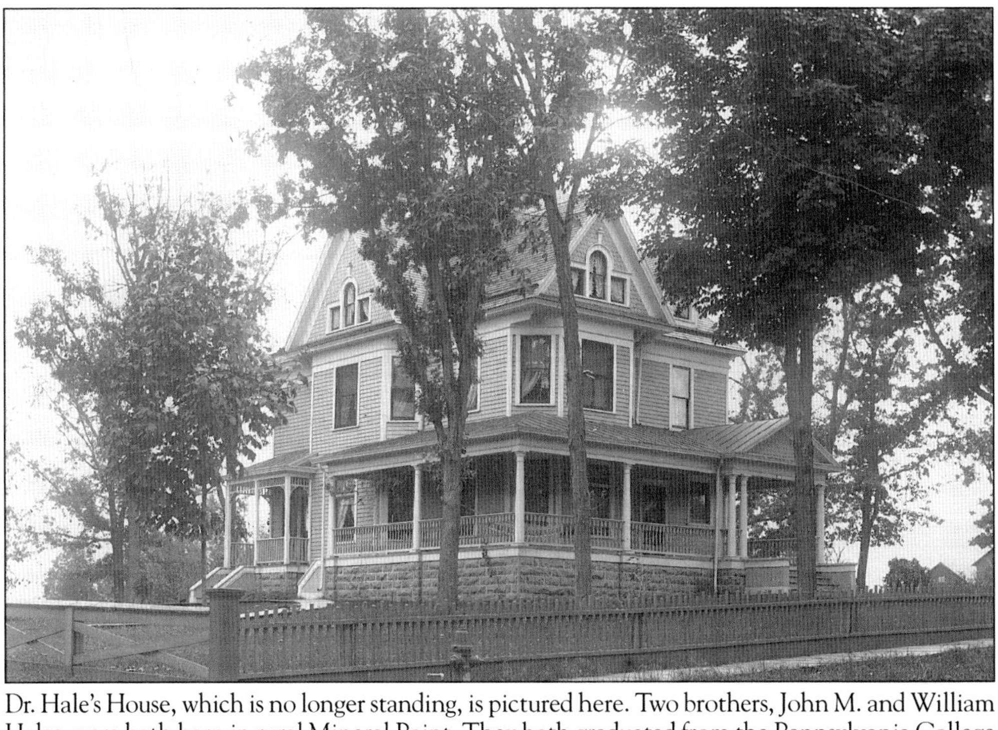

Dr. Hale's House, which is no longer standing, is pictured here. Two brothers, John M. and William Hales, were both born in rural Mineral Point. They both graduated from the Pennsylvania College of Dental Surgery in Philadelphia and practiced together in town for a time.

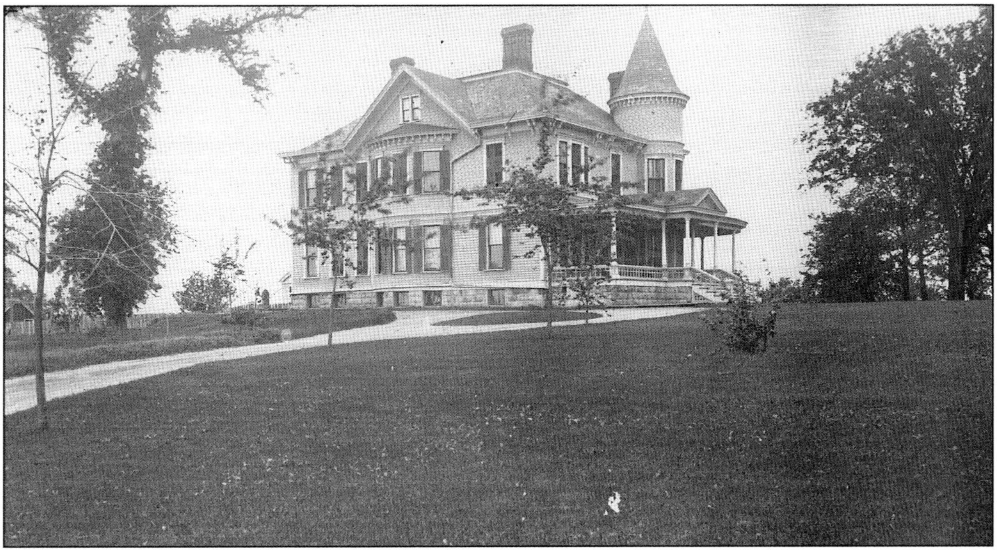

This is the Ross house on Ridge Street. The spectacular siting of this grand Queen Anne-style home matched the prominence and wealth of the Ross family, who had diversified interests in mines, smelters, stock farms, property, politics, and railroads; John J. Ross was on the board of directors of the Mineral Point Railroad. This site is now occupied by the Dairyland Motel.

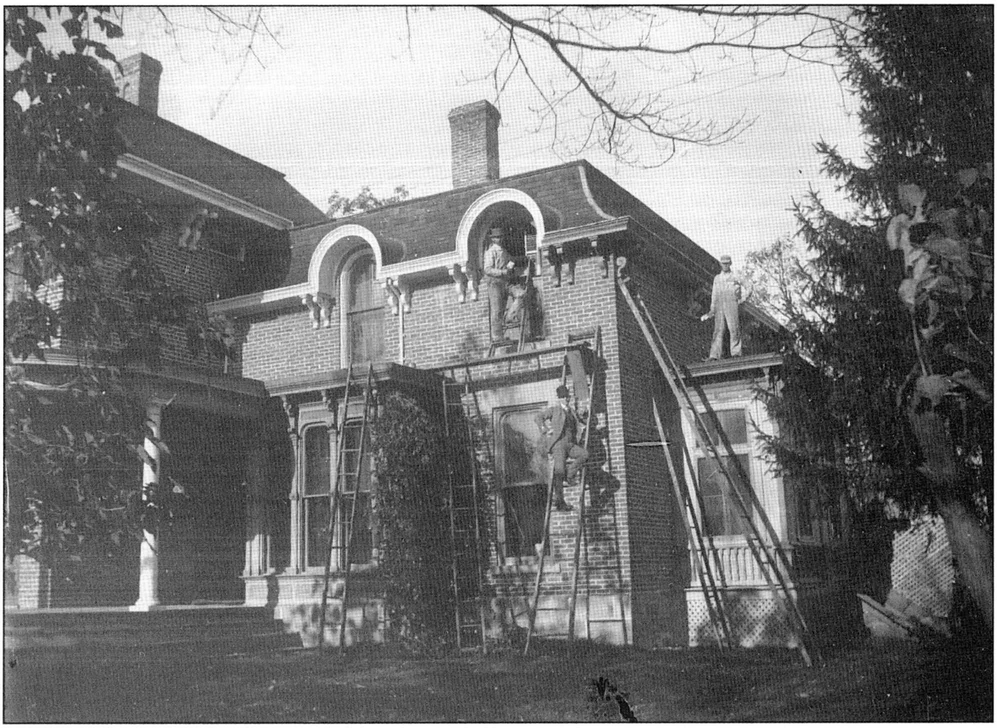

The Alexander Wilson House at 110 Dodge Street was constructed in 1868 in the Italianate style. Workers are pictured maintaining the lower and later Second Empire section of this house. Born in New York State, Wilson came to Mineral Point in 1855 to practice law and teach school. He then acted as the district attorney, the superintendent of schools, and from 1878–82 the attorney general for the State of Wisconsin.

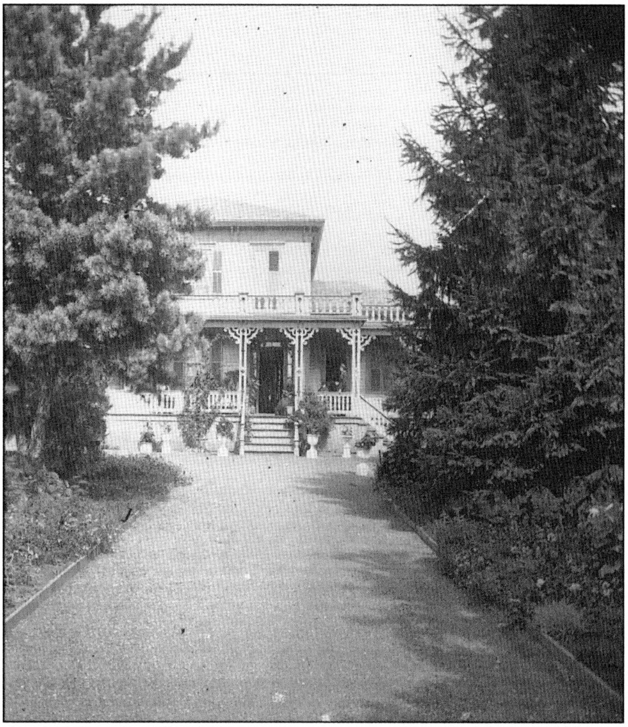

This Italianate-style house, which is no longer standing, has a particularly handsome drive and verandah.

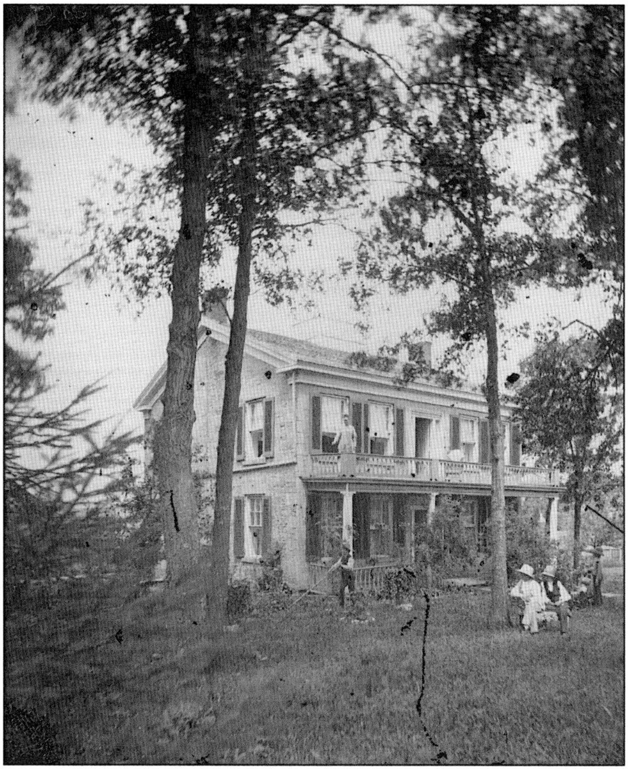

The Henry Plowman house at 115 Ridge Street was built in 1855. Made of local limestone, the two-story porch has since been removed. Plowman came to Mineral Point in the 1830s from Pennsylvania and established his newspaper, the *Miners Free Press*, with Henry B. Welsh.

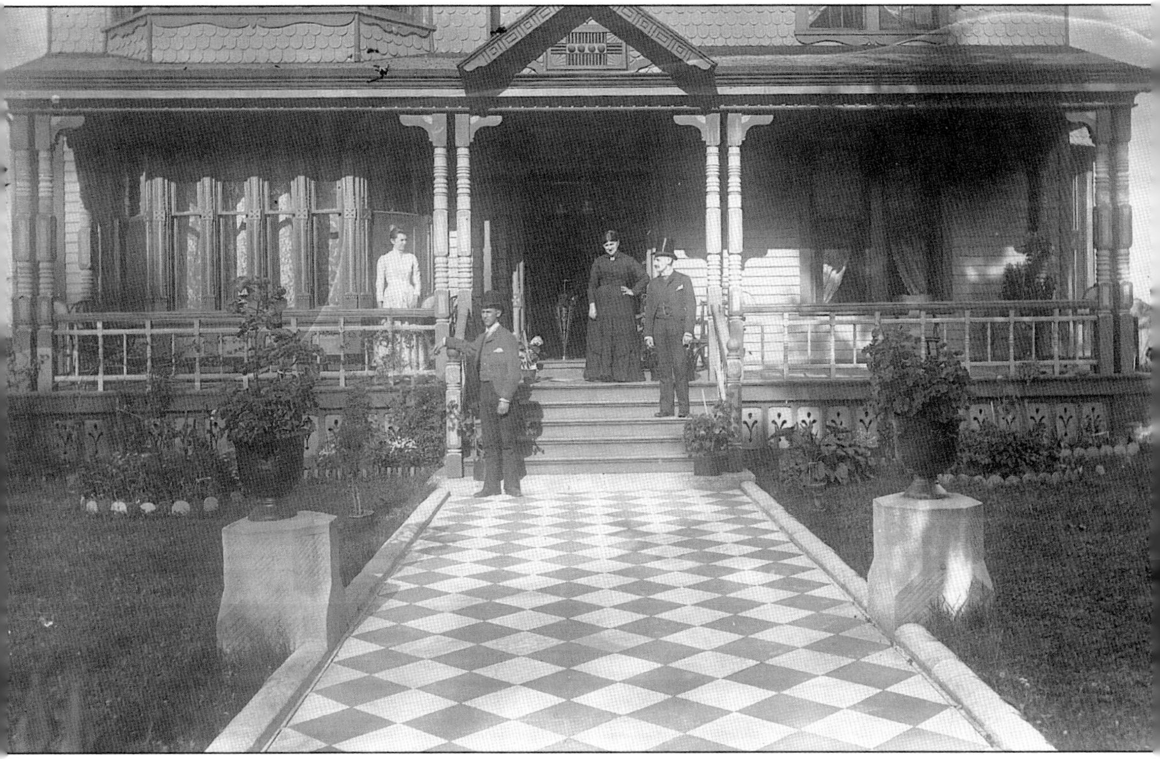

Built around 1883, the Joseph Deller House at 216 Iowa Street is a large and impressive Queen Anne-style structure. The checkered front walk, which is still present, is unique in Mineral Point.

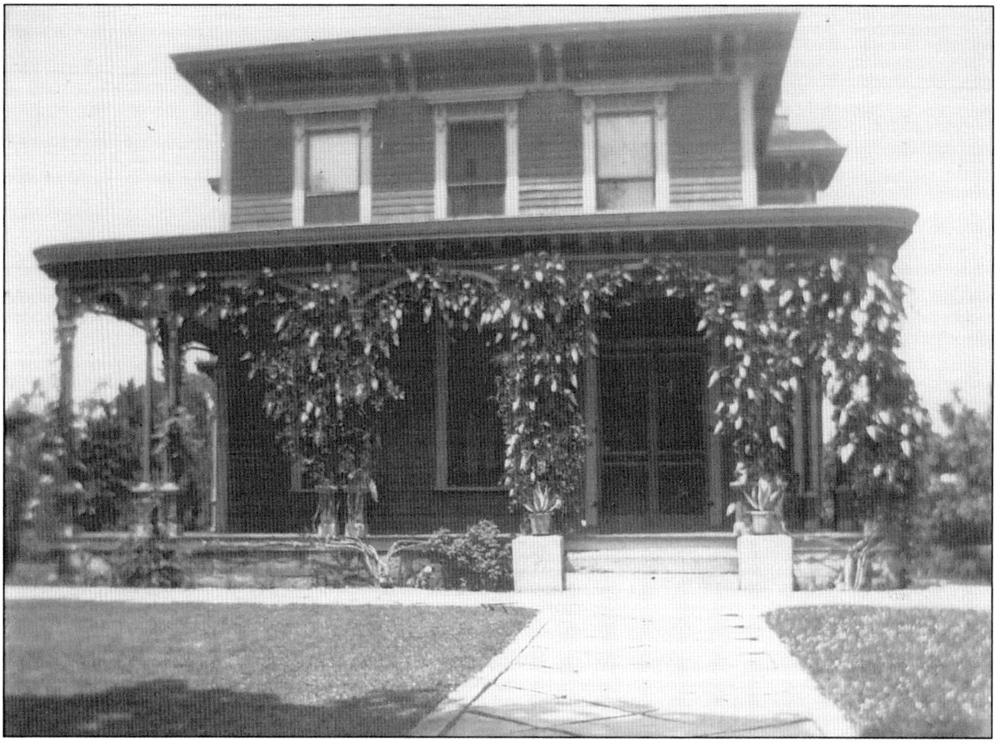

The John Gray house at 615 Maiden Street was constructed in 1855. Gray was the partner of Joseph Gundry in their very successful dry goods store, Gundry and Gray. Gray came to Mineral Point from Cornwall in 1844, and partnered with Gundry in 1850. The building formerly occupied by Gundry and Gray's store at 215 High Street is now the site of a delicatessen by the same name.

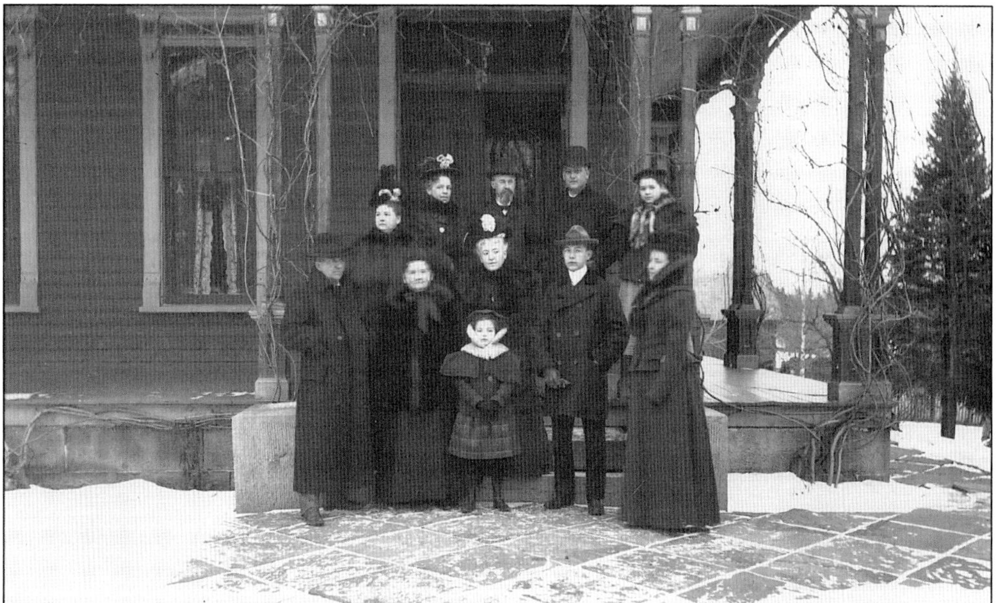

This scene in front of the Gray house was taken during Christmas of 1908.

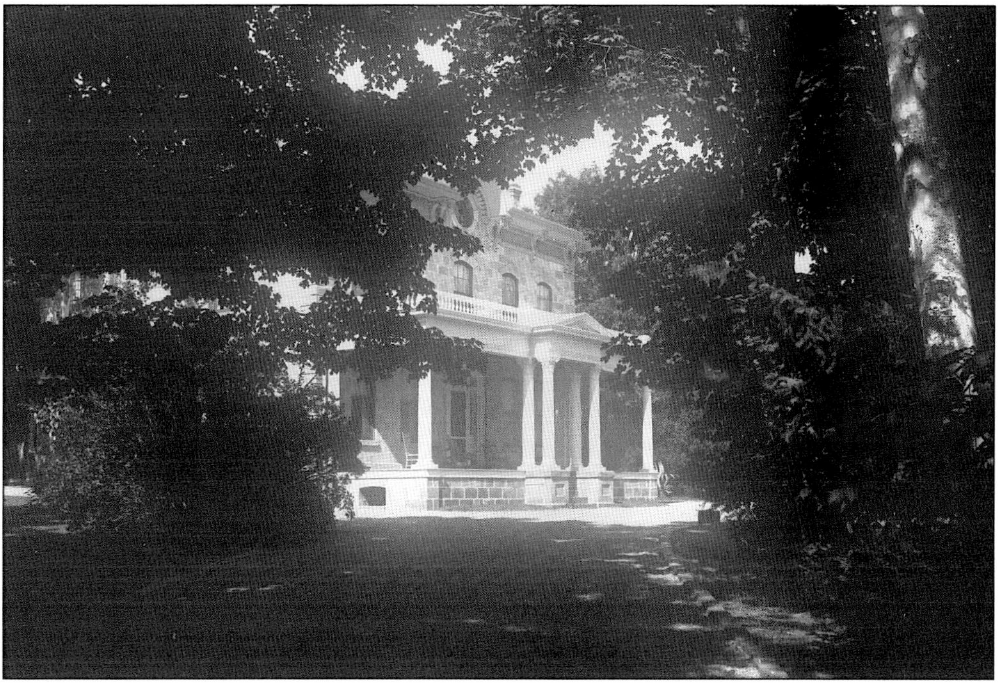

The Joseph Gundry estate, Orchard Lawn, included a house built in 1868, and extensive landscaped areas. Gundry came to Mineral Point from Cornwall in 1845, and made his fortune in land speculation, banking, mining, and especially in his dry goods business with John Gray. This house was saved from the wrecker's ball in 1939 by the fledgling Mineral Point Historical Society, which has maintained it as a museum. A recent matching grant to the society will allow for complete renovation of the building and expansion of its activities.

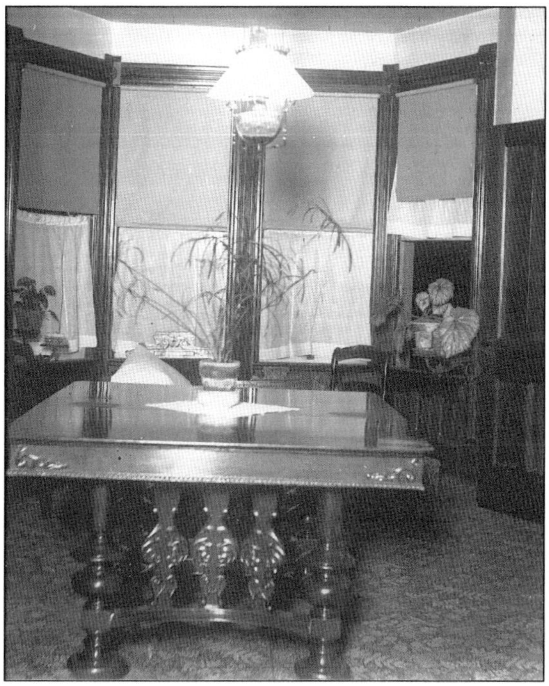

The interior of a Mineral Point home is pictured here. A handsome dining table is shown set in a window bay. Note the kerosene lamp above the table, with the heat shield above the lamp chimney and below the ball to prevent the hot vapors from scorching the ceiling.

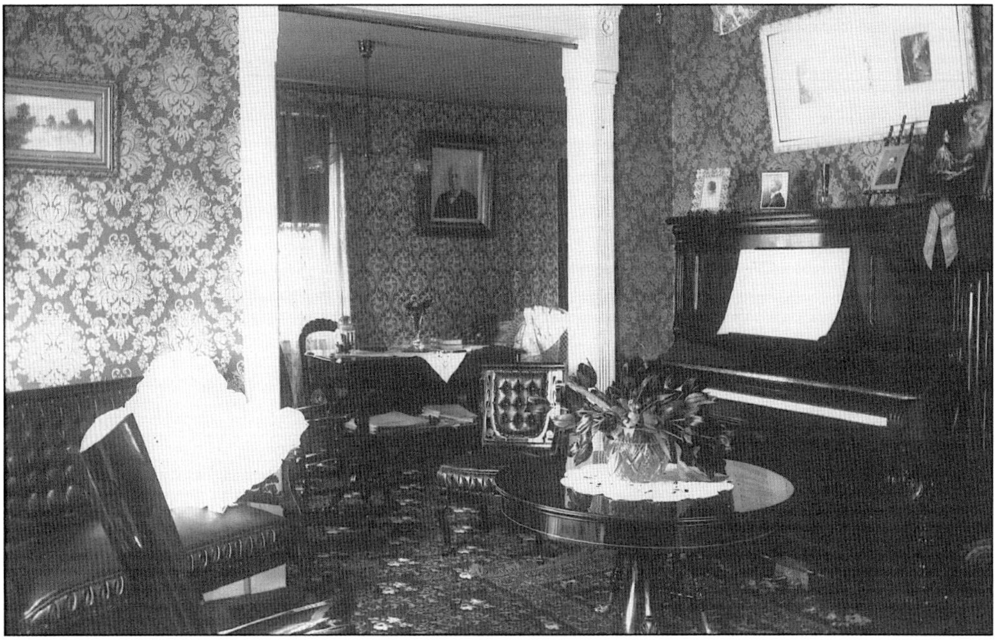

This is another interior view with flamboyant Victorian wallpaper and rugs. The presence of the piano is a reminder of the nature of home entertainment before radio, television, and players for records, tapes, and disks.

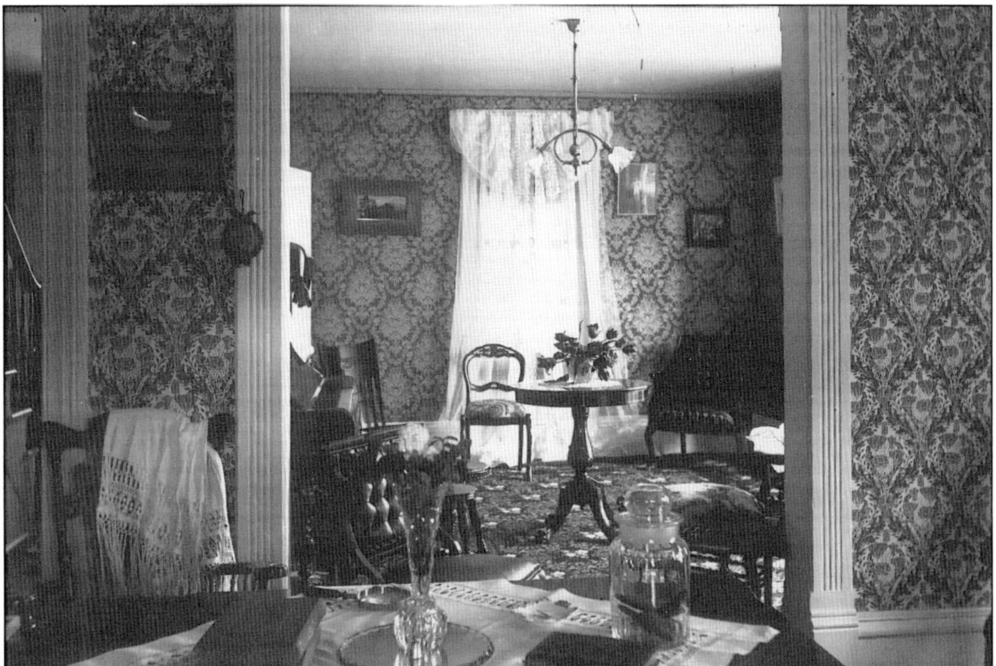

This is another interior view of the same house in the previous figure, but looking in the opposite direction. Here, electricity rather than kerosene is providing illumination. Although the first electric service was at the Mineral Point Zinc Company in 1891, the owners soon contracted to provide street lighting for the city.

Three

THE COMMERCIAL DISTRICT
HIGH AND COMMERCE STREETS

Following in the footsteps of the miners of the 1820s came those interested in trading and selling goods. At first, miners likely brought most of their own provisions for their seasonal diggings, often purchased at a larger center such as Galena, Illinois. Rather than interrupting their mining and risking the loss of a productive claim, they were soon able to purchase goods from enterprising men such as Erasmus Wright, John D. Ansley, and John F. O'Neill, who were all providing supplies by 1829. Soon Cornish miners were arriving with their families, the town was expanding, and the opportunities for commerce grew rapidly.

Not surprisingly, the commercial district originated near the hills where the miners worked and lived. The street running north and south at the base of the hills is Commerce Street, and the street running up the hill to the west is High Street, similar to England.

The fluctuating success of the commercial district followed the general prosperity of the town. In 1837, the estimated population of Mineral Point reached approximately one thousand, and by 1839 the town had three hotels, a bank, and a post office to add to the commercial ventures.

According to the 1859 Directory of the City of Mineral Point prepared by T.S. Allen in 1859, Mineral Point's population, including both the city and the town, soared to 5,800, making it larger than Chicago and Milwaukee. This publication also reports that Mineral Point was thriving with seventeen dry goods and grocery stores, nine boot and shoe stores, three harness stores, five wagon shops, two jewelry stores, one book and periodical depot, three hardware stores, and two furniture establishments. In addition, the town boasted two newspapers—the *Mineral Point Tribune* (est. 1847), which is still in existence as the *Democrat Tribune*, and the *Home Intelligencer* (est. 1859)—and one bank. There were also several hotels, and all of these buildings survive. These include the United State Hotel of 1853 (267 High Street), the Mineral Point Hotel which was often called the Walker House (1 Water Street) and opened in anticipation of the coming of the railroad in 1857, and the Globe Hotel (225–227 Commerce Street) of 1868 with an addition in 1876.

After the waning of the zinc industry after World War I and the hardships of the Depression in the 1930s, the commercial district thrives once again. It is now occupied by offices, numerous restaurants, and stores such as a pharmacy and a hardware store as well as a large selection of artists' galleries and antique stores.

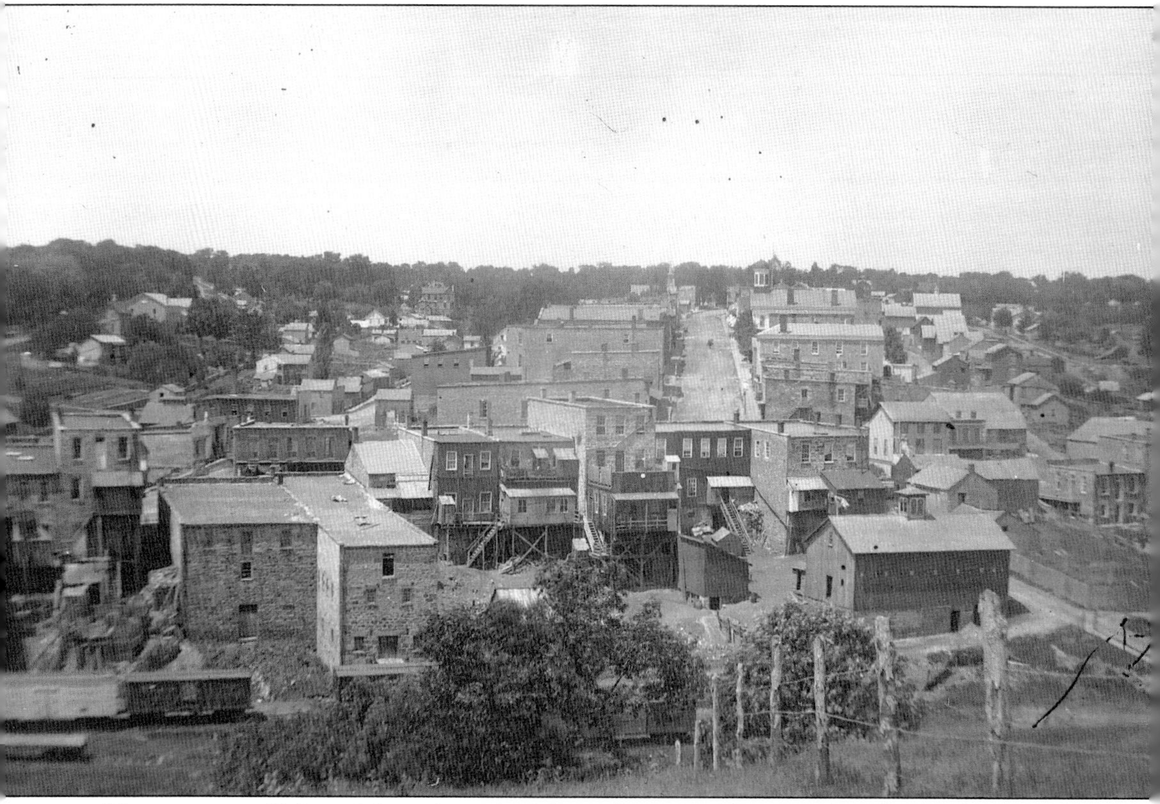

This is a view of Mineral Point from the hills to the east of the city where lead was first mined. The commercial district of Mineral Point started near this area and still continues along High and Commerce Streets. This photo looks up High Street. In the distance about halfway up the hill on the right side is the cupola of the former Iowa County courthouse completed in 1844, and at the top on the left is the steeple of the Presbyterian Church (both no longer standing). Commerce Street forms a "T" with High Street, running across the foreground of this photograph.

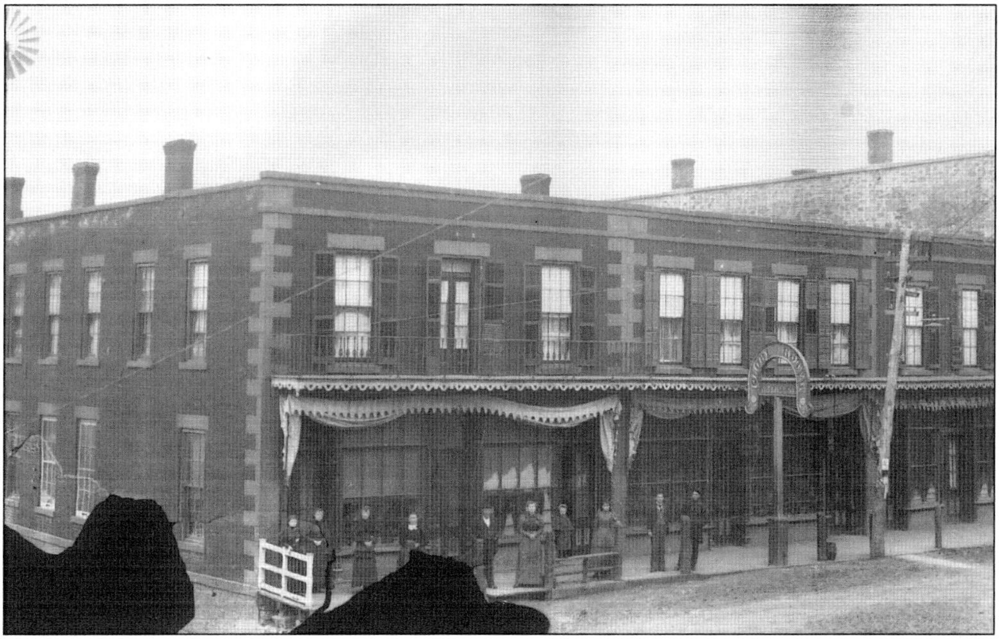

The buildings that once comprised the Globe Hotel still remain at 223–227 Commerce Street and now serve as the Mineral Point Clinic and Bruce Howdle's pottery studio. In 1868, Alfred Jenkin's Globe Hotel replaced an earlier hotel at #227. Purchasing the property in 1876, Nick Schillin added #225. In 1877–78, a meat market was built at #223, which was later used for the Globe Hotel Office and then the saloon. William McKinley, 26th president of the United States, visited the Globe Hotel in 1869. (From the private collection of Joyce P. Schaffer.)

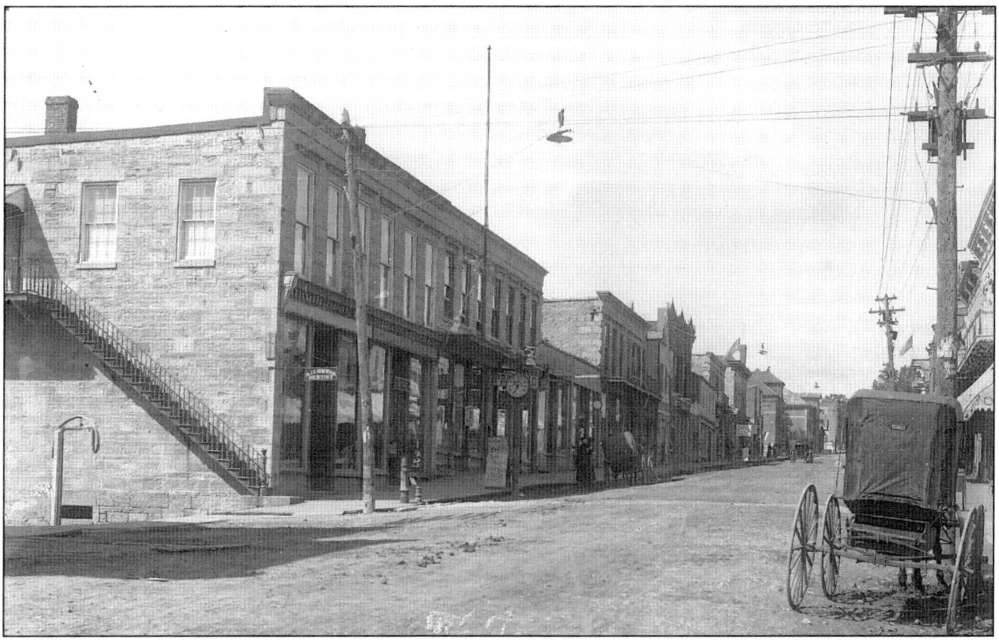

This view is looking up High Street from the corner of Chestnut Street. On the left is the office of Dr. C.G. Hubenthal, one of the several dentists practicing in Mineral Point. The building currently is part of the Ben Franklin Store.

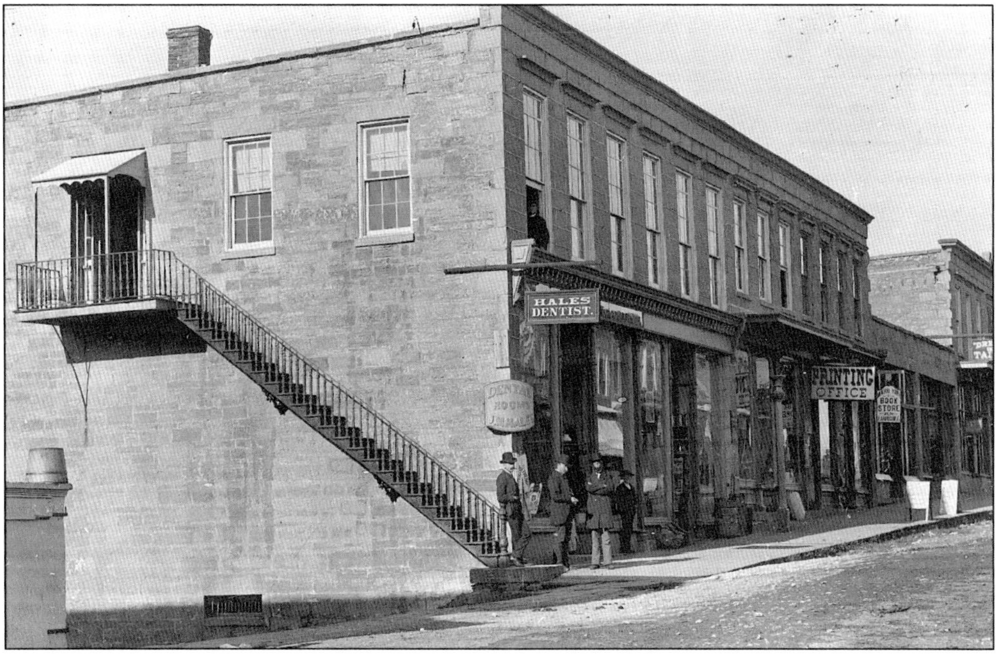

This photo is a closeup of the same corner building at High and Chestnut Streets. However, the dentist practicing is now one of the Hales Brothers who were both born in rural Mineral Point and both graduated from the Pennsylvania College of Dental Surgery in Philadelphia. They also both returned to Mineral Point where they practiced together until 1888. Dr. John M. Hales died at age 35 in Milwaukee in 1893. His brother, Dr. W.H. Hales, continued to live and practice in Mineral Point and died in 1935. (From the private collection of Joyce P. Schaffer.)

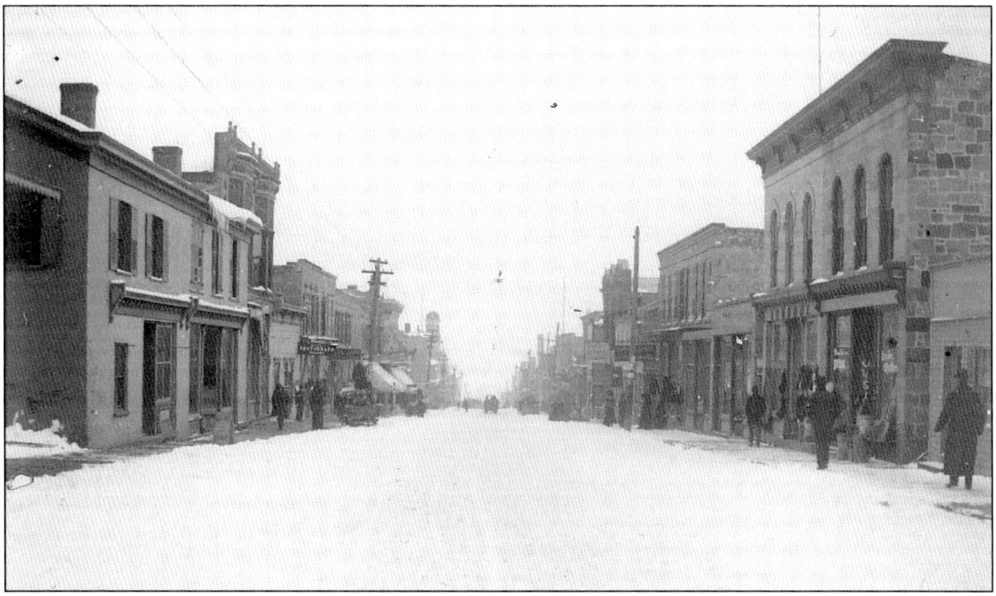

This image is looking down High Street in winter from a point close to the corner of Henry Street. The wooden sidewalks have been cleared for pedestrians, but the snow has been left on the street to accommodate horse-drawn sleighs.

High Street is decorated for the Fourth of July in this photo. In Mineral Point, this is a double celebration—in addition to the national holiday, the town also celebrates Territory Days when Colonel Henry Dodge was sworn in as the first governor of the new Territory of Wisconsin on July 4, 1836. Festivities now begin early with a road race, a parade down High Street, a chicken barbecue at the American Legion, a band concert and ice cream social, and conclude with fireworks.

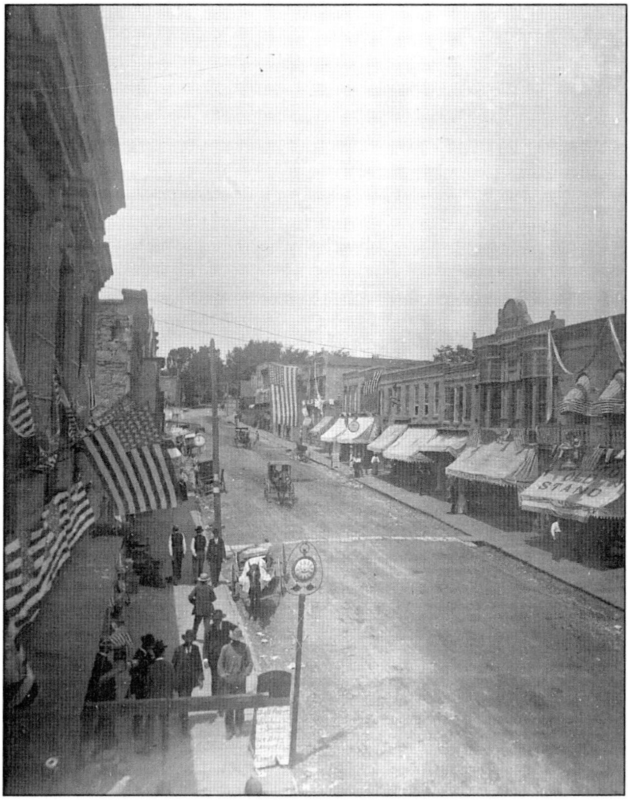

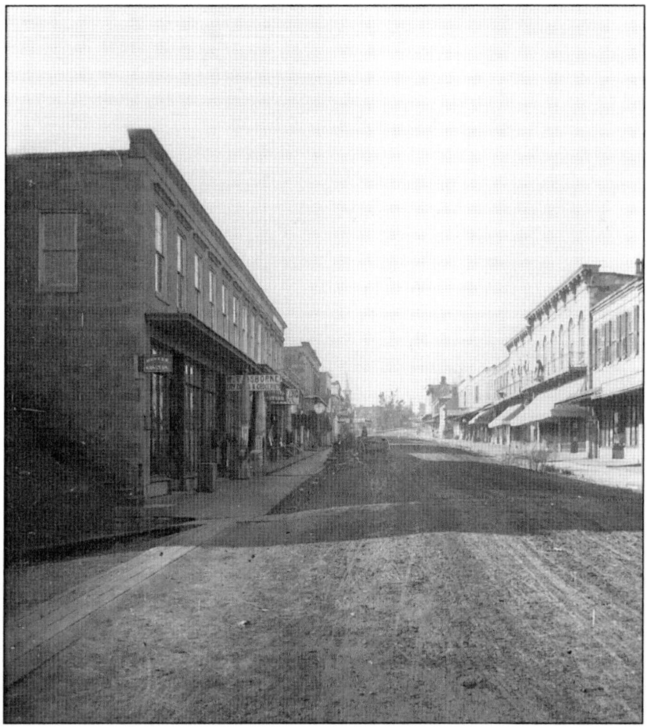

An almost deserted High Street as viewed from the corner of Chestnut Street is pictured here. Clearly visible are the wooden sidewalks for pedestrians and the packed dirt road suitable for horses and wagons.

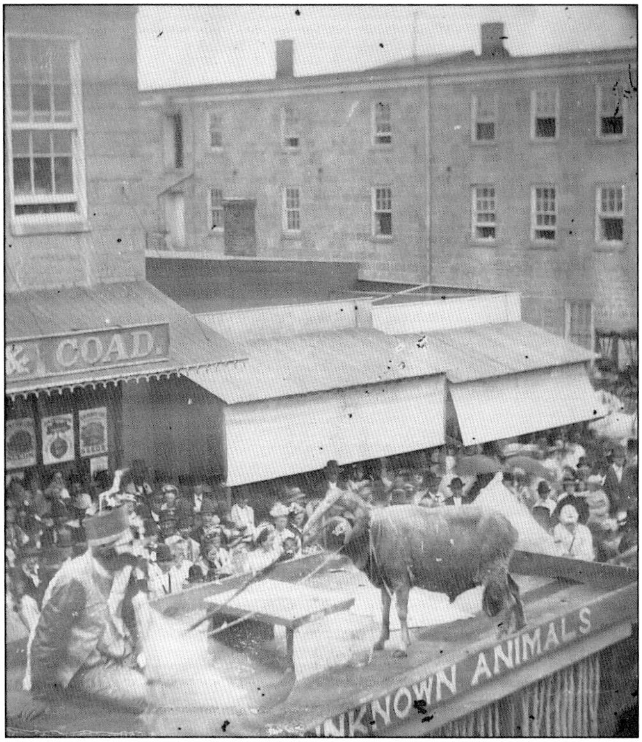

Pictured here is a circus parade on High Street with a member of the circus and an "unknown animal" on the top of a circus wagon. Circuses were an important, occasional part of life in small town America. The circus would host a parade to attract attention, put up tents, present a show, and leave for the next town after one or two performances. One of the earliest advertisements for a circus in Mineral Point is for the "Raymond and Company's Mammoth Menagerie" from 1848, indicating that unusual animals were a popular feature for many years.

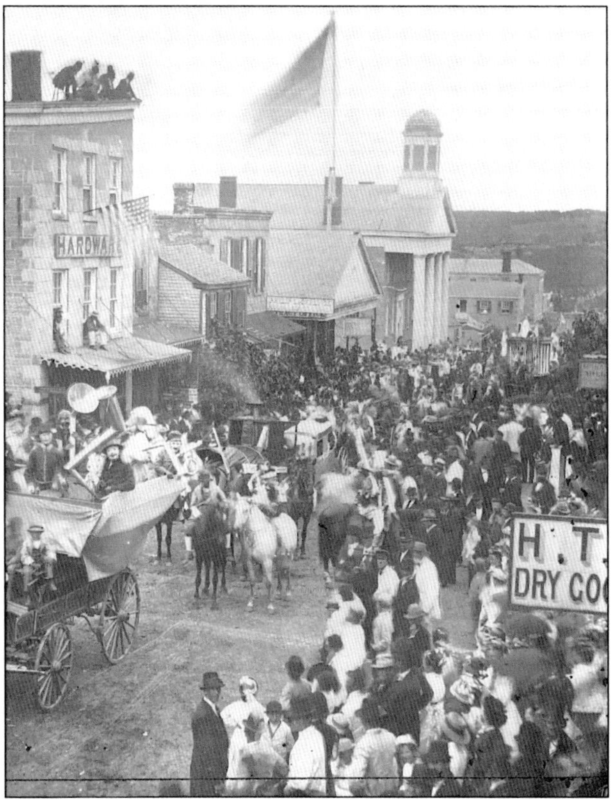

This is another view of the circus parade on High Street, which is attracting a large crowd of people. Some of the viewers have taken a precarious perch on the roof of the hardware store in order to see better.

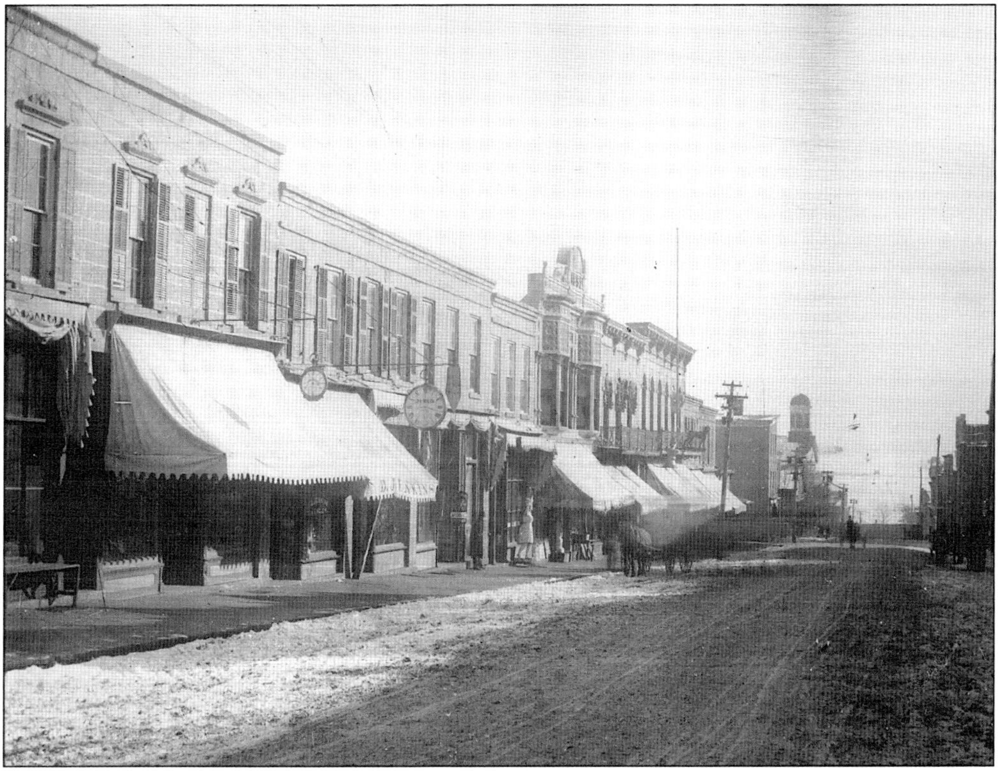

This view is looking down High Street on a late winter day with the street covered partly with snow and partly with mud.

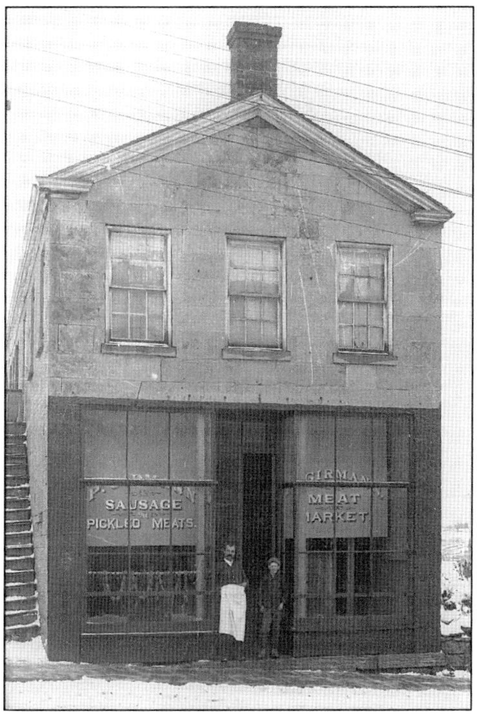

Girmann's Meat Market on Commerce Street is advertising meat, sausage, and pickled meats.

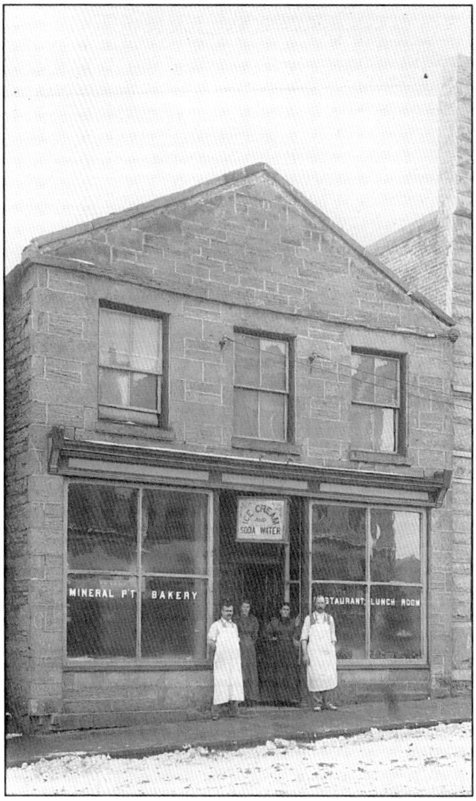

The Mineral Point Bakery included a restaurant and featured ice cream.

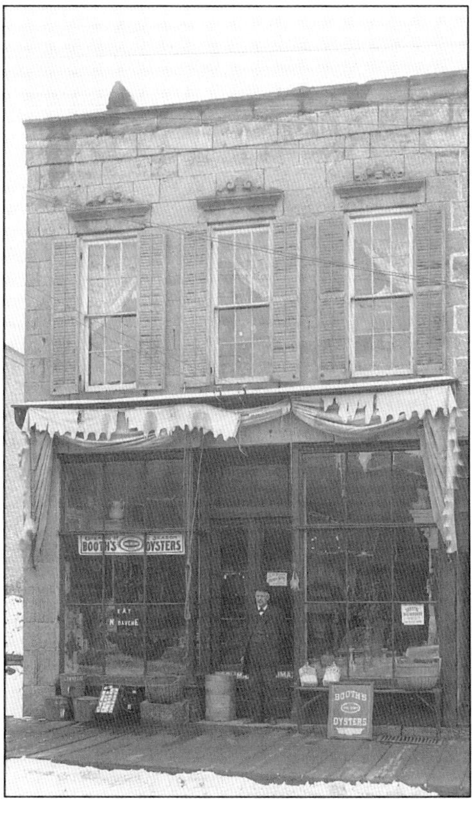

This grocery store also sold household necessities such as the "crystal washboards" advertised in the window. Oysters appear to have been a popular commodity in Mineral Point and were sold at a number of groceries in the town.

This store on High Street is fronted by the traditional symbol of a cigar store, a so-called wooden Indian.

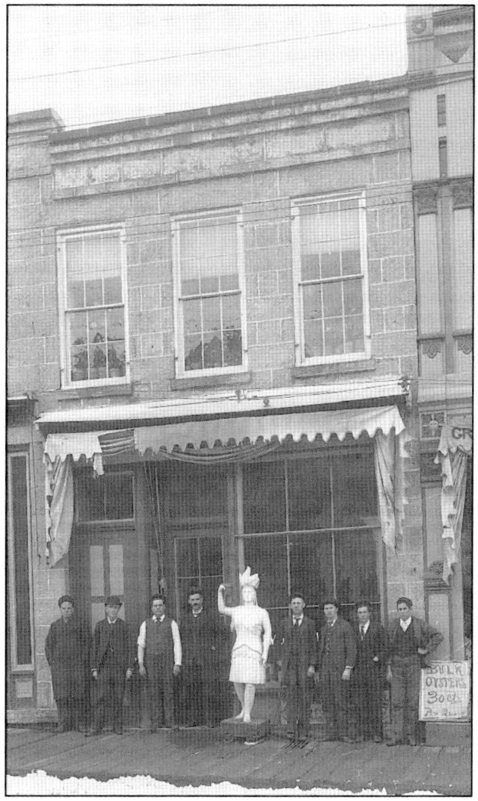

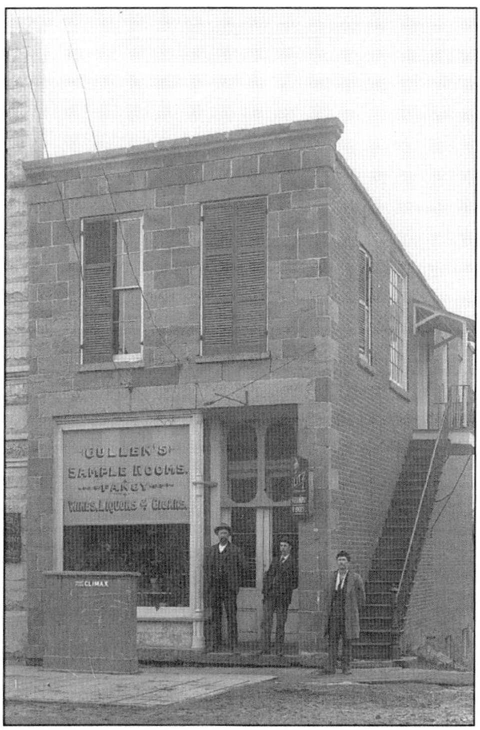

Gullen's Sample Rooms featured "fancy" wines, liquors, cigars, and Schlitz Beer, once the largest selling beer in America. This building is located at the corner of High and Chestnut Streets and is currently being renovated for commercial use once again.

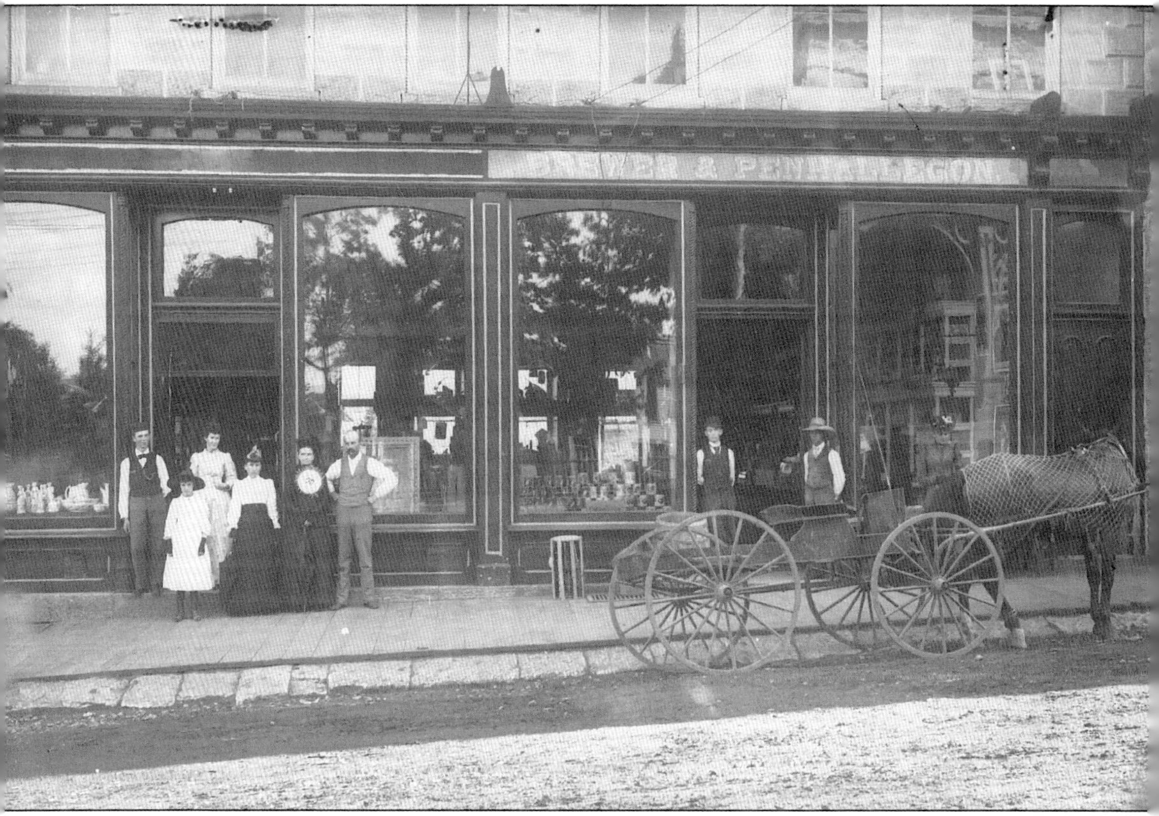

One of the most prominent grocery firms in Mineral Point was Brewer and Penhallegon, which was later called the James Brewer Grocery (114 High Street). It was founded in 1881 by James Brewer II and R.J. Penhallegon Jr., both of Cornish descent.

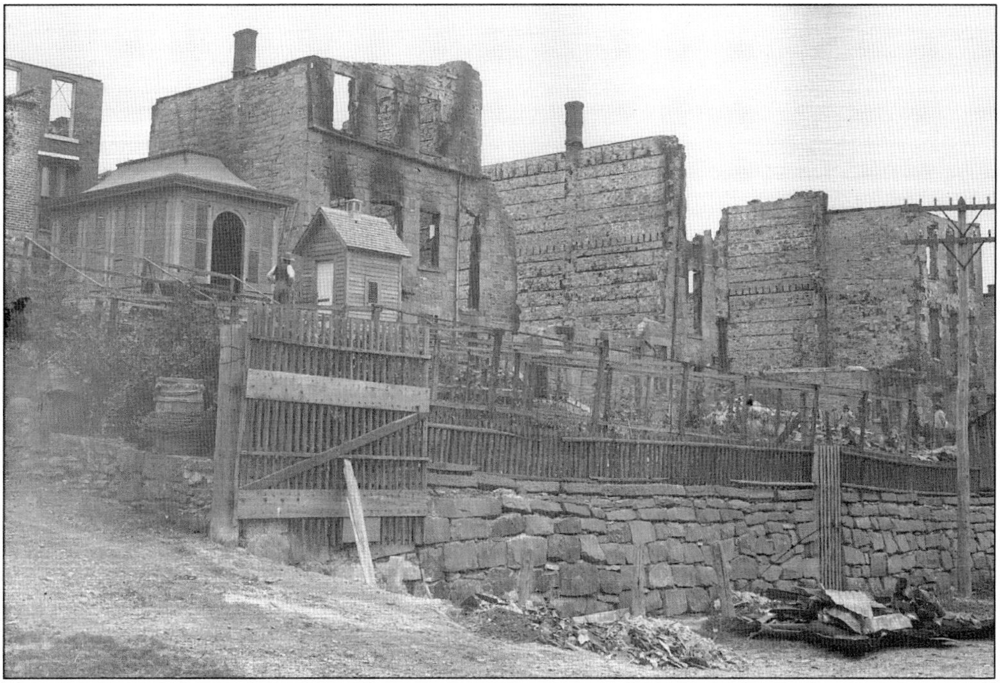

The aftermath of the May 1897 fire that destroyed several buildings on High Street is pictured here. This photo was taken from Fountain Street looking at the back of the burned buildings. Brewer and Penhallegon was one of the stores destroyed. The local newspaper, the *Mineral Point Tribune* entitled their May 6, 1897 article "Mineral Point Scorched," explaining that $40,000 worth of property was consumed in a few hours when half a business block burned. The fire was discovered by several members returning from a meeting of the International Order of Odd Fellows. Fred Vivian and Fred Penhallegon discovered that the basement of the double store of Brewer and Penhallegon was on fire. They soon raised the alarm, and the fire was eventually checked. Also advertised in that day's paper were fire sales offering "hot bargains!"

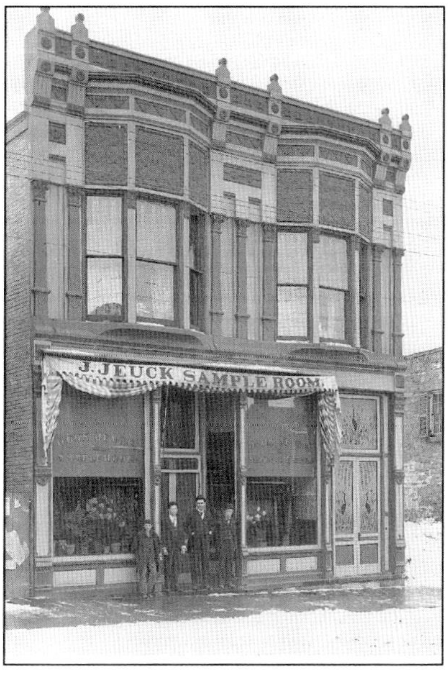

The J. Jeuck Sample Room was on High Street at the location which now houses the Mitchell floor covering shop. Notice the beautifully etched design in the frosted glass on the doorway to the right, which would have led upstairs to apartments. This arrangement continues in Mineral Point, and many residents still live above shops. This mixed use of downtown buildings significantly contributes to the activity and engagement of the residents and the community to the center of town and to town life.

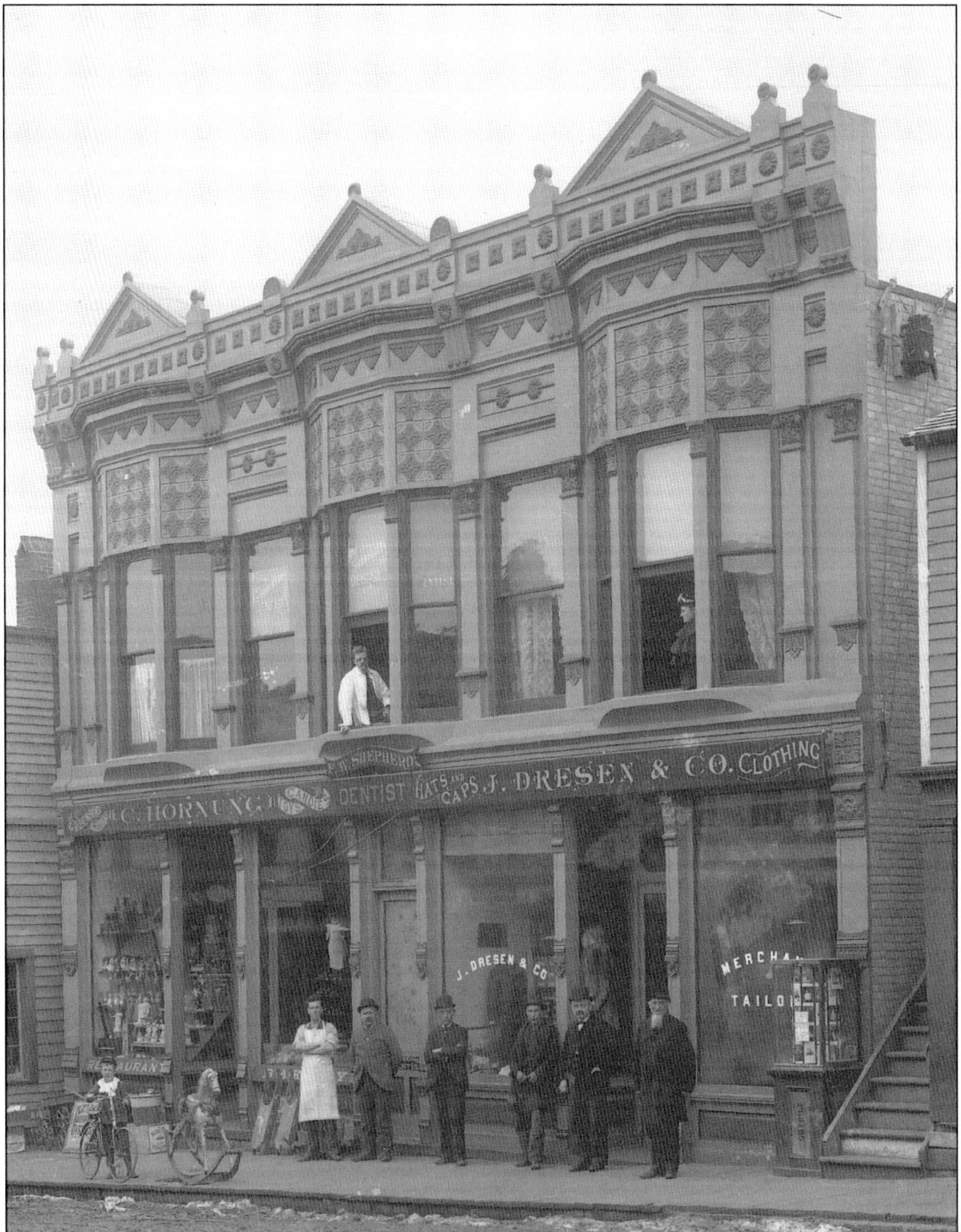

Two shops in one High Street building (236–240 High Street)—C. Hornung's shop advertising groceries, fruit, candy, and toys; and J. Dresen's for clothing and tailoring—are pictured. In 1897, Dresen advertised in the *Mineral Point Tribune*, "…to all gentlemen who appreciate good fitting clothes well tailored and made from GOOD materials GIVE ME A CALL…." The central portion of the upper floor is occupied by F.W. Shepherd, another Mineral Point dentist, who is most likely the man in the white coat sitting in the window. Also in the upper floor flanking the dentist's office are curtained windows, one with a woman standing in view, which frames what were most likely used as residences.

A tavern in Mineral Point featuring Pabst Beer, another product of the Milwaukee brewing industry, is pictured.

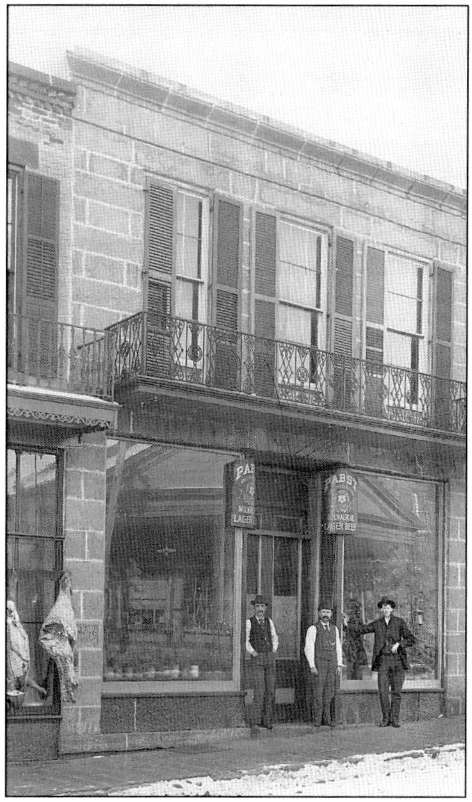

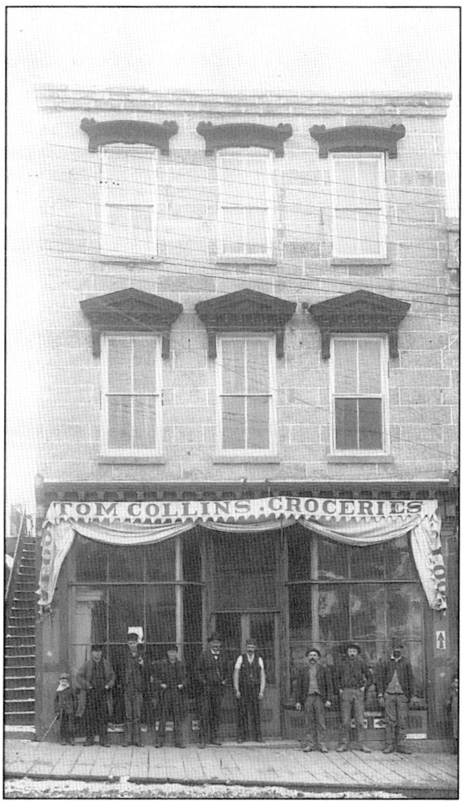

Another Mineral Point grocery, Tom Collins Groceries, is pictured here. The outside stairway at the left in the photo would have served as an entrance to the residence above.

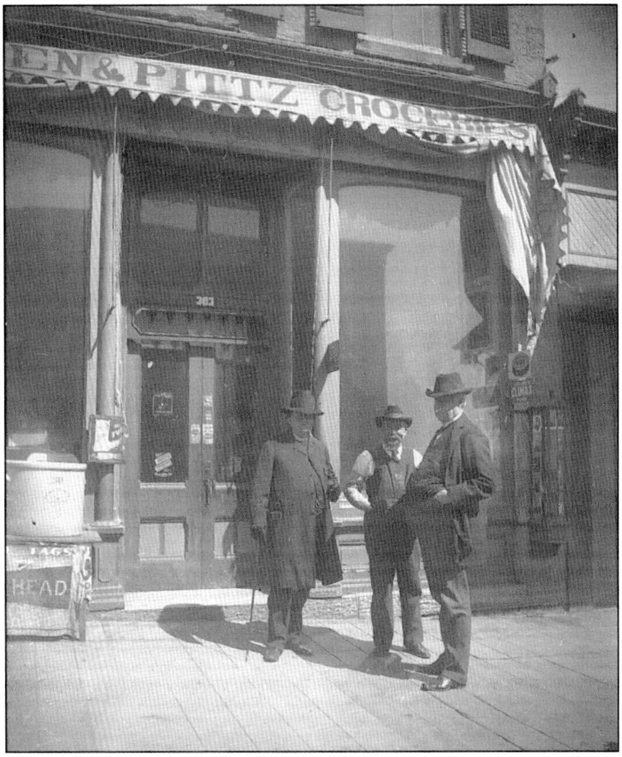

Gorgen and Pittz Groceries at 303 High Street. A huge pickle crock stands next to the doorway, and three unidentified men are in front on the wide wooden sidewalk.

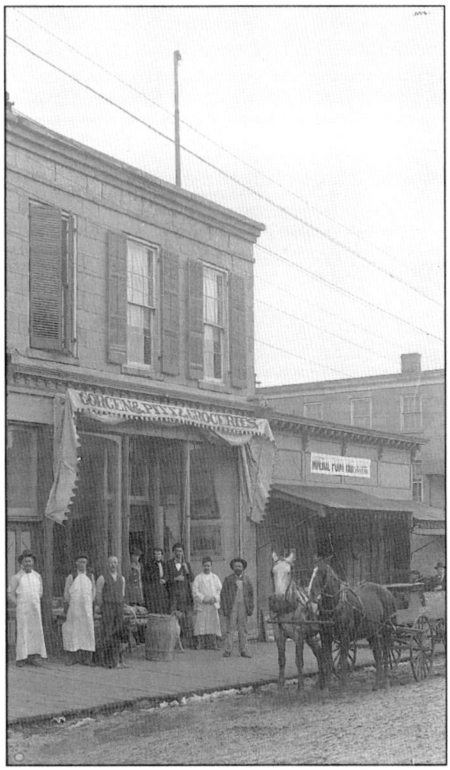

Another view of Gorgen and Pittz Groceries is pictured at right. Notice the advertisement for the Mineral Point Fair for September 1894, on the adjacent building. The fairs were another popular activity beginning around 1857, and continue now as the Iowa County Fair in Mineral Point every September.

J.R. Osborne on High Street sold horse goods, trunks, and valises as well as warm coats for riding in a carriage on a cold winter day.

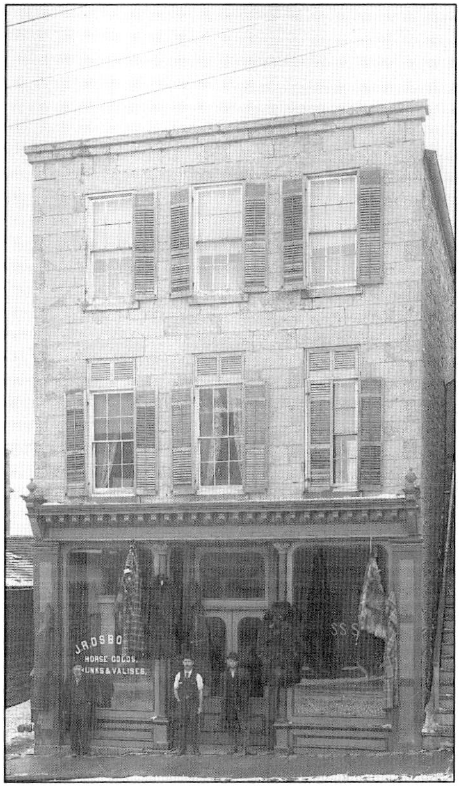

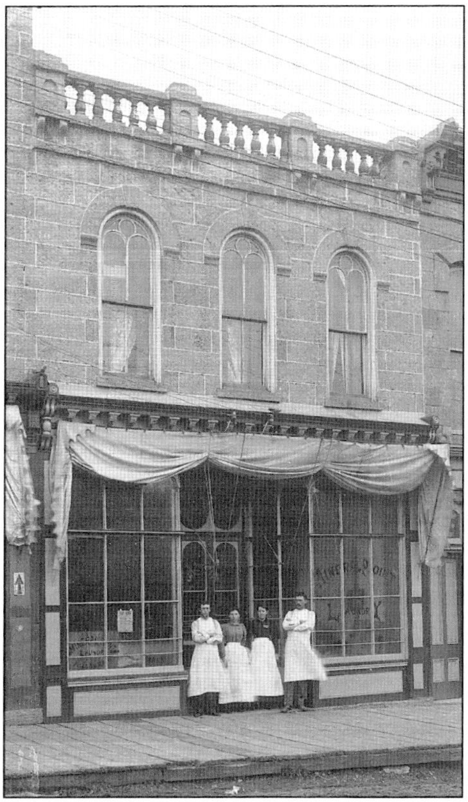

The Mineral Point Laundry on Commerce Street is shown with four of the workers, two women and two men. Women were beginning to work more outside the home, but only a few professions such as milliners in local shops and schoolteachers were acceptable.

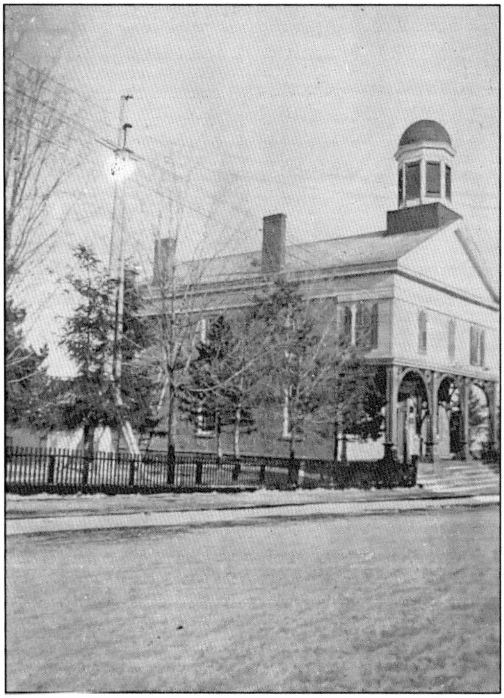

The former Iowa County courthouse on High Street was completed in 1844 when Mineral Point became the seat of Iowa County. In 1861, a three-year struggle called the "county seat war" concluded with Dodgeville, a town 8 miles north, becoming the county seat after the boundaries of the county had been changed. This handsome building was renovated several times and served as the Mineral Point City Hall until it was demolished in 1913.

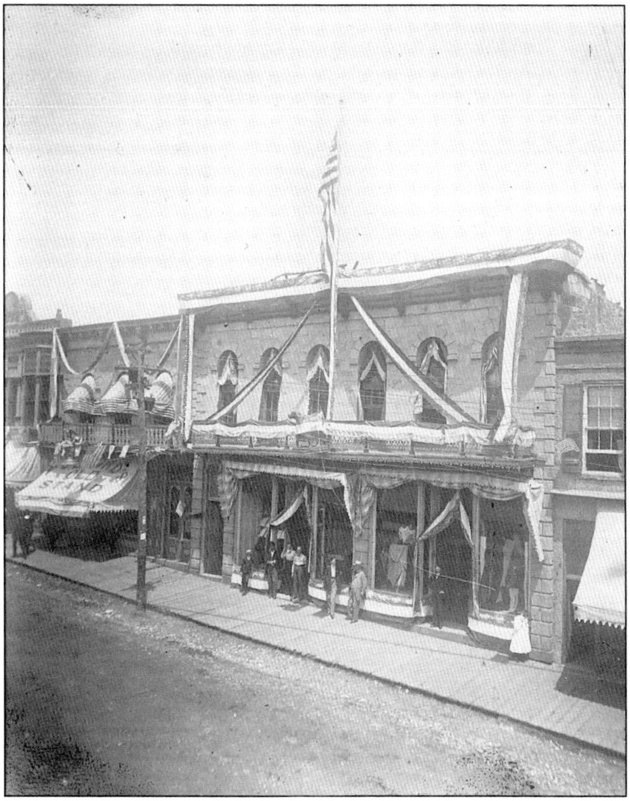

Gundry and Gray's clothing store at 215 High Street is decorated for July 4th. The store was Mineral Point's most notable retail establishment, and the building still looks much the same and is operated as a delicatessen. The earlier owners, John Gray and especially Joseph Gundry, built fine houses in town. Gundry's house is now owned and maintained by the Mineral Point Historical Society.

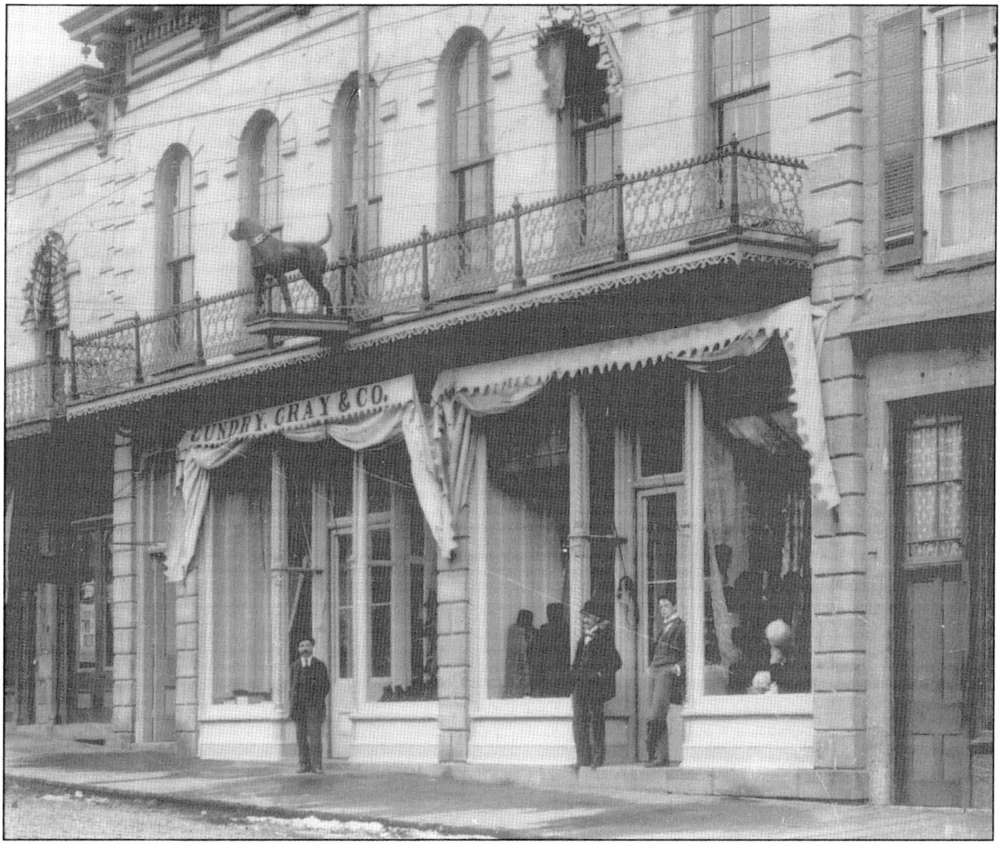

This is another view of Gundry and Gray. This photograph clearly depicts the sculpture of the pointer dog, which has become the town's symbol and remains poised on the building. The dog is cast in zinc to celebrate Mineral Point's most important industry at the time.

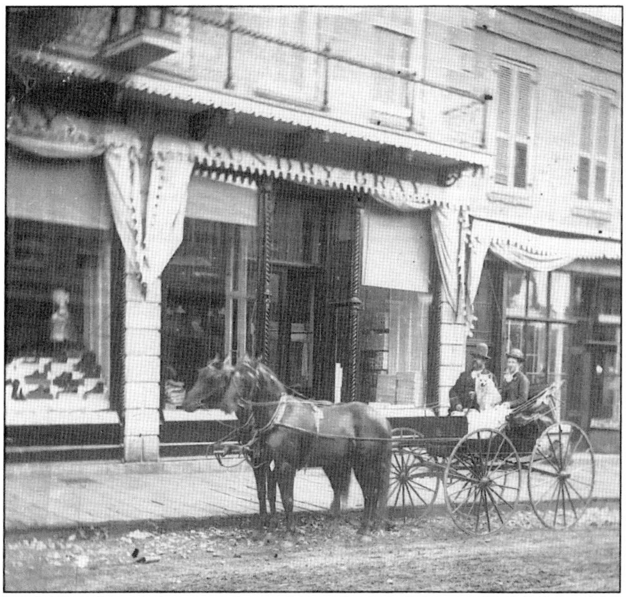

This photo was taken in front of Gundry and Gray's store of an unidentified man and woman with a dog in her lap in a carriage.

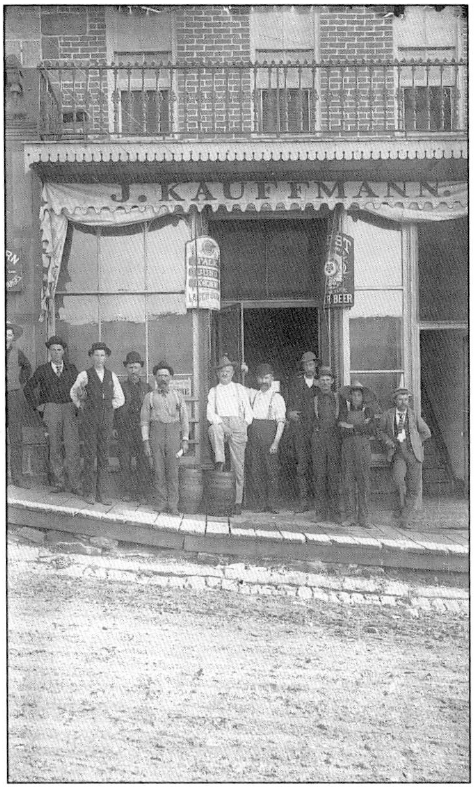

Kaufmann's Tavern on High Street featured Pabst as well as Falk, Jung, and Borchert Lager Beer. A beer keg in the front is functioning as a handy footstool for one of the customers.

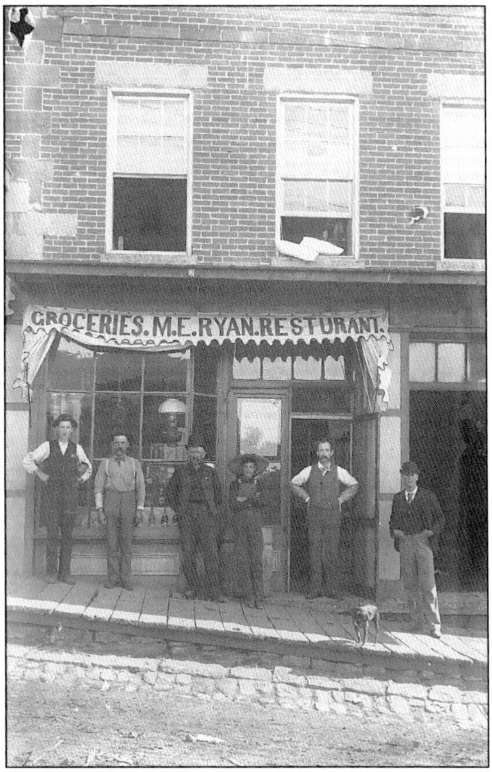

Ryan's Groceries and Restaurant on High Street is pictured here. Notice that some of the gentlemen in this photograph are shown in the former photo of Kaufmann's Tavern.

This is the Fiedler Building (est. 1891) at the corner of High and Vine Streets. The second story of this building has since been removed, and the remaining first story is now occupied by The Sweet Shop (60 High Street), a restaurant and ice cream parlor.

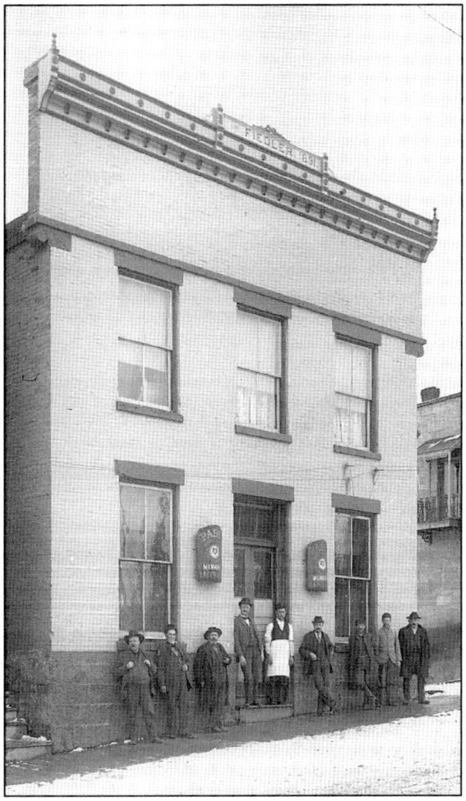

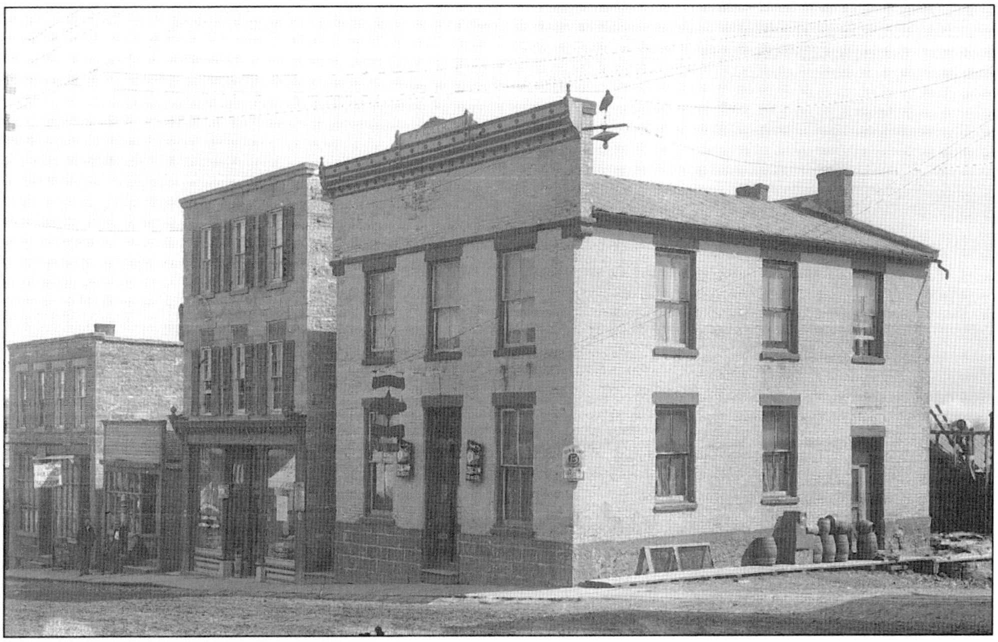

This view is looking down High Street from the corner of High and Vine Streets with another view of the Fiedler Building, apparently functioning as a tavern on the first floor, with its beer kegs in the foreground.

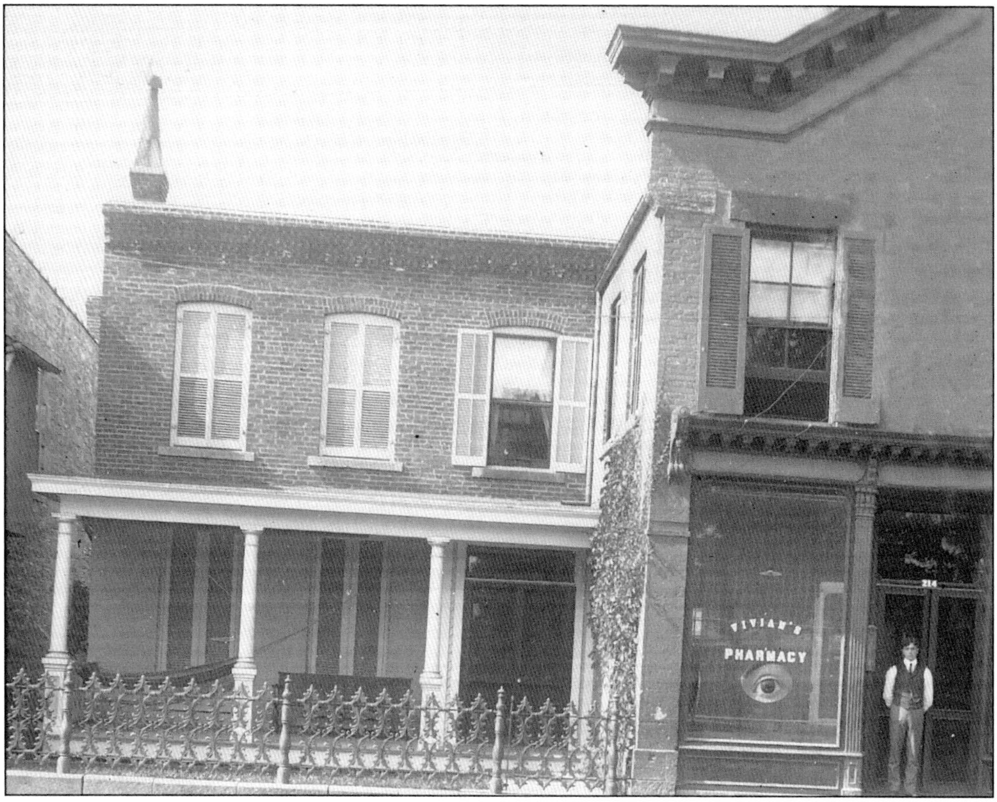

This image depicts the building at 128 High Street, which became a drug store in 1848 with a window advertisement for Vivian's Pharmacy. In 1905, the pharmacy was purchased from the heirs of John Vivian by Charles Ivey, who had worked as the druggist there since 1902. Today it is still Ivey's drug store, and one of the pharmacists is Harry Ivey, the son of Charles. It is believed to be the oldest continuously operating pharmacy at its original location in the state of Wisconsin.

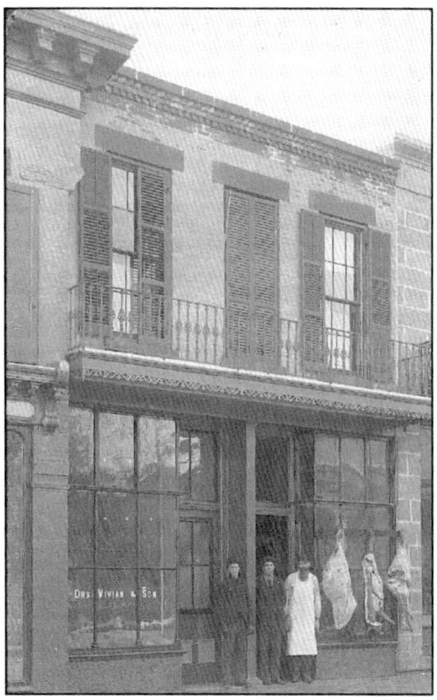

The offices of Dr. John H. Vivian and his son were located next to a meat market. In 1847, John H. Vivian, who had been born in Cornwall and studied medicine there, came to Mineral Point and initially opened his practice using the upper levels of the buildings at 128 High Street and later also at 130 High Street. The Drs. Vivian located their offices in the downtown area like many of the other physicians and dentists in town in the nineteenth century and even today.

This is an advertisement for Dr. John H. Vivian's service from the 1859 Directory of the City of Mineral Point compiled by T.S. Allen.

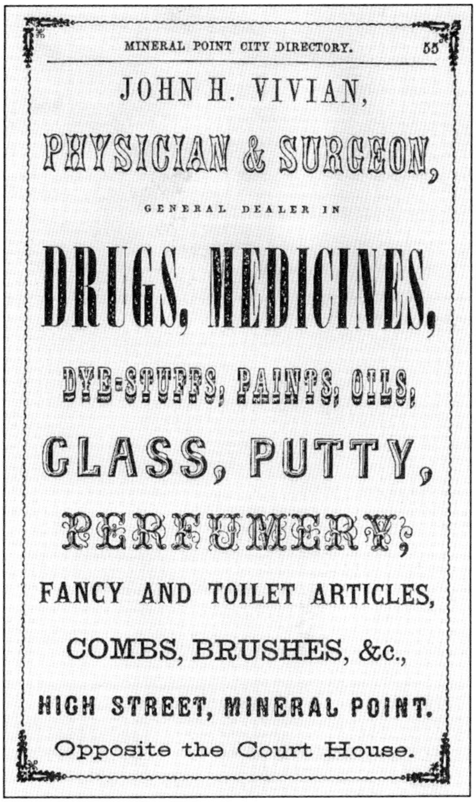

MINERAL POINT CITY DIRECTORY. 55

JOHN H. VIVIAN,

PHYSICIAN & SURGEON,

GENERAL DEALER IN

DRUGS, MEDICINES,

DYE-STUFFS, PAINTS, OILS,

GLASS, PUTTY,

PERFUMERY;

FANCY AND TOILET ARTICLES,

COMBS, BRUSHES, &c.,

HIGH STREET, MINERAL POINT.

Opposite the Court House.

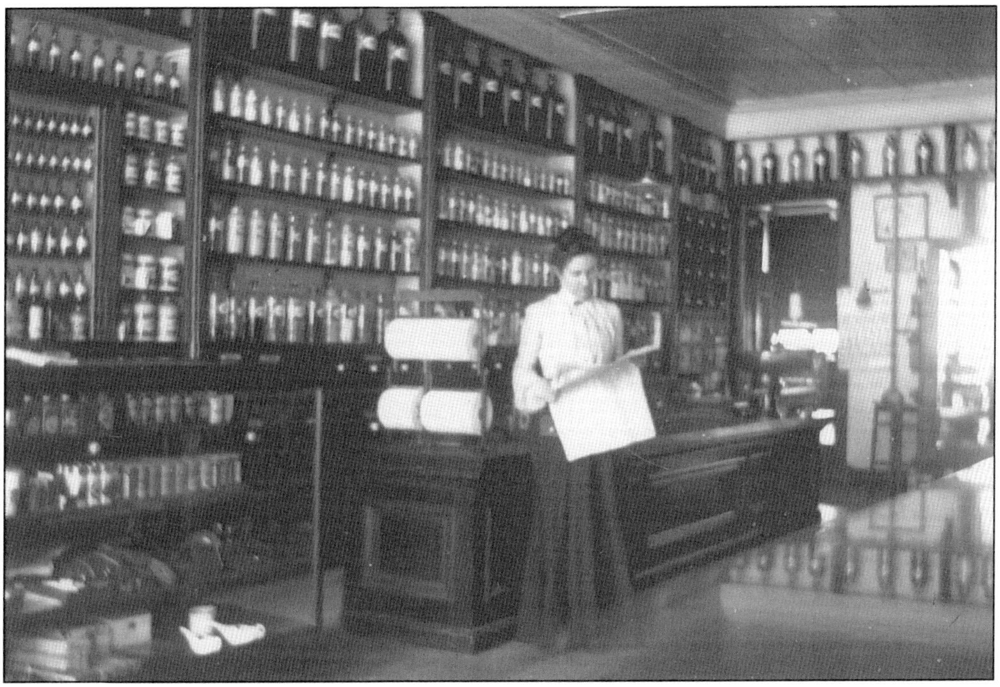

A drugstore interior is pictured with an unidentified woman occupied reading the paper.

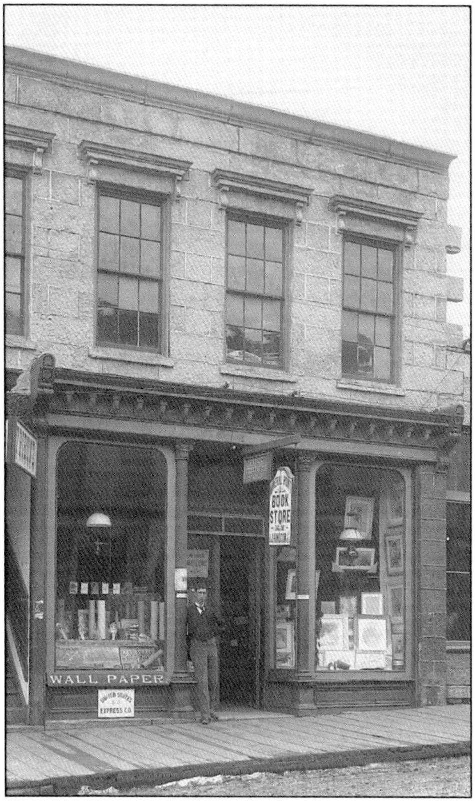

This is the Mineral Point Bookstore on Commerce Street—J.J. Hanscom, proprietor. This store also sold wallpaper and was the agency for the United States Express Company and the telephone company.

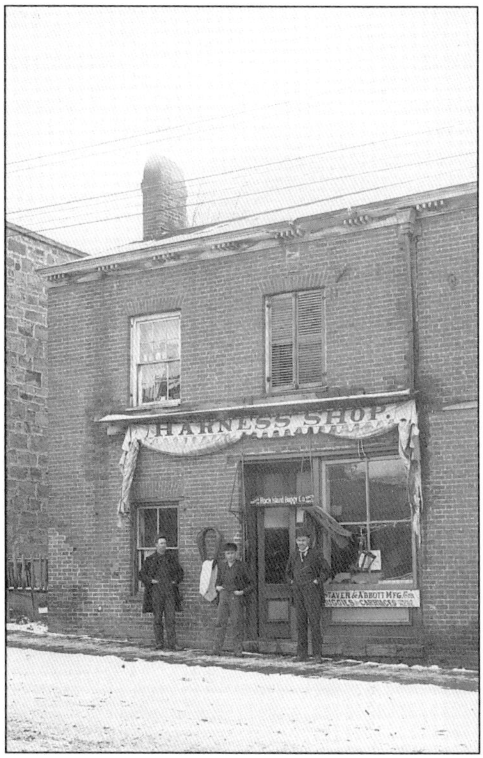

This is a harness shop on High Street specializing in buggies and carriages made by the Rock Island Buggy Company and Staver and Abbott.

Hats for sale! The Ziegin and Wearne Millinery Shop on High Street. As a milliner a woman could find acceptable employment outside the home. The upper story is still recognizable above the Mitchell Hardware Store at 250 High Street. Miss Wearne, milliner, was burned out in the fire on High Street in 1897, and she likely reopened later with a partner further up the street.

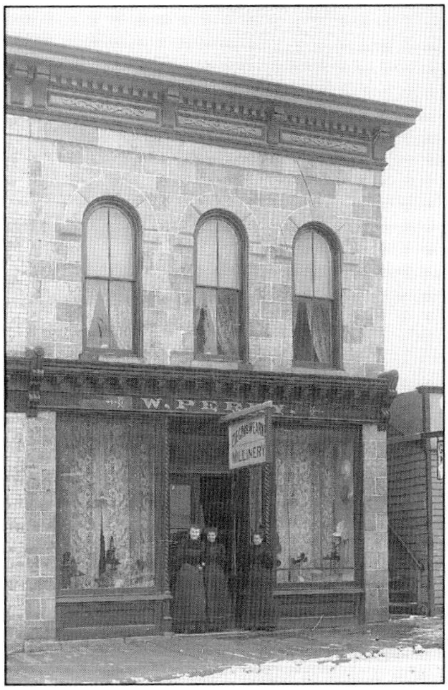

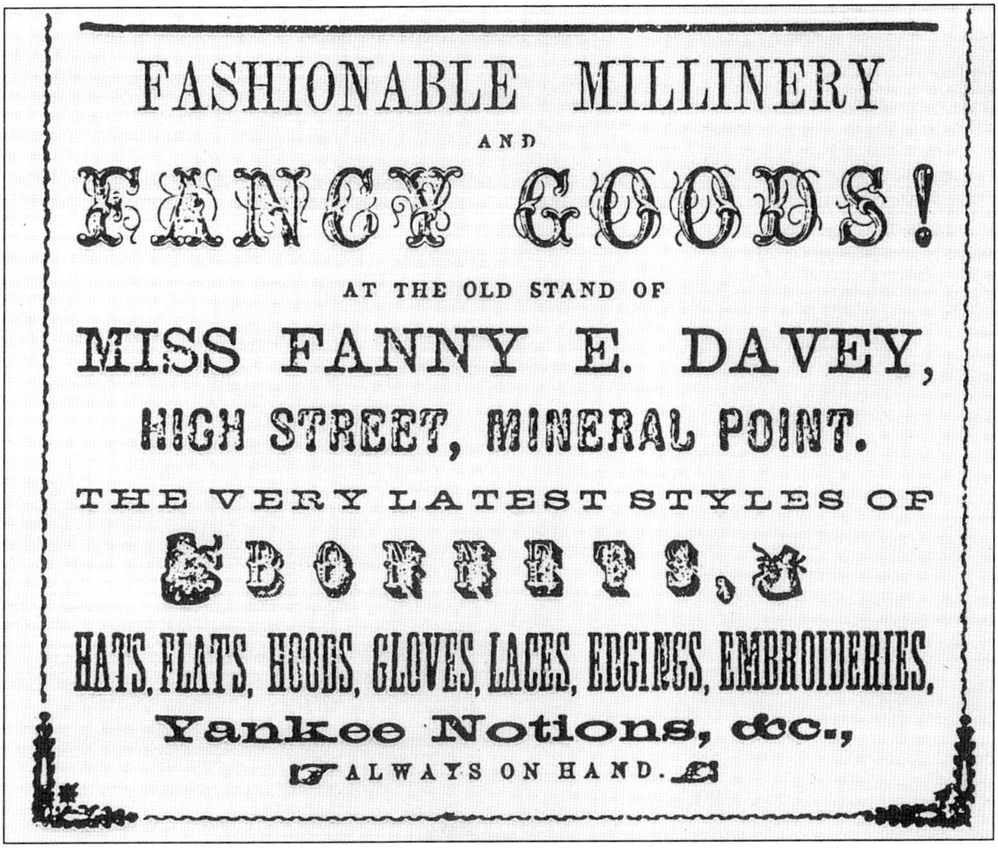

This is an ad from the Directory of the City of Mineral Point from 1859. There were numerous millinery shops in Mineral Point attesting to the popularity hats and notions once had.

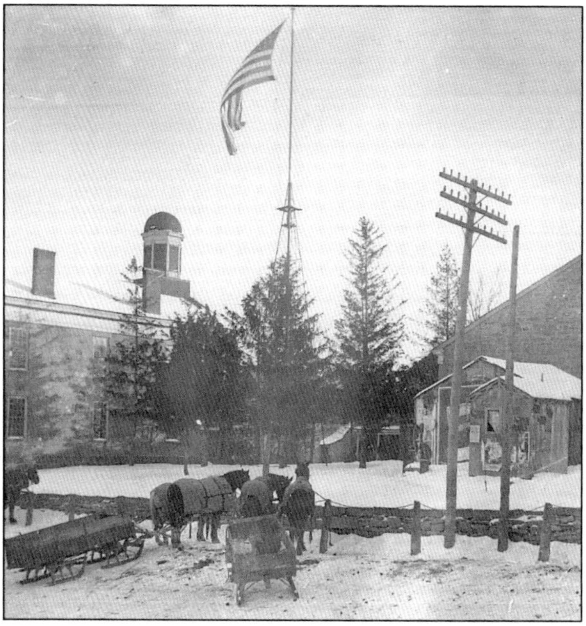

This view is looking toward High Street from Jail Alley with the former Iowa County courthouse prominent in this photograph. Jail Alley was named as such because of the old county jail that was once adjacent to this small street running parallel to High Street. Jail Alley still bears the same name and is now a delightful street with private residences and antique and craft shops.

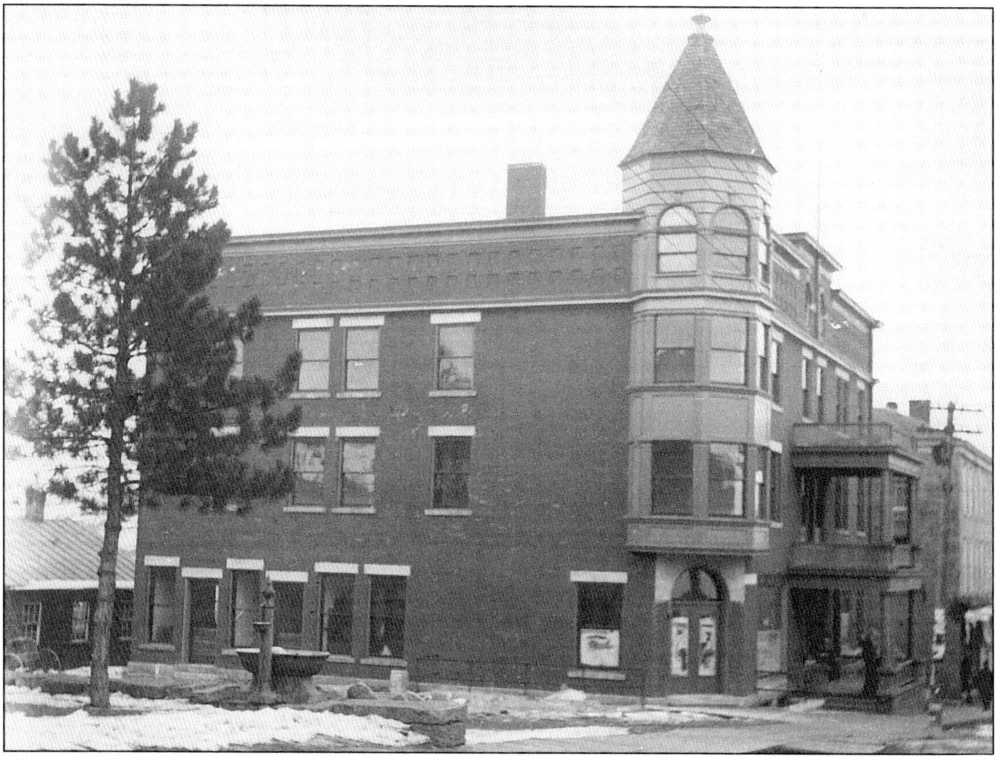

The Royal Hotel of 1900, on the corner of High and Vine Streets across from the Fiedler Building remains a fine example of the commercial interpretation of Queen Anne-style architecture with its contrasting materials, shapes, decorative elements, and asymmetrical façade. A corner of Library Park, a green space still preserved on High Street, is visible in the left foreground.

H.H. Chandler leather and cloth goods at 37 High Street is pictured here. Their wares, including boots, shoes, handbags, and towels or blankets, are displayed outside by the male and female clerks.

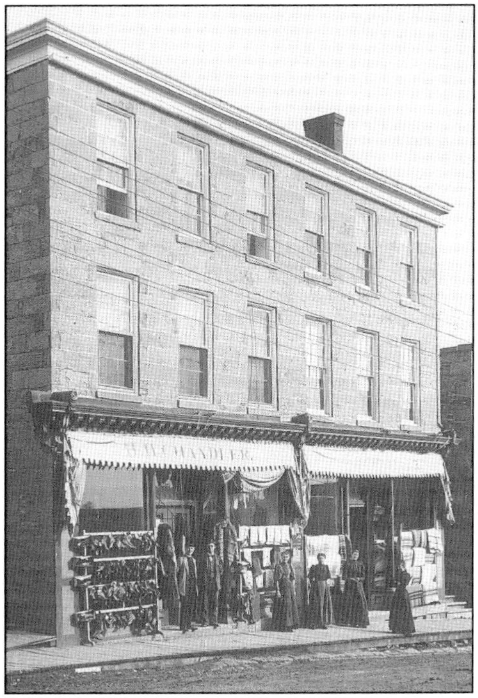

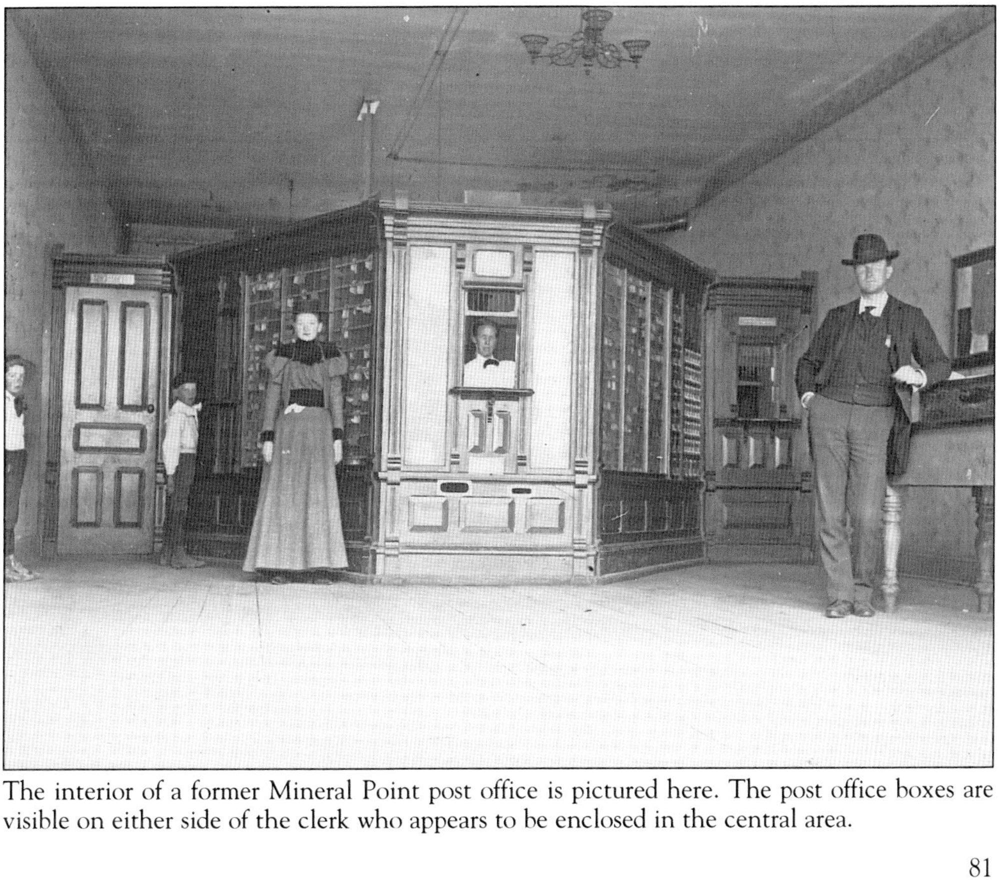

The interior of a former Mineral Point post office is pictured here. The post office boxes are visible on either side of the clerk who appears to be enclosed in the central area.

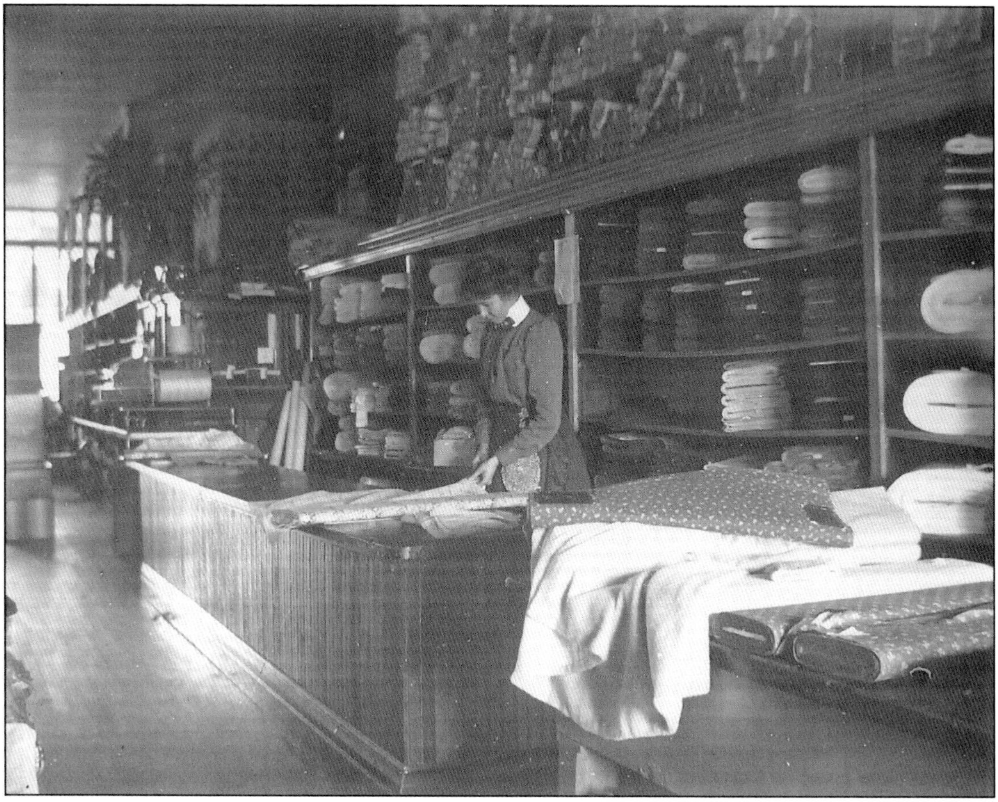

Cloth is for sale by the yard. The female clerk is depicted cutting a purchase from a bolt. This may be the interior of Gundry and Gray's store.

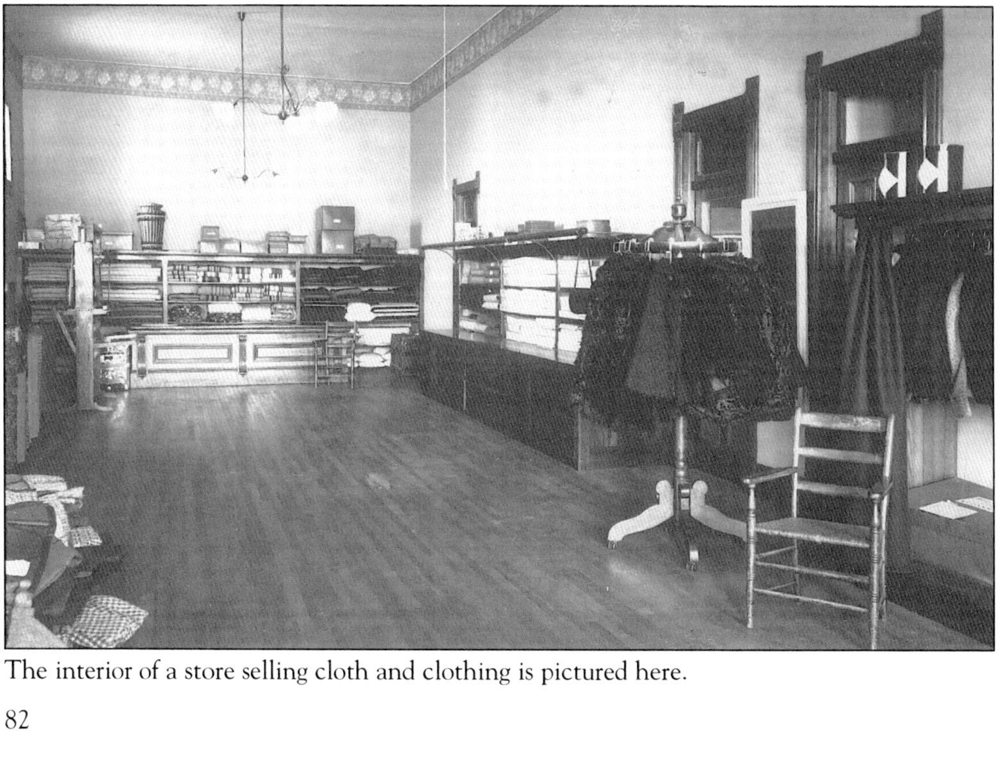

The interior of a store selling cloth and clothing is pictured here.

Four

GOVERNMENT, CHURCHES, SCHOOLS, AND PRIVATE ORGANIZATIONS

The arrival of permanent settlers to Mineral Point also meant the establishment of their churches, schools, and organizations. The town's early governance was under the territorial system of the Northwest Ordinance of 1787, then part of Illinois Territory in 1804, Michigan Territory in 1834, and as Wisconsin Territory in 1836, and the State of Wisconsin in 1848. Incorporated as a city in 1857, Mineral Point was the county seat of Iowa County until 1861 and participates in the strong system of county government in Wisconsin.

The makeup of the early religious organizations, including circuit-riding ministers, missions, and churches, reflected the ethnic background and religious heritage of those first groups of settlers. The nineteenth-century churches in Mineral Point included those of several Methodist groups, Catholics, Episcopalians, and a Lutheran church in 1939.

Historically, the earliest schools in Mineral Point were quasi-public schools—the first documented in 1829—funded by subscriptions and fees, and many were established by the town's churches at the primary and secondary levels. Intermittent public education became secure when the town opened a new public school in 1850 in response to the education laws identified in the new state's constitution of 1848. The incorporation of Mineral Point as a city in 1857 gave further stability to the public school program here with its own school district and superintendent. Linked to the concept of public education was the incorporation of the Free Public Library of Mineral Point in 1895, which was preceded by the Mineral Point Library Association of 1860, and George W. Bliss's private reading room of 1854.

Other social and political organizations in Mineral Point include the International Order of the Odd Fellows (IOOF) Lodge No.1 (1835) and the women's auxiliary of the IOOF, the Daughters of Rebekah (1872), Mineral Point Lodge No.1 of the Free and Accepted Masons chartered in 1841, and many women's clubs—the most popular of which was affiliated with the Wisconsin Federation of Women's club founded in 1896. In the twentieth century, the American Legion Post organized in 1919, the Mineral Point Historical Society formed in 1939, and several movements advocating for temperance and women's suffrage began their existence at various times.

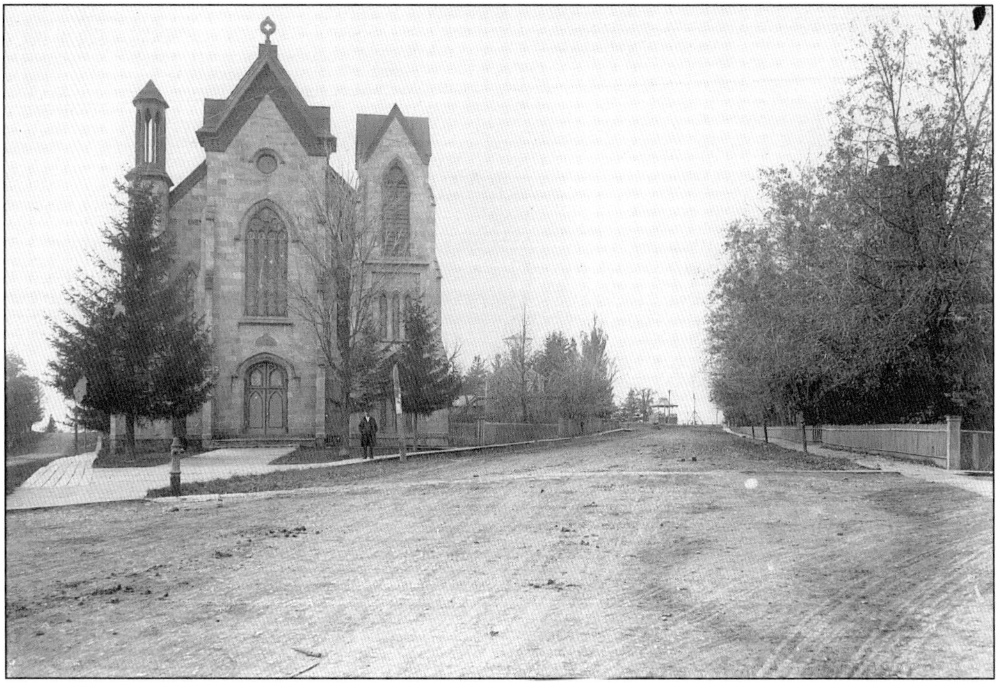

The present Mineral Point Methodist Episcopal Church was consecrated in 1871, and is the third structure erected by this congregation. It is located at the top of the hill of High Street at 400 Doty Street. Organized in 1834, the Methodist Episcopal Church is one of the oldest Protestant congregations in Wisconsin. The original church on Commerce Street constructed of logs no longer stands. They built another structure to serve as their church and day school, which was dedicated in 1838, expanded in 1845, and stood on the site of the Gothic Revival-style home on the corner across the street (402 Doty Street).

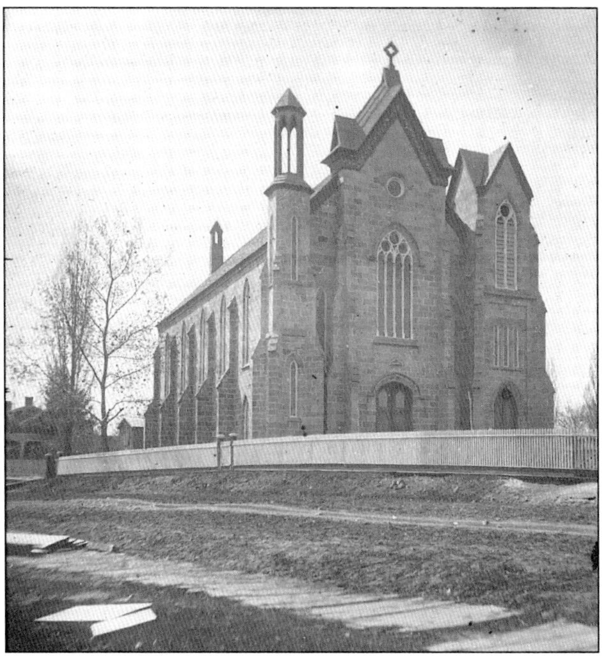

This is another view of the Methodist Episcopal Church of 1871. This Gothic Revival-style church features strong vertical lines, pointed arches, and asymmetrical towers, and is constructed of St. Peter's sandstone from a local quarry.

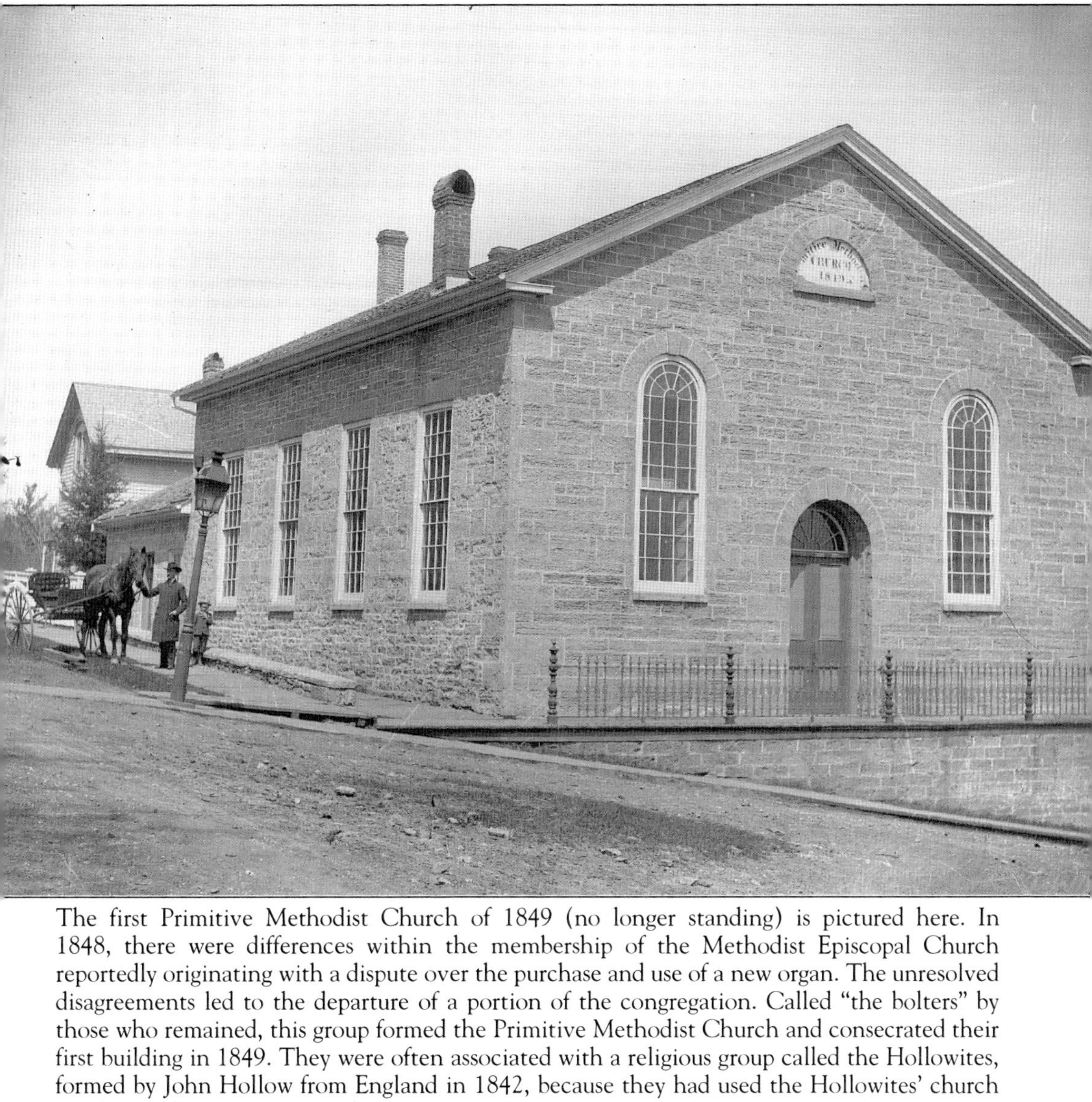

The first Primitive Methodist Church of 1849 (no longer standing) is pictured here. In 1848, there were differences within the membership of the Methodist Episcopal Church reportedly originating with a dispute over the purchase and use of a new organ. The unresolved disagreements led to the departure of a portion of the congregation. Called "the bolters" by those who remained, this group formed the Primitive Methodist Church and consecrated their first building in 1849. They were often associated with a religious group called the Hollowites, formed by John Hollow from England in 1842, because they had used the Hollowites' church building before moving into their own.

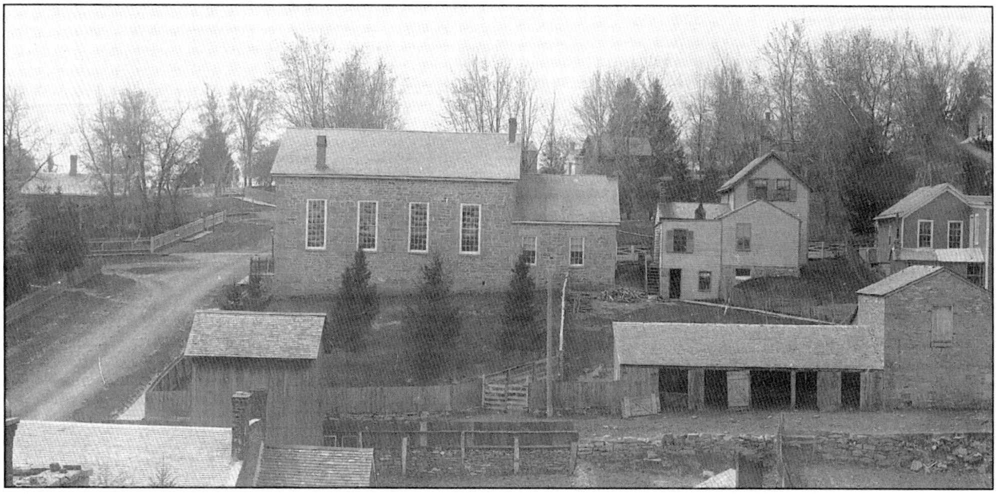

The Primitive Methodist Church was located at the corner of Chestnut and Maiden Streets on the site of the present United Church of Christ (315 Maiden Street). This view of the Primitive Methodist Church was taken looking up Chestnut Street toward the old cemetery near the crest of the hill.

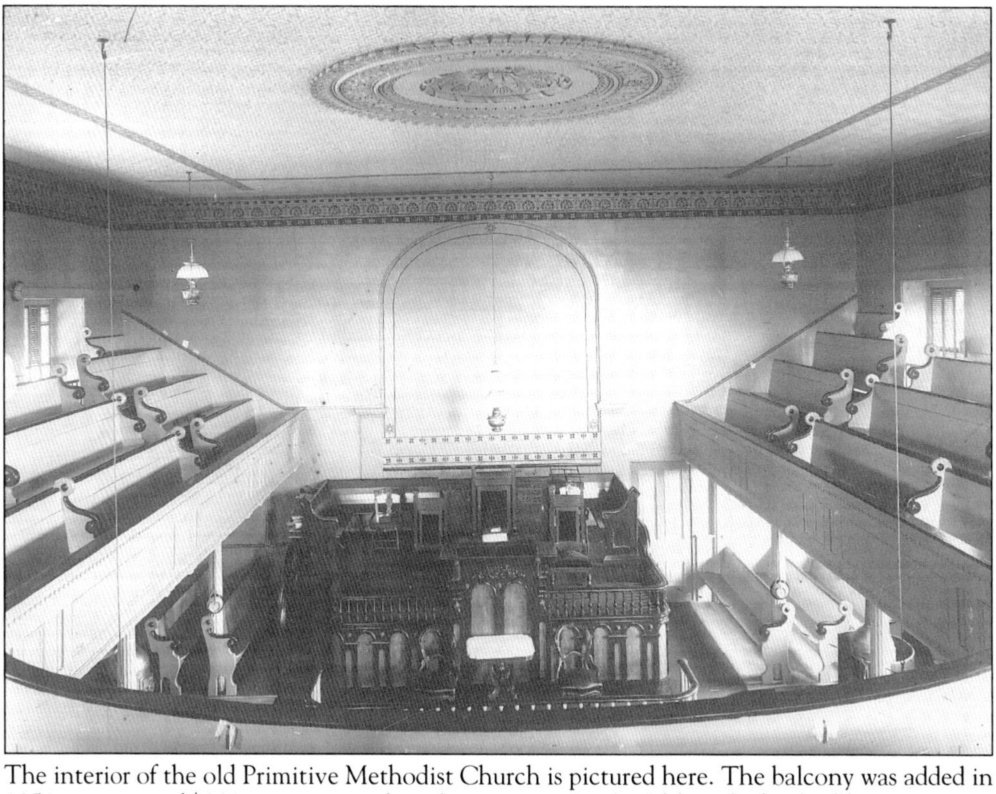

The interior of the old Primitive Methodist Church is pictured here. The balcony was added in 1851, at a cost of $800 to accommodate the growing parish. Although this building no longer stands, the interior and exterior of this building are very similar to the Methodist Church in nearby Linden which is still in use, except that the Linden church has a tower. The Linden church also constructed an additional balcony for a growing congregation at approximately the same time.

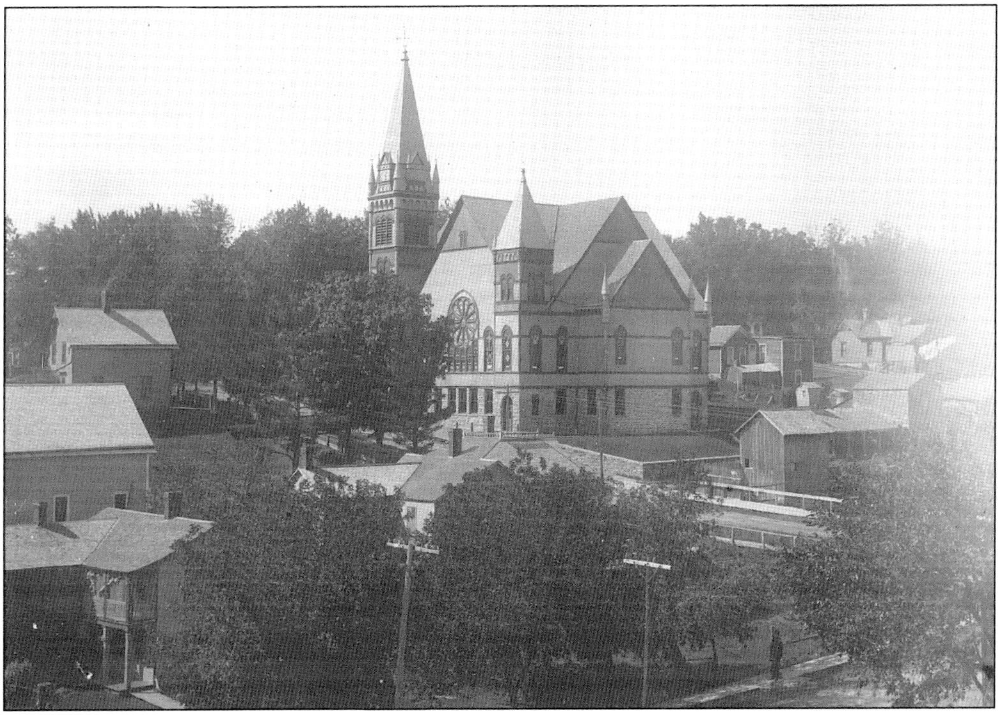

By 1893, the Primitive Methodist Church had grown enough that this new church was built as a replacement in the site of the old structure reportedly costing just over $22,000. In 1912, the congregation shifted its affiliation to the Congregational Church under the guidance and influence of their minister, Reverend W.J.C. Bond, who was a Congregationalist himself. The shift was likely due to concerns regarding the lack of financial and administrative support from the Primitive Methodists who had no central organization.

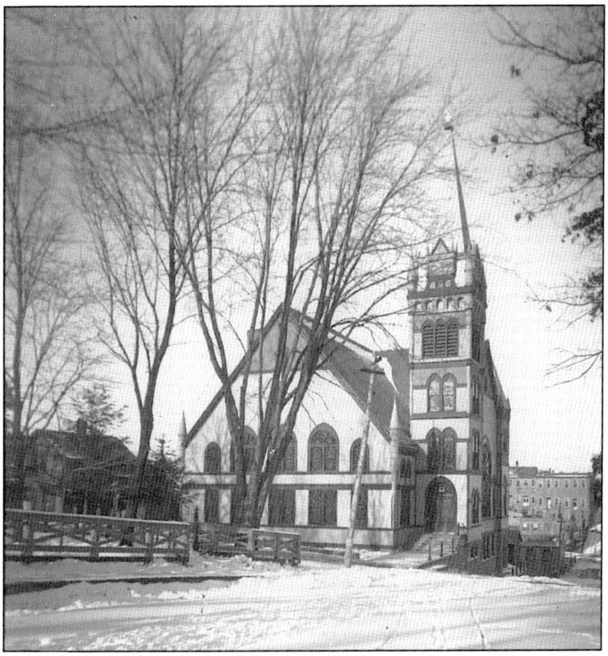

The new Primitive Methodist Church (by then a Congregational Church) is pictured in winter looking down Chestnut Street toward the business district. In 1912, the spire atop the tower and turrets around the church were removed as an economical measure, since their maintenance was judged to be too expensive.

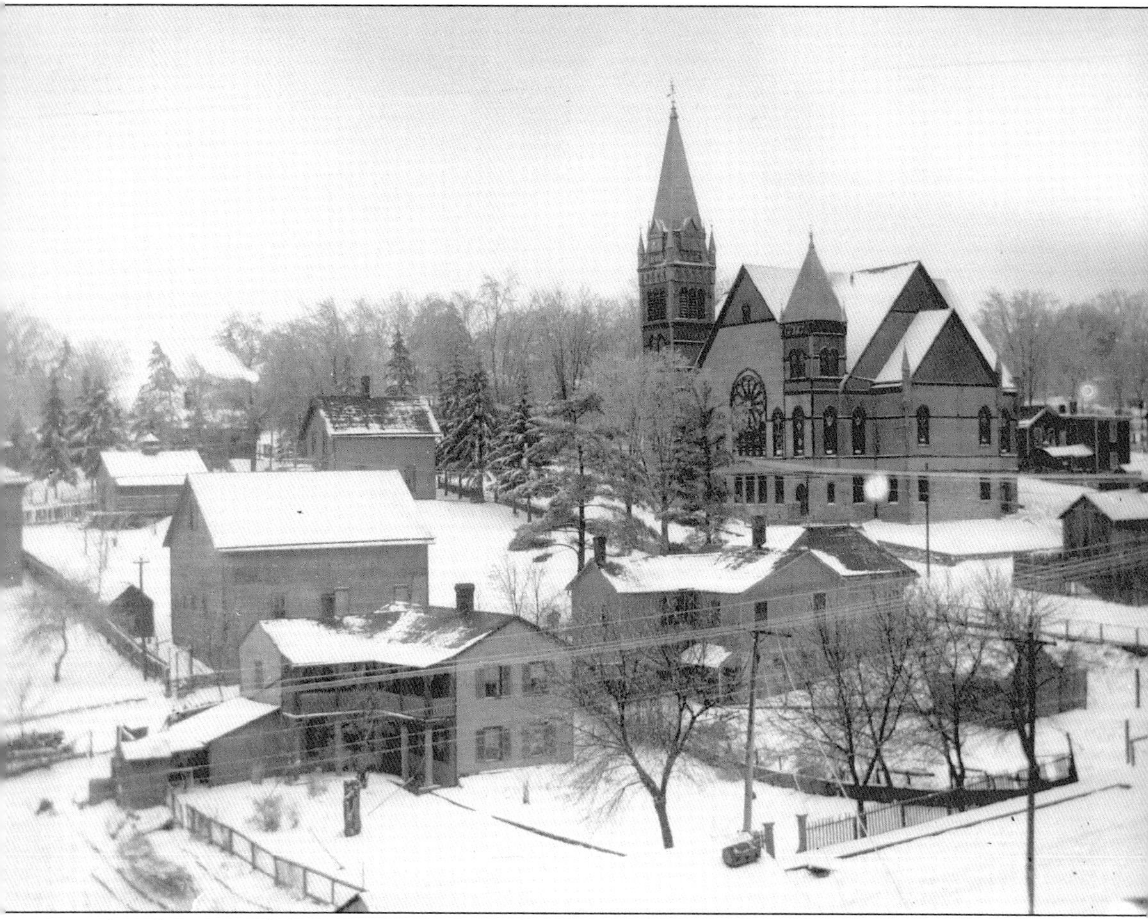

Another view of the new Primitive Methodist is shown here. In 1913, the church added a new pipe organ, reportedly at a cost of $2,000. This church still has an active congregation and accepted the constitution of the United Church of Christ in 1961.

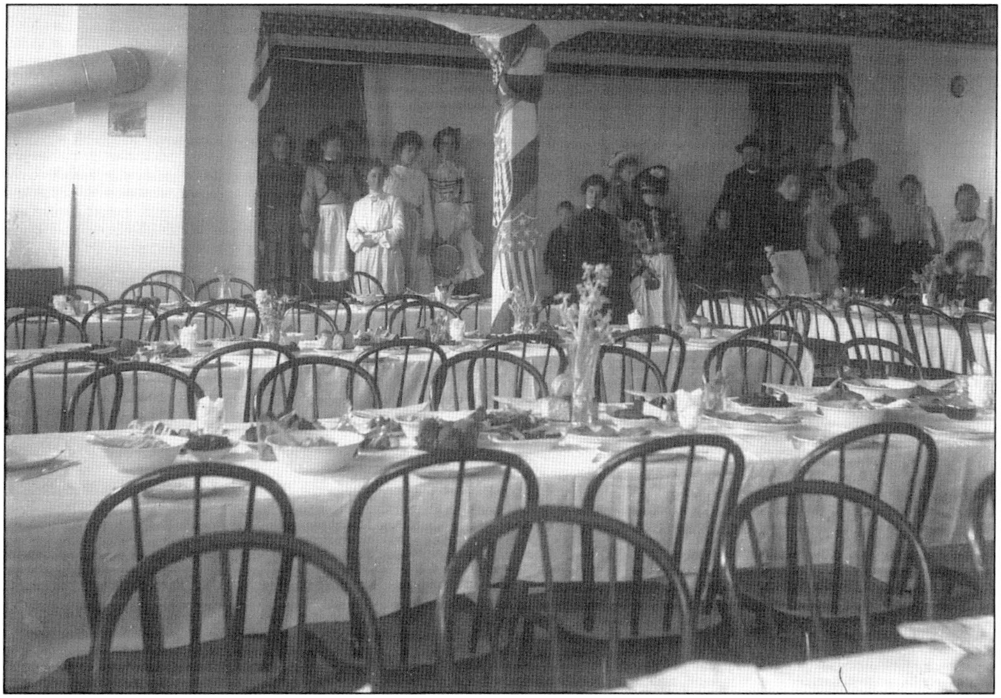

This is the lecture room in the new Primitive Methodist Church. A feast for a considerable number of people has been prepared. Church suppers are still popular in Mineral Point and in the surrounding area and continue to be held regularly by the local congregations.

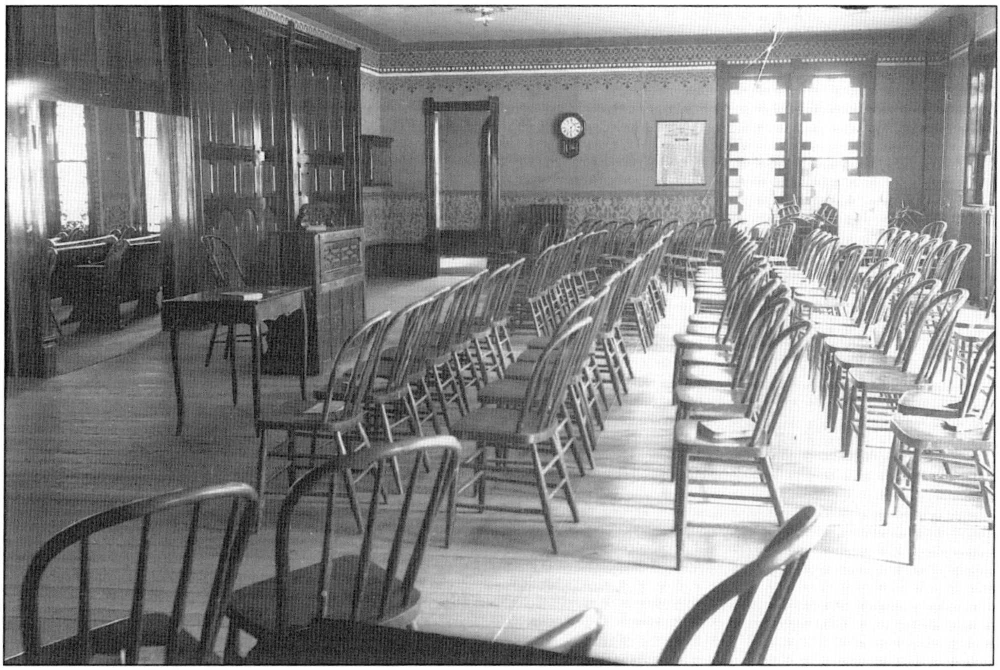

This is another room in the new Primitive Methodist Church. The sliding wooden panels on the left side of the photograph separate this room from the chapel. Some of the pews of the chapel are visible through the opened panel.

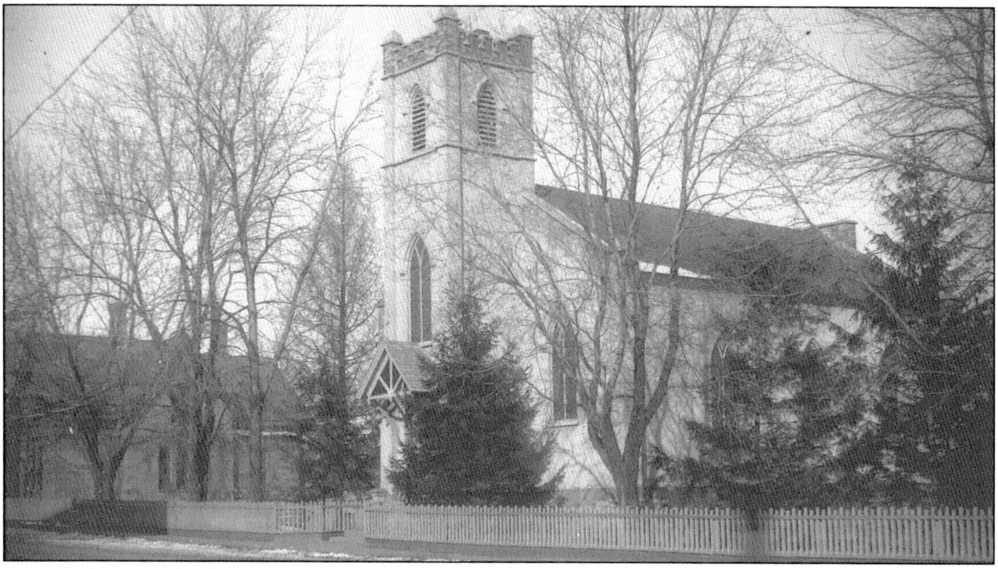

Trinity Episcopal Church in Mineral Point at 409 High Street is pictured here. This parish was formed in 1835–36, and the actual building was constructed in 1845, and is believed to be the oldest continuously operating church building still standing in the state of Wisconsin. The building was consecrated by Bishop Jackson Kemper in 1855, and members of the first vestry included Colonel Henry Dodge, later governor of the Territory of Wisconsin; Henry Hamilton, son of Alexander Hamilton; and Moses M. Strong, an influential Wisconsin lawyer. Constructed of local red brick with a limestone foundation, it is in a Gothic Revival style with strong vertical lines and pointed arches. Note its central tower and symmetrical façade.

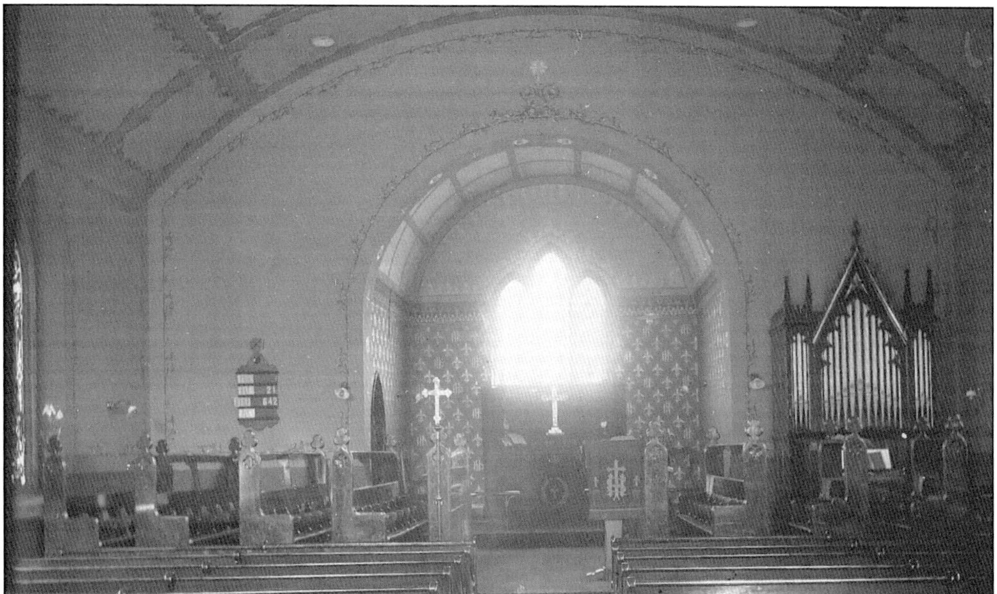

The interior of Trinity Episcopal Church is pictured here. One of the stained glass windows in this church comes from the studio of William Comfort Tiffany. Since this photograph was taken, the pipe organ has been replaced by a much larger instrument, but the church remains much the same on the interior and exterior.

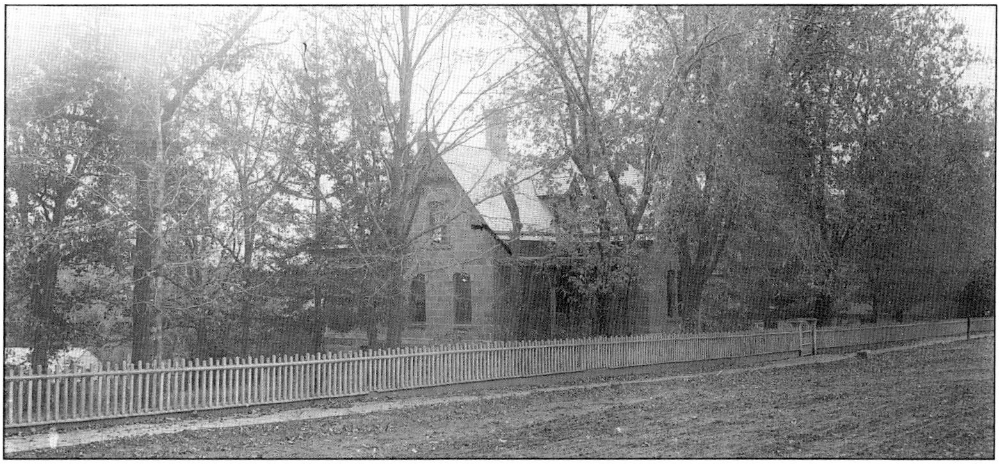

According to parish records, the rectory of Trinity Episcopal Church was begun in 1866. It is located at 409 High Street, next to the church building. This house is the outstanding example of a Gothic Revival-style residence executed in stone in Mineral Point at a reported cost of $6,700. A small school had been operating in the basement of the church since 1858, and in 1866, the church built a parish school at a cost of $2,875. It was a simple one-story building, which could hold 150 pupils. The building no longer stands. Mrs. Lyman Phelps, wife of the Episcopal minister, served as the first teacher. Shortly after her death, the school closed in 1874 but reopened in 1879, and was leased to the City of Mineral Point as a public primary school in 1889.

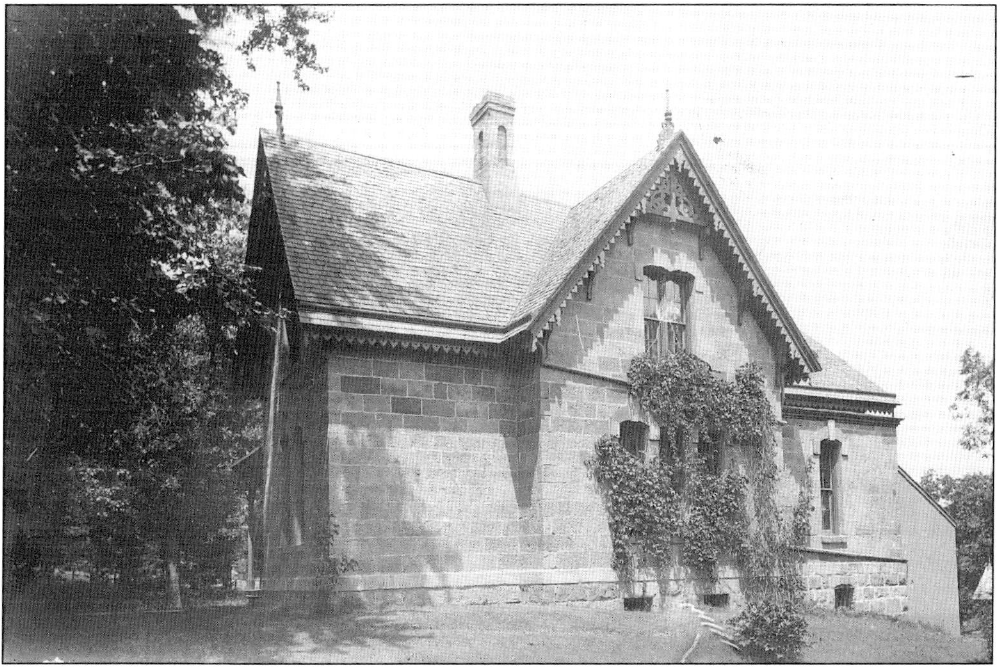

This is another view of the Trinity Church Rectory. Constructed of local sandstone with a limestone foundation, one can see the stonemasons' skill and attention to details such as the slightly protruding arches above the windows with their prominent keystone (central stone in the arch). Much of the wooden detail work also survives in the decorative barge boards following the roofline.

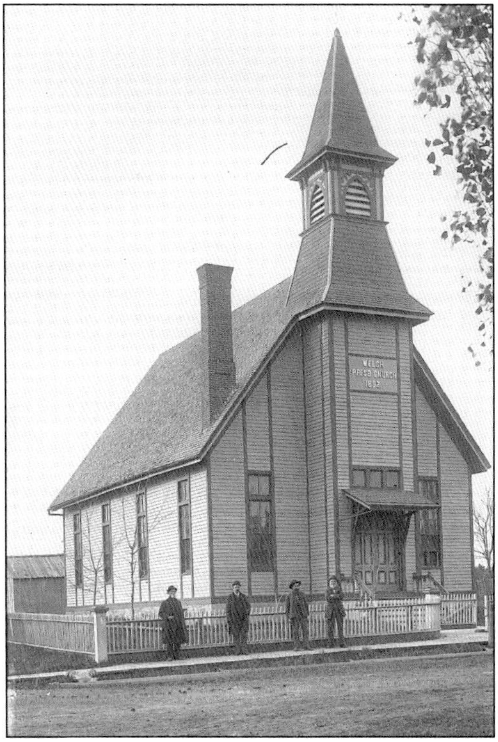

Pictured here is the more successful Welsh Presbyterian Church of 1882 in nearby Dodgeville, which drew many of its congregation from immigrants from Wales. The Presbyterian Church in Mineral Point had a relatively short existence having been formed in 1839, and dissolved in 1885, for lack of money and parishioners. The Cornish were the principal nationality in Mineral Point throughout this period, and the majority of them were Methodists. One of the prominent early parishioners at the Mineral Point Presbyterian Church who later became a deacon was William A. Jones, who was born in Wales and immigrated to the United States in 1851. One of his three influential sons, his namesake—William Arthur Jones, remained in Mineral Point. He held many offices, the most notable being Commissioner of Indian Affairs in Washington D.C, for eight years. His large home at 215 Ridge Street still stands and is presently a bed and breakfast.

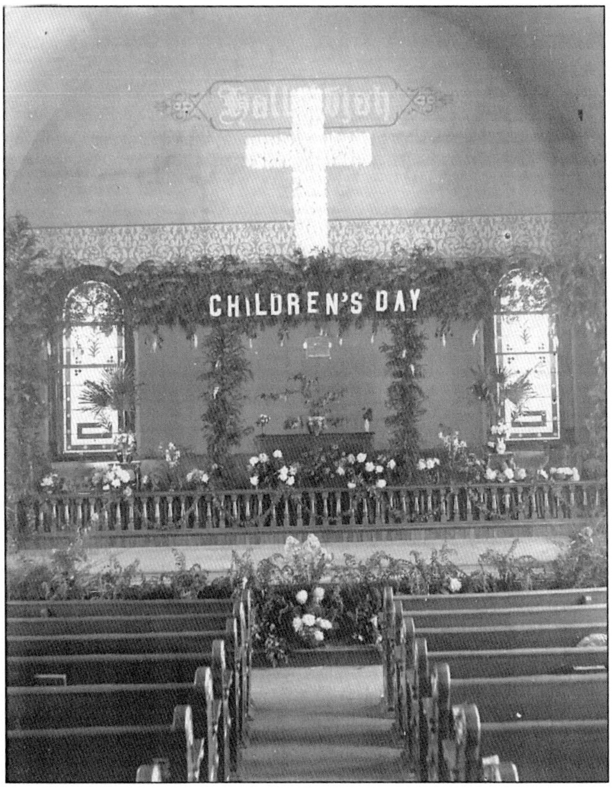

This scene in one of the Protestant churches in Mineral Point has not been identified. The church is nicely decorated for "Children's Day."

"Old" St. Paul's Catholic Church at 414 Ridge Street is pictured here. This photo depicts two of the buildings formerly used by the Catholic congregation organized in 1838, and now known as St. Paul's. The early, small stone building of 1842 was originally called St. Charles'. It is linked to the missionary activity of the Reverend Samuel Mazzuchelli, who preached, baptized and performed Mass in Mineral Point during the 1830s and 1840s. A Dominican missionary born in 1806 in Milan, Italy, he came to the United States and was ordained by Bishop Edward T. Fenwick in 1830. Fr. Samuel served in Green Bay and then came to the lead region, and continued his missionary work in the present states of Wisconsin, Illinois, and Iowa. There he founded several other Catholic churches and schools as well as the Dominican Mother House at Sinsanawa prior to his death in 1864. The larger building in this photo was used from 1860 until 1910, when it was demolished for construction of an even larger building.

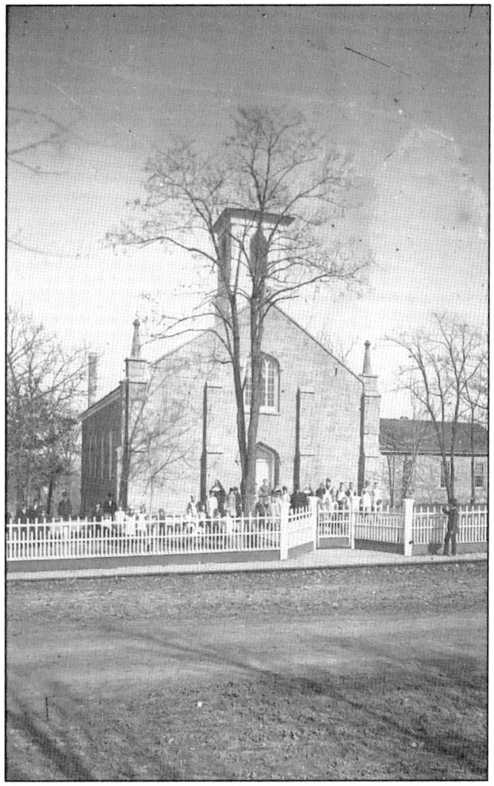

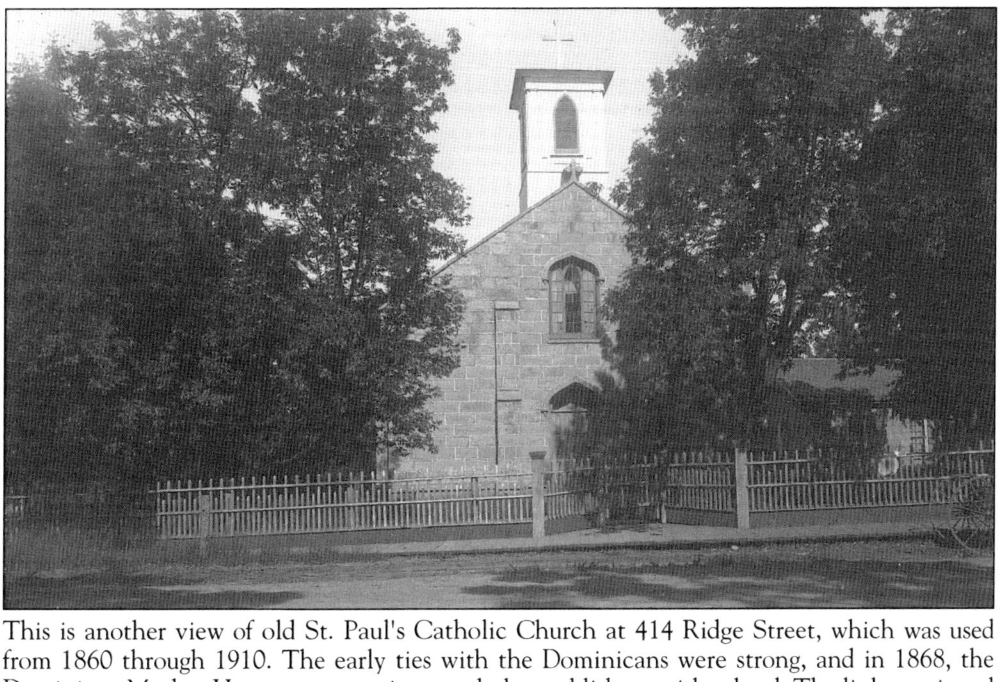

This is another view of old St. Paul's Catholic Church at 414 Ridge Street, which was used from 1860 through 1910. The early ties with the Dominicans were strong, and in 1868, the Dominican Mother House sent two sisters to help establish a parish school. The link continued until July of 1883. St. Paul's early congregation was primarily made up of Irish immigrants who were later joined by Italian immigrants to Mineral Point.

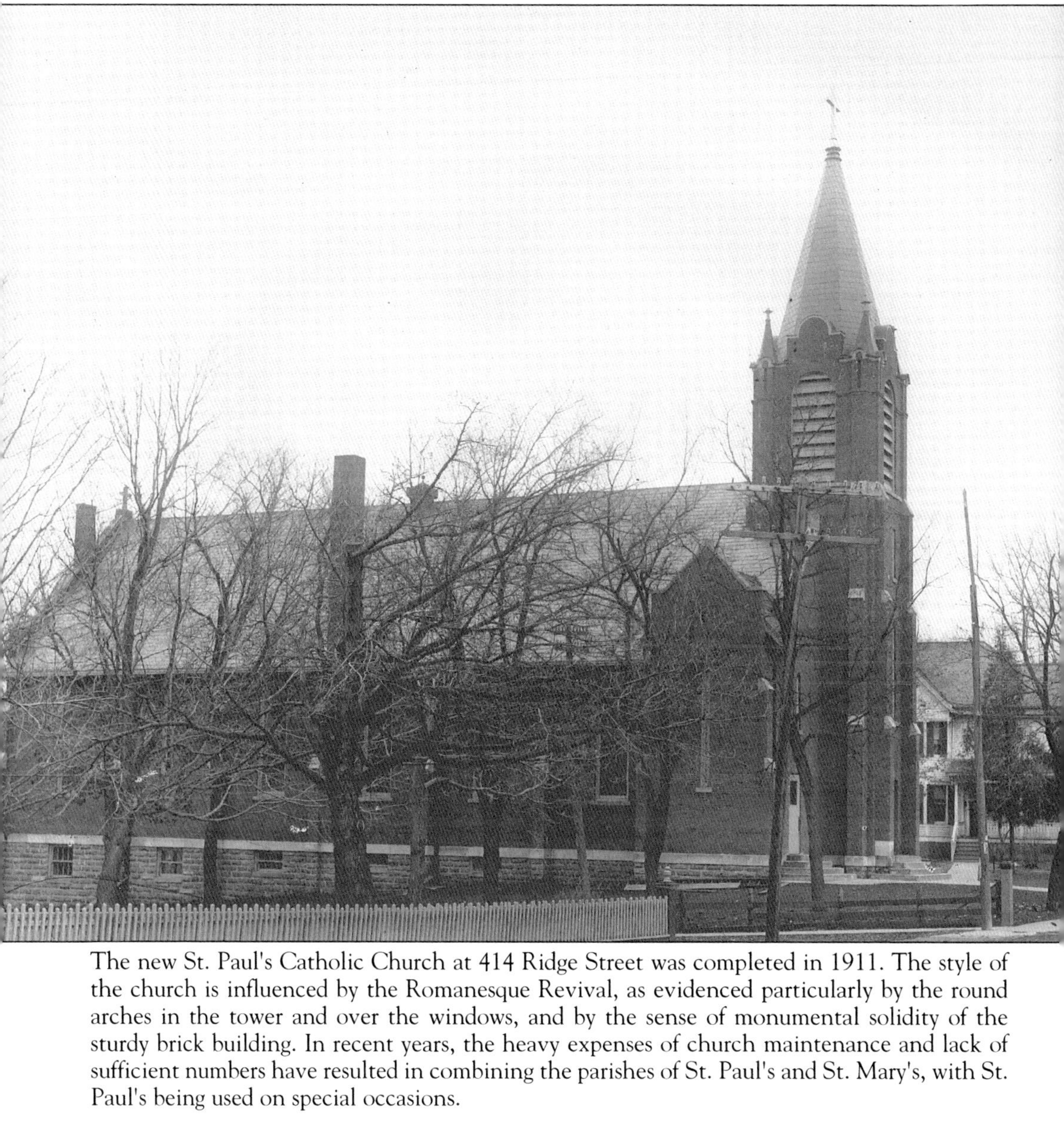

The new St. Paul's Catholic Church at 414 Ridge Street was completed in 1911. The style of the church is influenced by the Romanesque Revival, as evidenced particularly by the round arches in the tower and over the windows, and by the sense of monumental solidity of the sturdy brick building. In recent years, the heavy expenses of church maintenance and lack of sufficient numbers have resulted in combining the parishes of St. Paul's and St. Mary's, with St. Paul's being used on special occasions.

Old St. Mary's Catholic Church was constructed in 1870 in the northeast area of town but is no longer standing. This parish was formed by Catholics of German extraction who had originally belonged to St. Paul's and then decided they wanted their own church. In 1871, St. Mary's opened a school—a two-story structure which no longer stands.

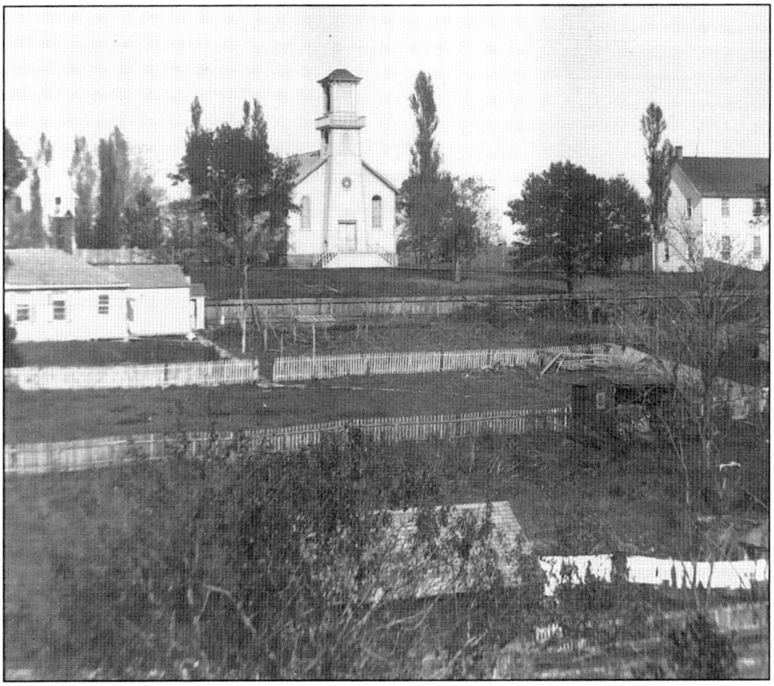

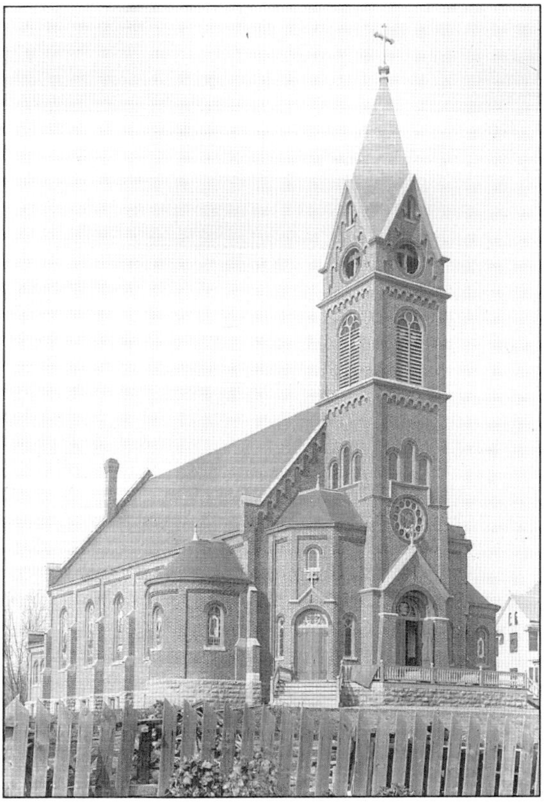

The new St. Mary's Catholic Church at 224 Davis Street was constructed in 1901 of red Menominee pressed brick. The Romanesque Revival style of this church is noted in the rusticated stone of the foundation and in the abundant use of arches over all the windows and doors and as decorative features with strings of miniature arches under the eaves of the front facade and on the tower. St Mary's also built a new school in 1904, a large two-story brick structure at 216 Davis Street. It featured a high stone foundation and intersecting gabled roofs surmounted by an octagonal cupola. Ornamentation consisted of white stone lintels and foundation contrasting with the red brick of the structure in keeping with the Victorian penchant for constructional coloration. St. Mary's school was substantially renovated and expanded in the 1960s. The school operated successfully for almost one hundred years. It closed in 1969–70, and the last teaching sisters left at that time.

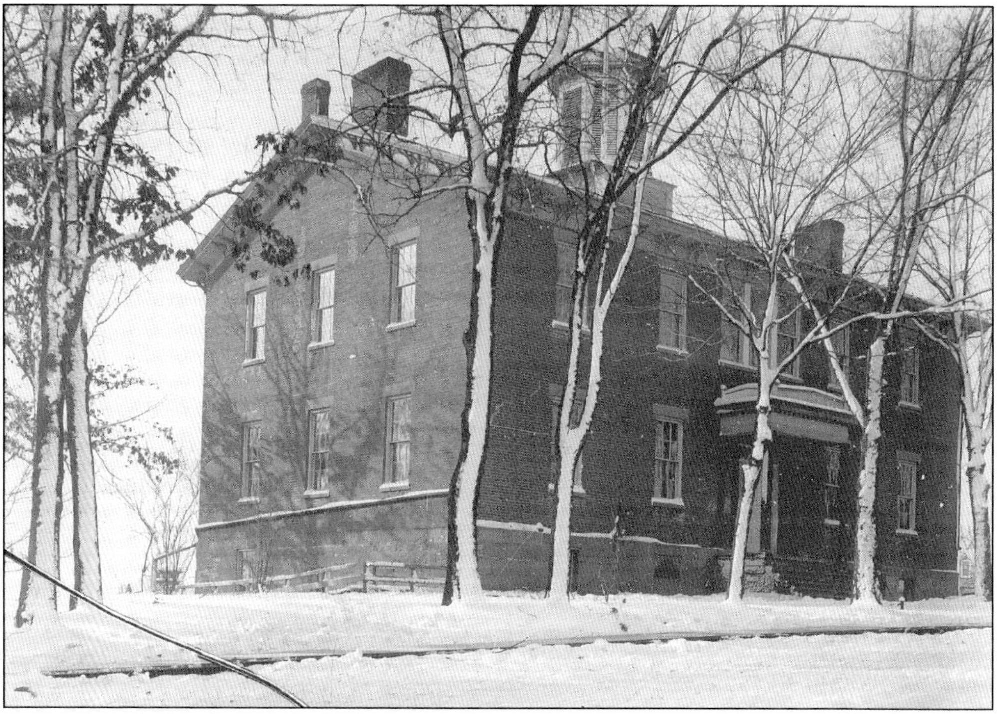

An unidentified, substantially-built two-story brick school with a stone foundation is pictured here. It is a side-gabled structure accented by a cupola.

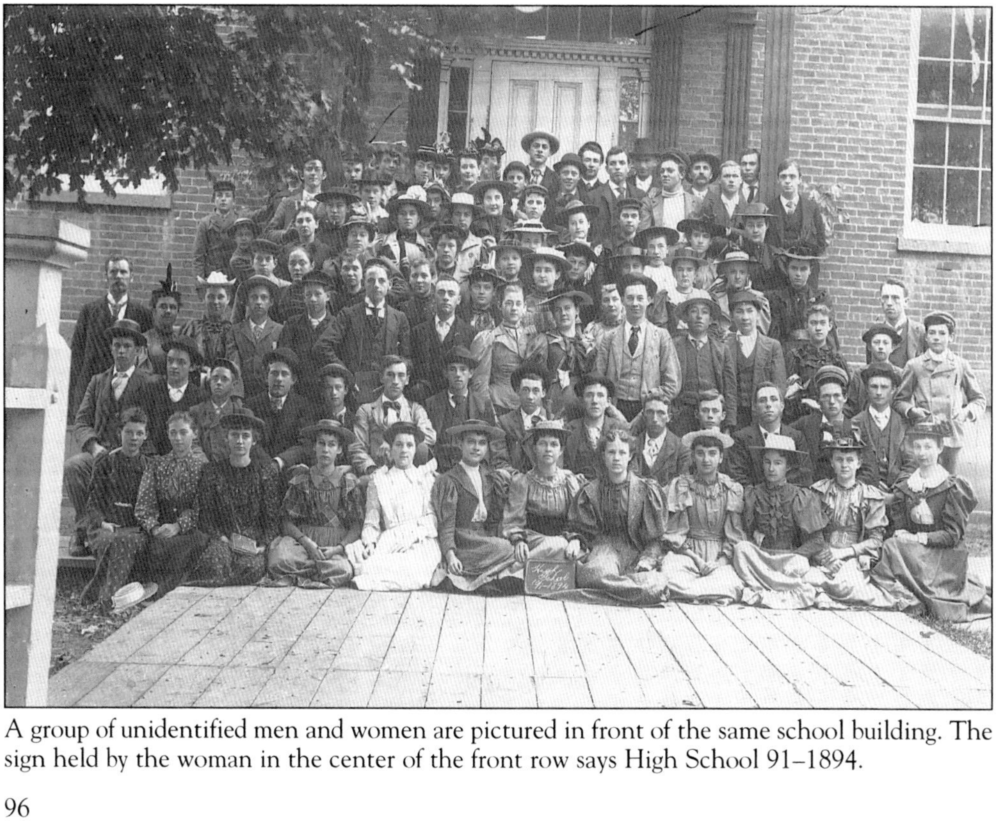

A group of unidentified men and women are pictured in front of the same school building. The sign held by the woman in the center of the front row says High School 91–1894.

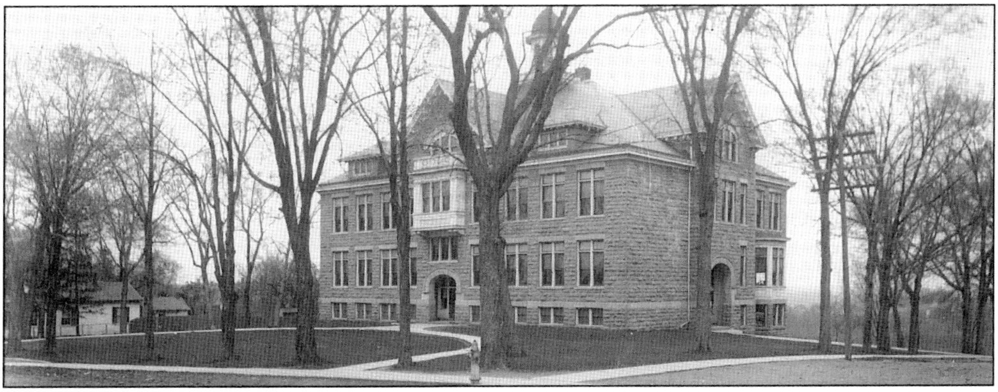

The former Mineral Point High School opened in 1904 at 530 Maiden Street. Early attempts to provide a high school education in Mineral Point were established by private academies, churches, and individuals offering private lessons. For example, in 1848 Miss E. Phillips opened a school for young ladies, in 1854 Miss Caroline Jacobs opened a school in the basement of the Episcopal church, and in 1856 the Methodist Episcopal church opened a seminary. With the formation of the State of Wisconsin, the first public school was opened in 1850, in response to laws organized in the constitution of the new state. In 1861, Mineral Point created its official public high school program.

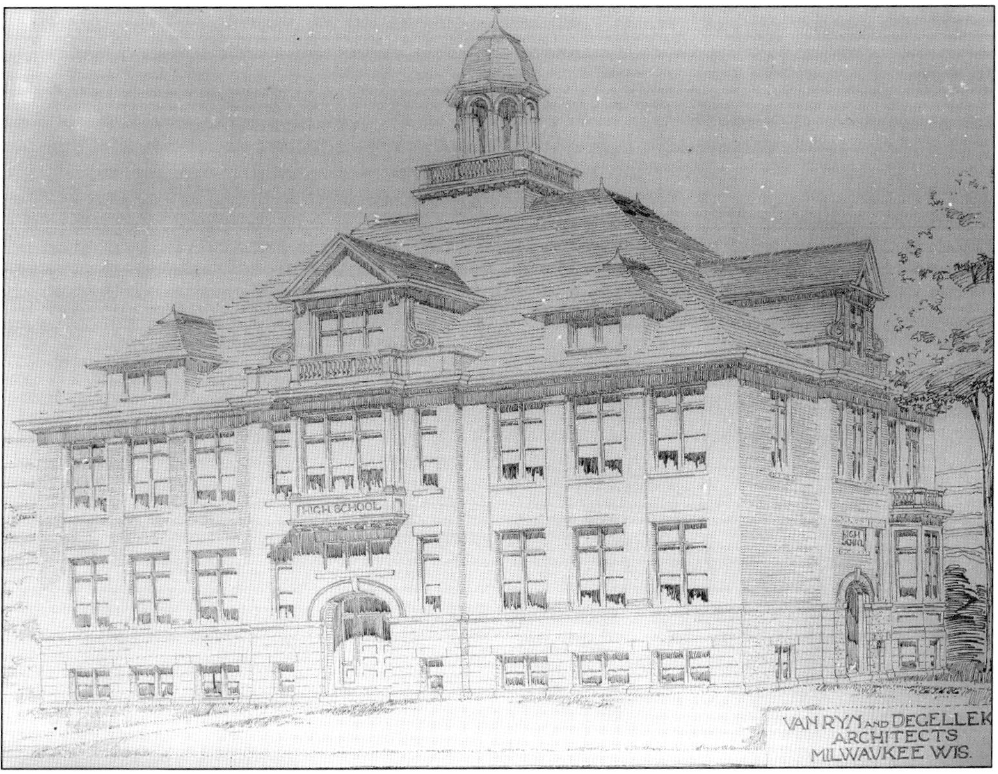

This is a photo of the architects' drawing of the former Mineral Point High School, which was designed by the Milwaukee firm of Van Ryn and Degelleke. This building was constructed of beautifully cut limestone by local builders Charles Curtis, S. Jenkin, and Herman Enzenroth. This building later became an elementary school, a middle school, and has now been sold to a private developer and divided up into apartments.

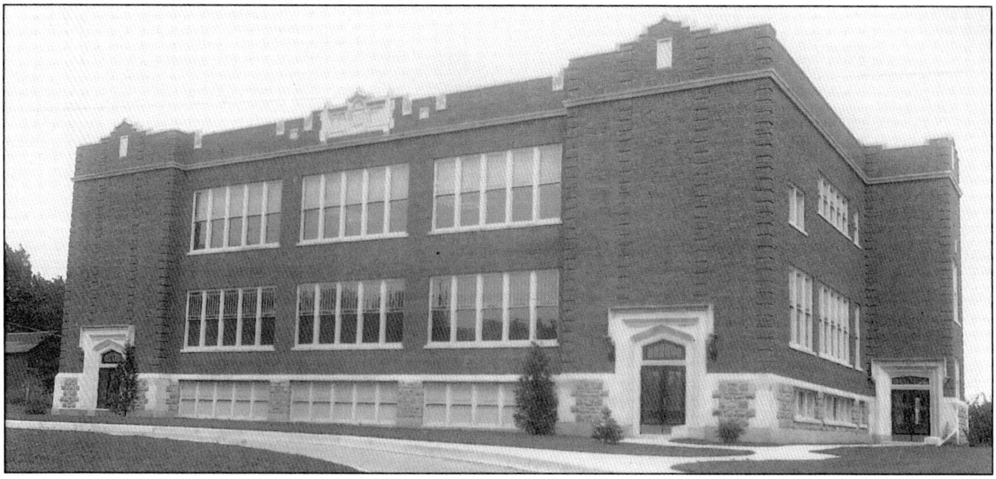

This Mineral Point High School building at 706 Ridge Road, which opened in 1925, superseded the building shown in the preceding photograph. It has since been succeeded by a new high school and middle school which opened in the fall of 1997. This building has been sold by the city and currently houses several businesses.

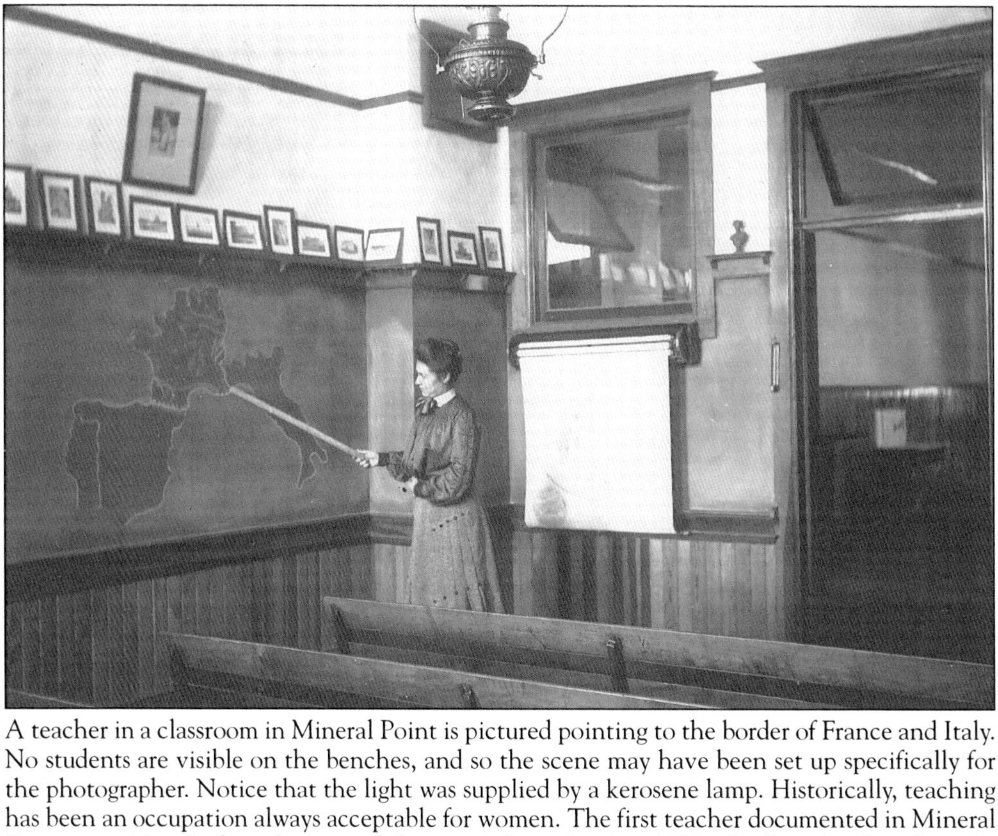

A teacher in a classroom in Mineral Point is pictured pointing to the border of France and Italy. No students are visible on the benches, and so the scene may have been set up specifically for the photographer. Notice that the light was supplied by a kerosene lamp. Historically, teaching has been an occupation always acceptable for women. The first teacher documented in Mineral Point was a Mrs. Harker who opened the town's first school in 1829, which is also thought to be the first school opened for non-Native Americans in what is now Wisconsin. Reportedly there were eight students in Mrs. Harker's school—most of them belonging to the Nolton family.

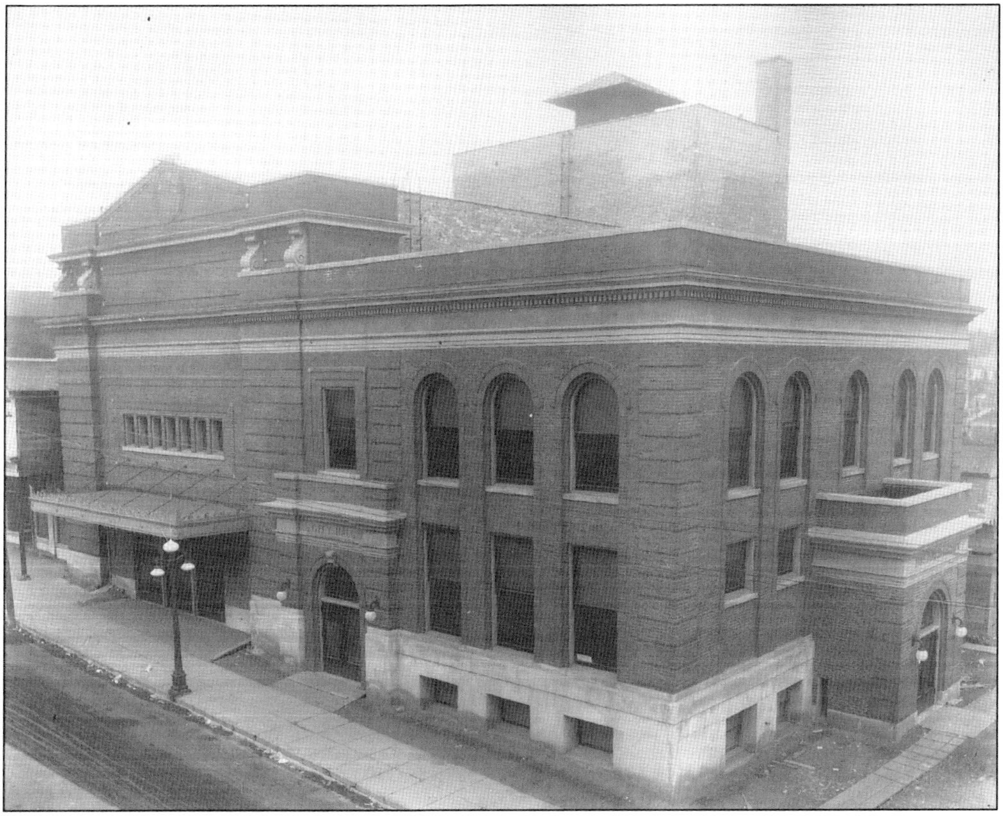

The Mineral Point Municipal Building at 137–139 High Street was built in 1913 by the architectural firm of Claude and Stark. The history of libraries in Mineral Point begins with George W. Bliss establishing a private reading room in 1854. This was followed by the Mineral Point Library Association in 1860, and the Free Public Library of Mineral Point in 1895. The library is presently housed in the Mineral Point Municipal Building with the entrance to the library on the right side of the building. This structure also housed the city hall and the Municipal Theater, which is now called the Opera House.

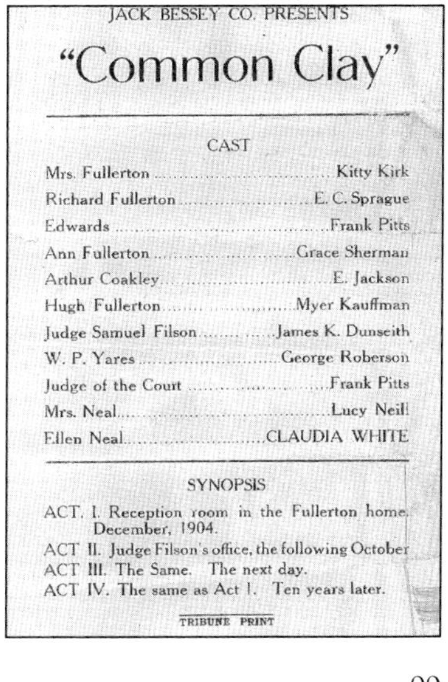

JACK BESSEY CO. PRESENTS

"Common Clay"

CAST

Mrs. Fullerton	Kitty Kirk
Richard Fullerton	E. C. Sprague
Edwards	Frank Pitts
Ann Fullerton	Grace Sherman
Arthur Coakley	E. Jackson
Hugh Fullerton	Myer Kauffman
Judge Samuel Filson	James K. Dunseith
W. P. Yares	George Roberson
Judge of the Court	Frank Pitts
Mrs. Neal	Lucy Neill
Ellen Neal	CLAUDIA WHITE

SYNOPSIS

ACT. I. Reception room in the Fullerton home, December, 1904.
ACT II. Judge Filson's office, the following October
ACT III. The Same. The next day.
ACT IV. The same as Act I. Ten years later.

TRIBUNE PRINT

A playbill for the Municipal Theatre on High Street is shown here.

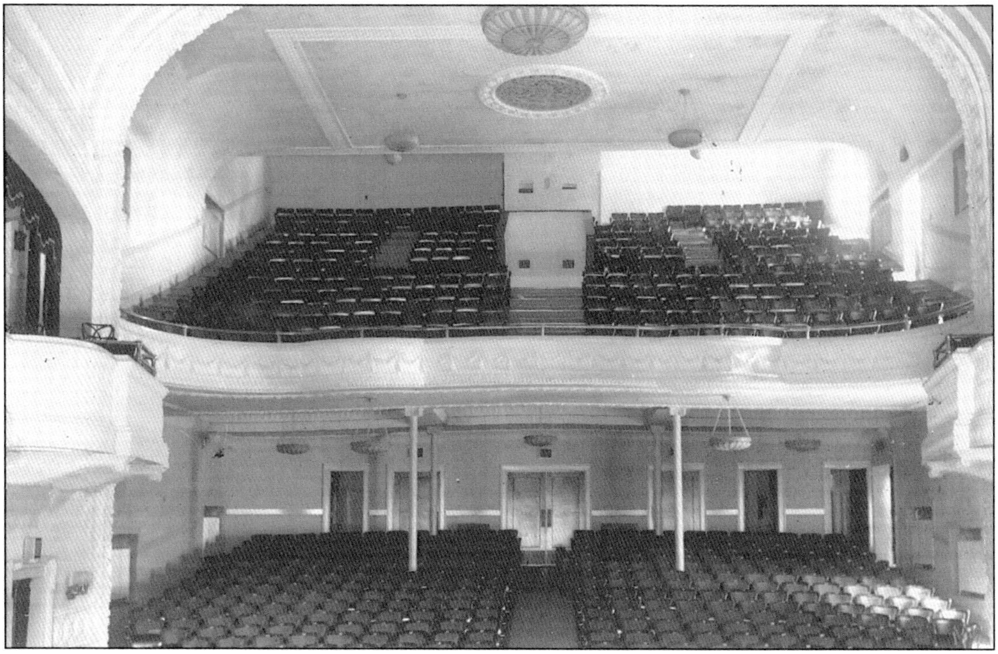

Mineral Point Municipal Building on High Street houses the library, city offices, and a large theater. The theater interior of the Mineral Point Opera House includes a full proscenium, box seats, and a commodious balcony—excellent sight lines from every seat and elaborate plaster cast decorations as are visible in this photograph.

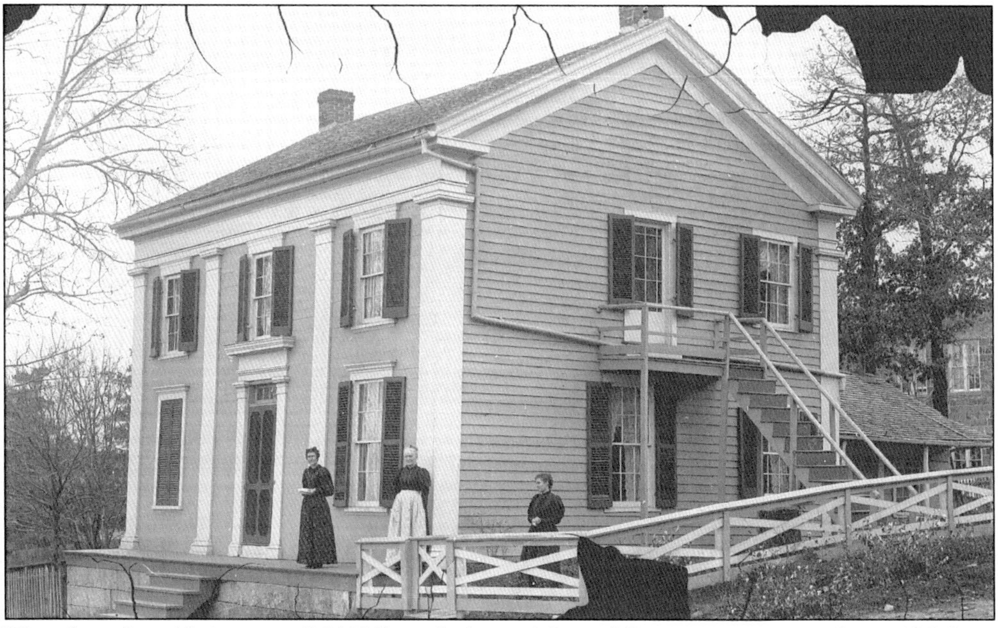

The idea of establishing an Odd Fellows lodge in Mineral Point was conceived in 1835, by a group of miners from Pottsville, Pennsylvania, who had been members there. The lodge shown here was constructed in 1838, and is the oldest Odd Fellows lodge west of the Alleghenies. This frame building in a Greek Revival style with a low-pitched roof and Doric pilasters still stands at 112 Front Street, and is currently the Wisconsin Odd Fellows Museum.

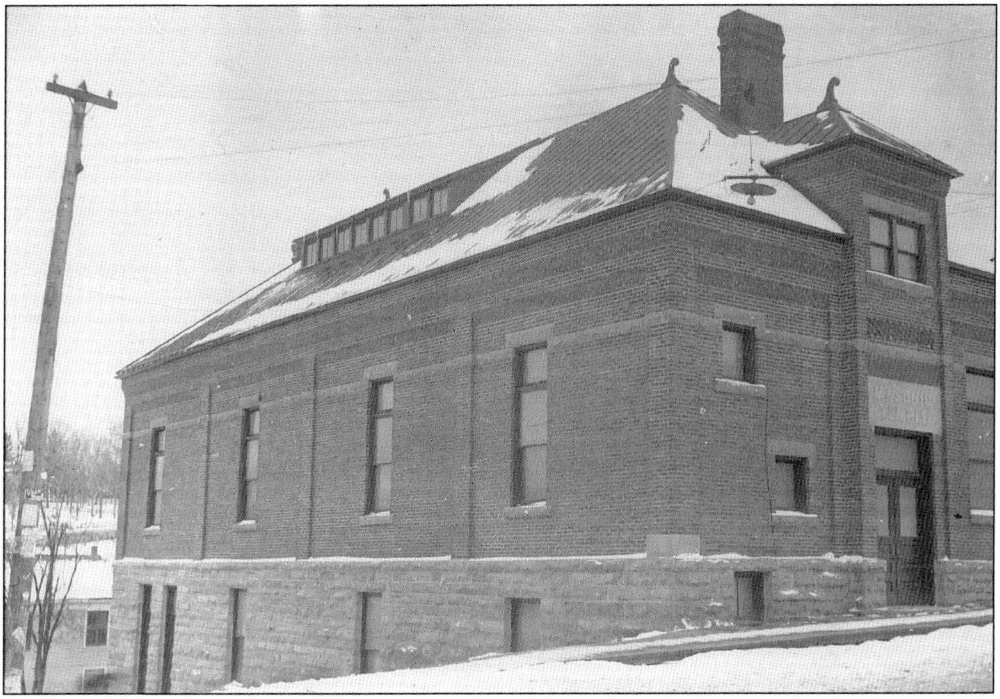

In 1841, Lodge No. 1 of the Free and Accepted Masons was established in Mineral Point, and many prominent men of the community were members. The present building at 306 High Street was constructed in 1897 to replace an earlier lodge which had been destroyed by a fire on High Street earlier in the same year. This building was expanded in 1920 with a brick addition to its right. The building still stands, and the organization continues to meet, although currently there is a small membership.

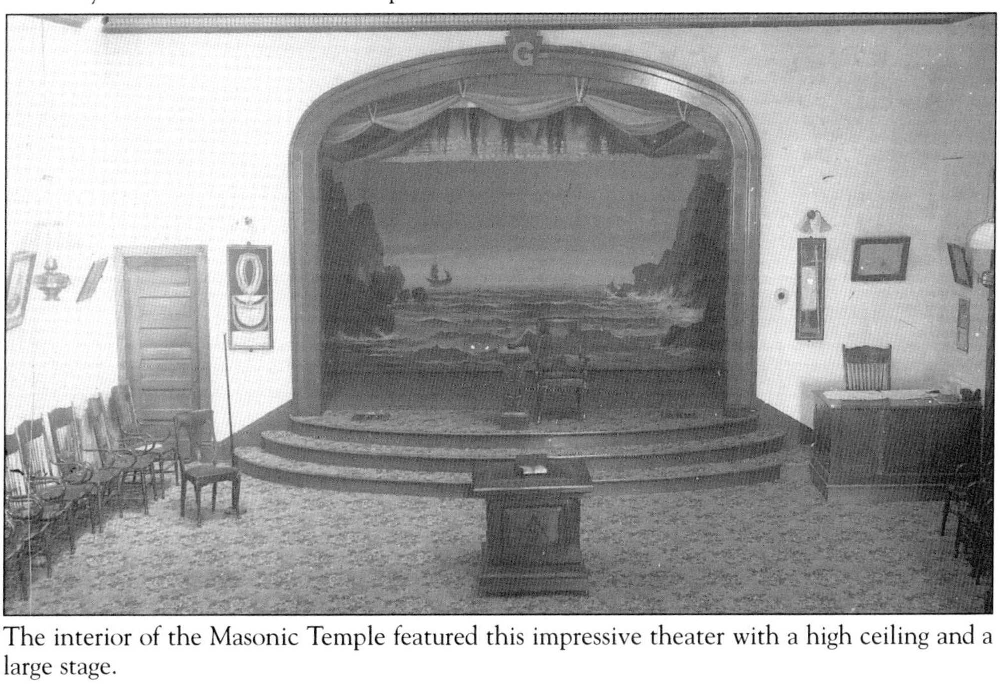

The interior of the Masonic Temple featured this impressive theater with a high ceiling and a large stage.

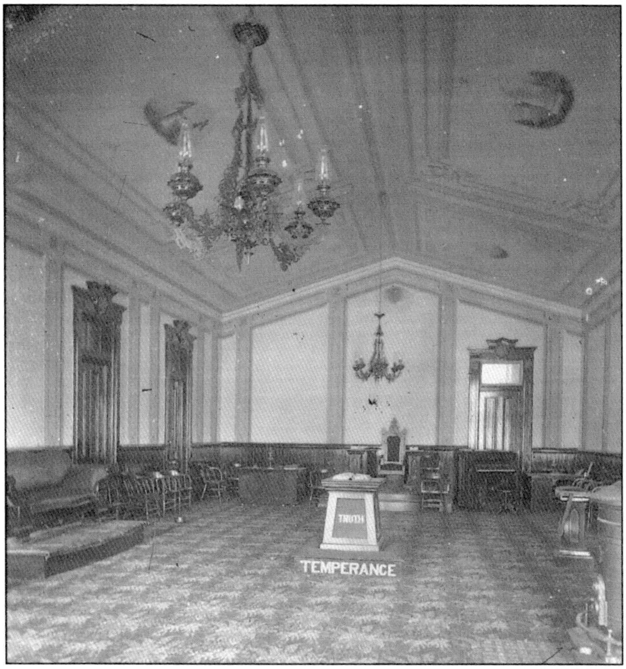

This room, reportedly located inside the Masonic Temple, has elaborate carpeting and two fine chandeliers for kerosene lamps. The virtues of truth and temperance are featured on the lectern in the center of the room. There is a long history of temperance movements in Mineral Point, including one as early as 1845 called the Sons of Temperance and one in 1856 organized by the town's women to promote temperance in the home and in social circles. The latter was appropriately called the Cold Water Union, No. 9 D.T. (Daughters of Temperance), and like most of the other temperance groups, seemed to be short-lived.

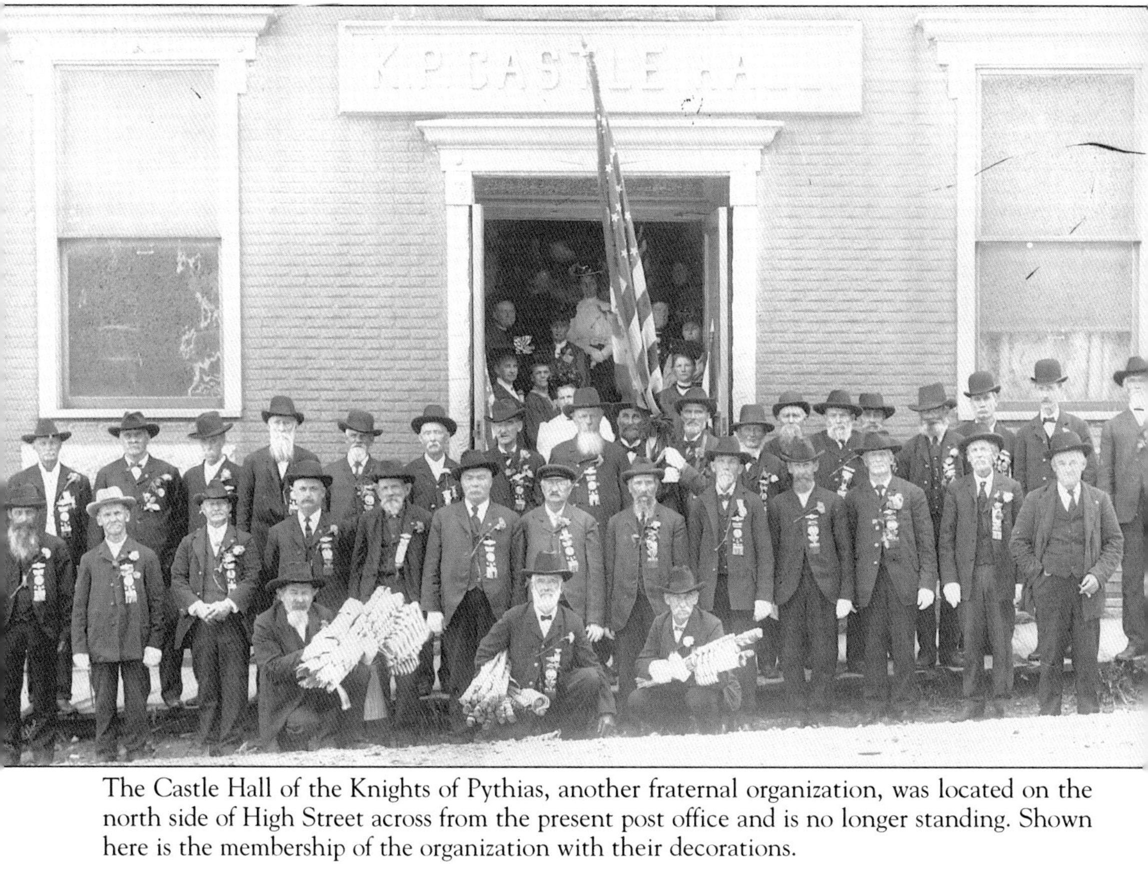

The Castle Hall of the Knights of Pythias, another fraternal organization, was located on the north side of High Street across from the present post office and is no longer standing. Shown here is the membership of the organization with their decorations.

Five

The People of Mineral Point

The history of Mineral Point is certainly a history of the people who came to prospect, to settle, and to raise their families and build a community. In the 1820s, men and a few women from the United States came north drawn by lead deposits. New opportunities for mining and owning land attracted increased numbers of settlers, miners, and land speculators after the so-called Blackhawk War of 1832. At that time the decimated Sauk and Fox tribes of Chief Blackhawk were permanently removed from the lead region and resettled across the nearby Mississippi River on the western side.

The waves of immigrants coming to Mineral Point initially were directly connected to the lead and zinc mining industry. The early arrivals came from the fledgling country of America, mainly from what are now the states of Missouri, Kentucky, Tennessee, and Illinois, with a strong representation also from New England, New York, and Ohio. In 1836, Colonel Henry Dodge, who had come to mine and settle and also fought in the Blackhawk War, was sworn in as the first governor of the Territory of Wisconsin in Mineral Point on July 4, 1836. By 1837, the town's population swelled to one thousand.

An influx of European immigrants came, and the early censuses of 1850 and 1860 indicated that the majority of households were English-speaking but foreign-born. The 1850 census counted 508 households including 311 English—the majority of whom were Cornish—108 American, 49 Irish, and 28 German. Most of those listed as American were then from Pennsylvania and New York, because many of those from the southern states had been transient miners. A significant wave of Italian immigrants arrived late in the nineteenth century to work in the zinc mines and zinc works.

Like people everywhere, those in Mineral Point worked, built homes, raised families, founded organizations—sacred and secular—and enjoyed recreation as well. It is the Cornish population who left the most indelible stamp on the town with their characteristic use of limestone and sandstone for construction, their fascinating myths and legends, and their traditional foods such as the pasty, tea biscuits, and saffron cakes, which are still sold in many area restaurants.

While many former mining towns collapsed along with the industry, the resilient people of Mineral Point have continued to adapt. The town currently has an increasingly diverse population of around 2,500 with a strong commitment to the town's historic past and a vision for the future.

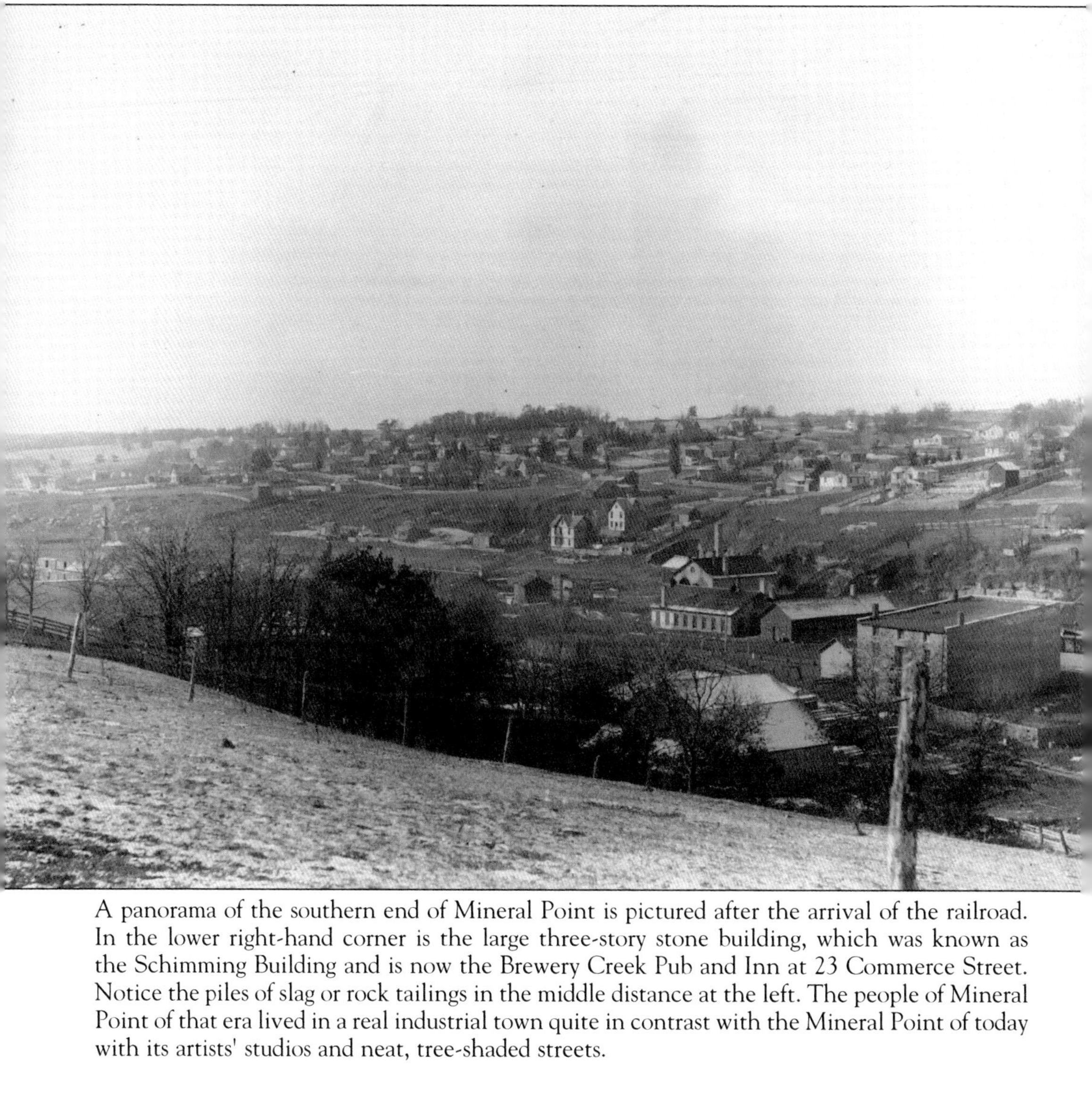

A panorama of the southern end of Mineral Point is pictured after the arrival of the railroad. In the lower right-hand corner is the large three-story stone building, which was known as the Schimming Building and is now the Brewery Creek Pub and Inn at 23 Commerce Street. Notice the piles of slag or rock tailings in the middle distance at the left. The people of Mineral Point of that era lived in a real industrial town quite in contrast with the Mineral Point of today with its artists' studios and neat, tree-shaded streets.

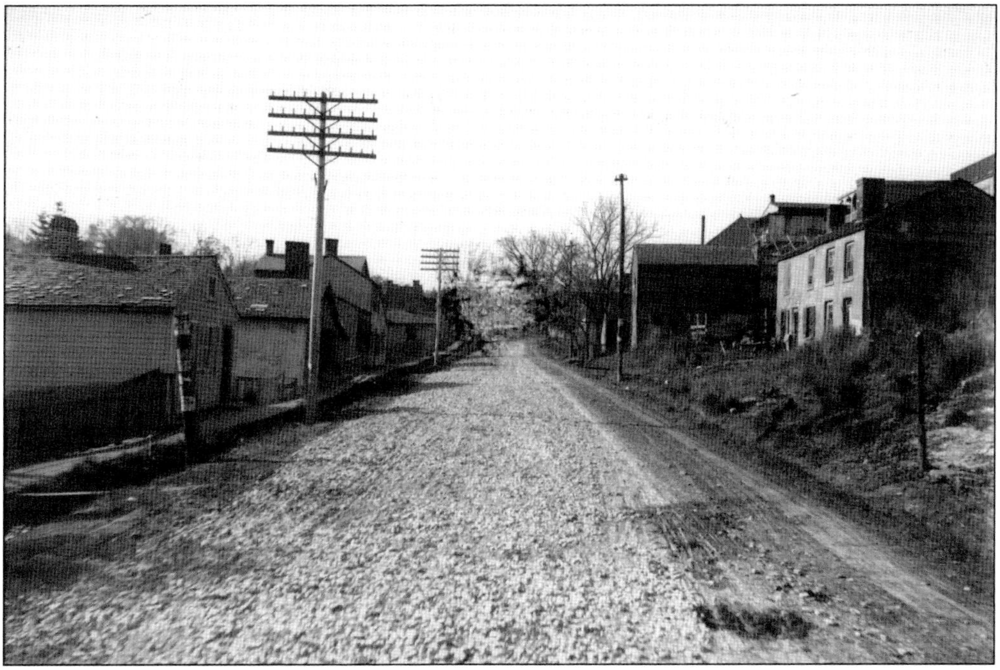

This is a view up Fountain Street from the corner of Chestnut Street. The backs of the buildings on High Street are visible on the right. The residences on the left side of the street are, for the most part, very modest.

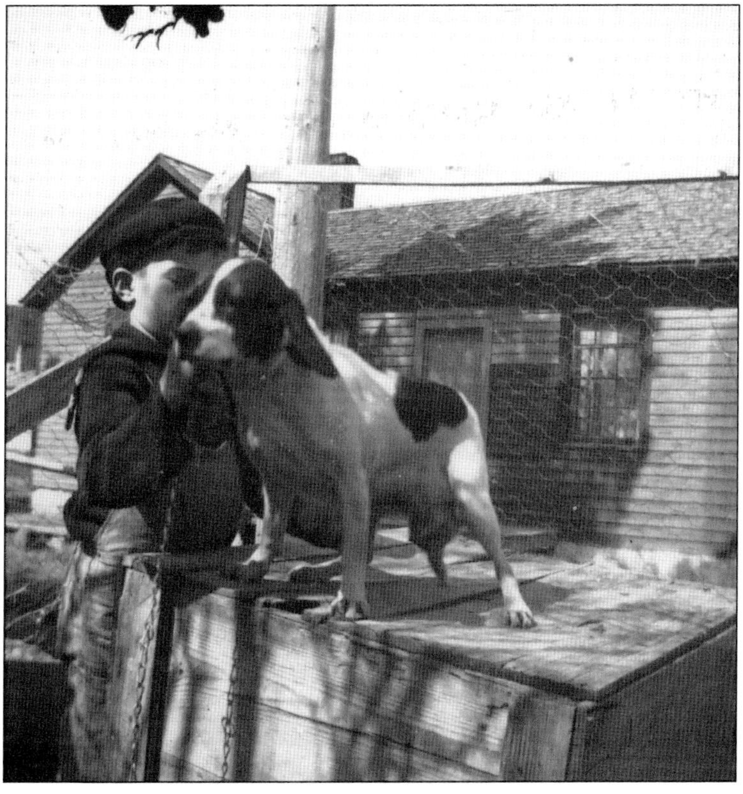

A boy and his dog are pictured with a small frame house in the background.

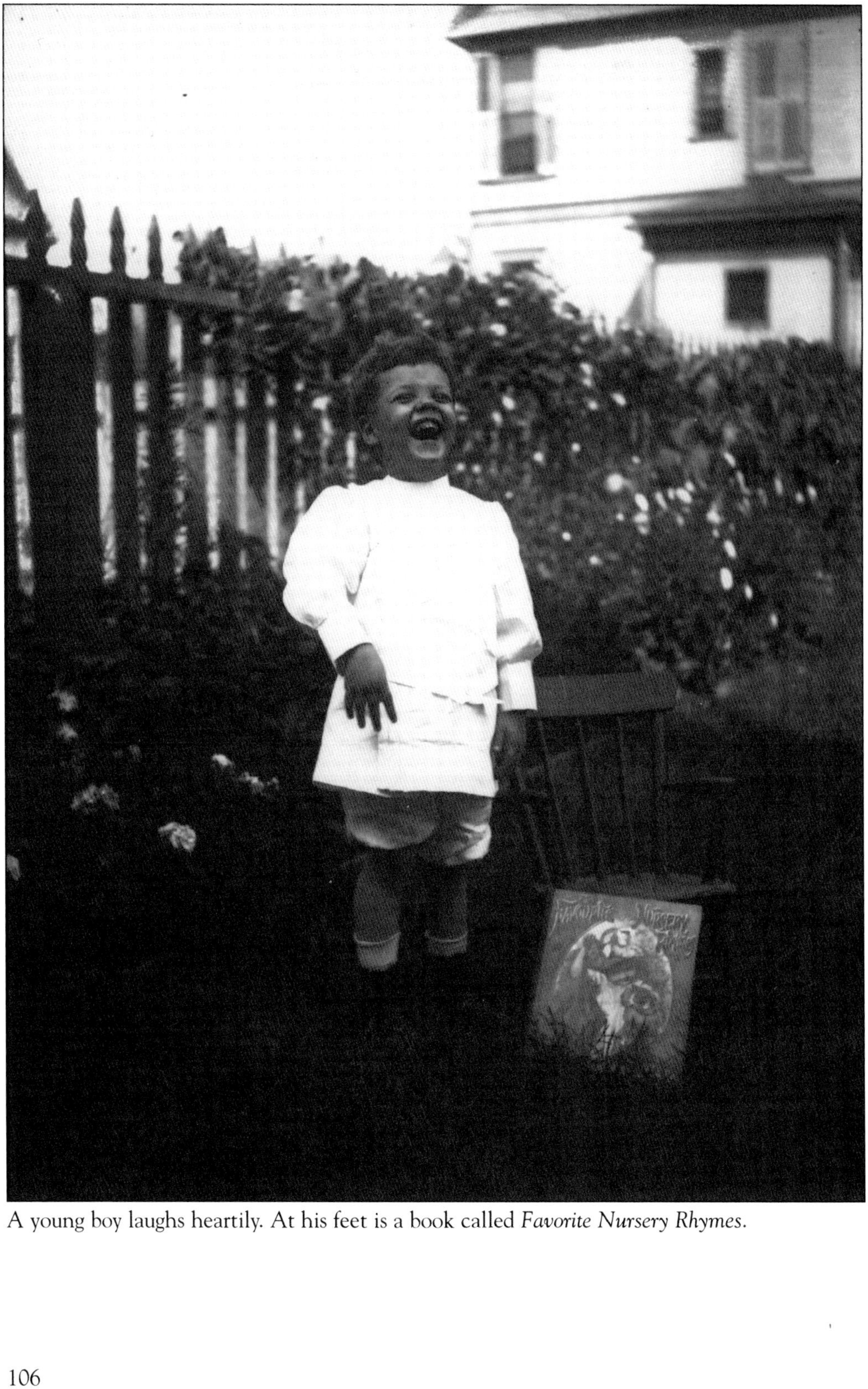

A young boy laughs heartily. At his feet is a book called *Favorite Nursery Rhymes*.

This is a photo of three young children in the garden of their home.

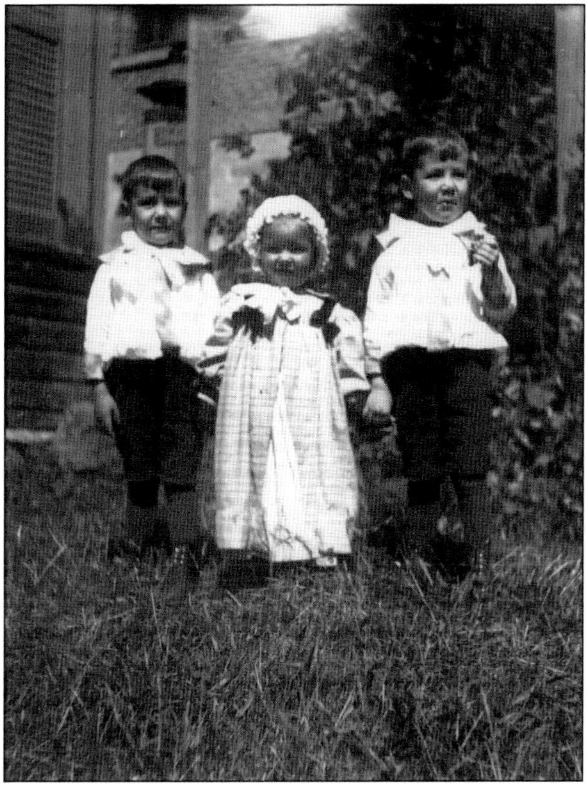

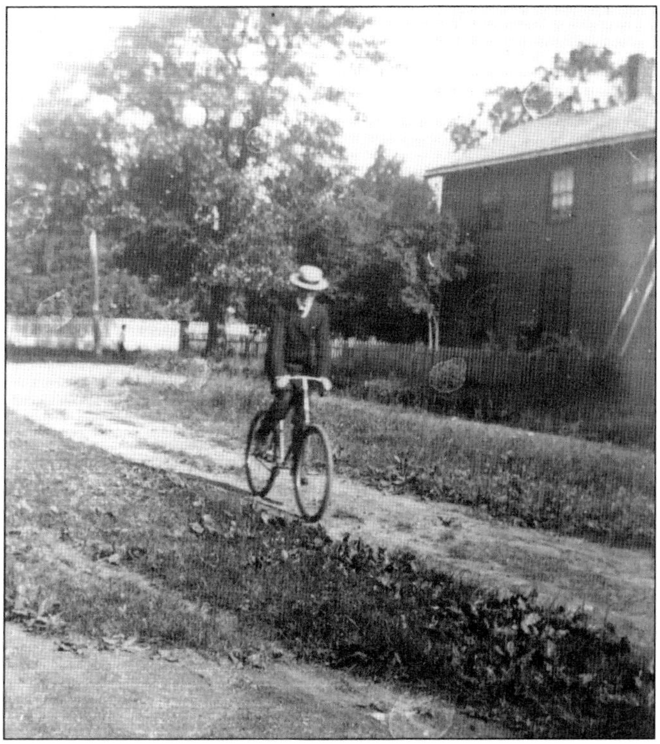

This is a photo of a man on a bicycle in Mineral Point. Early bicycles were soon improved, with many of the innovations taking place in France. They quickly gained popularity as being a relatively inexpensive and fast means of transport. The ninth edition of the *Encyclopedia Britannica* in 1876 gives some sage advice on riding a bicycle, warning that "Falls are inevitable at first, and they are best avoided by slightly turning the driving-wheel in the direction the machine is inclining...."

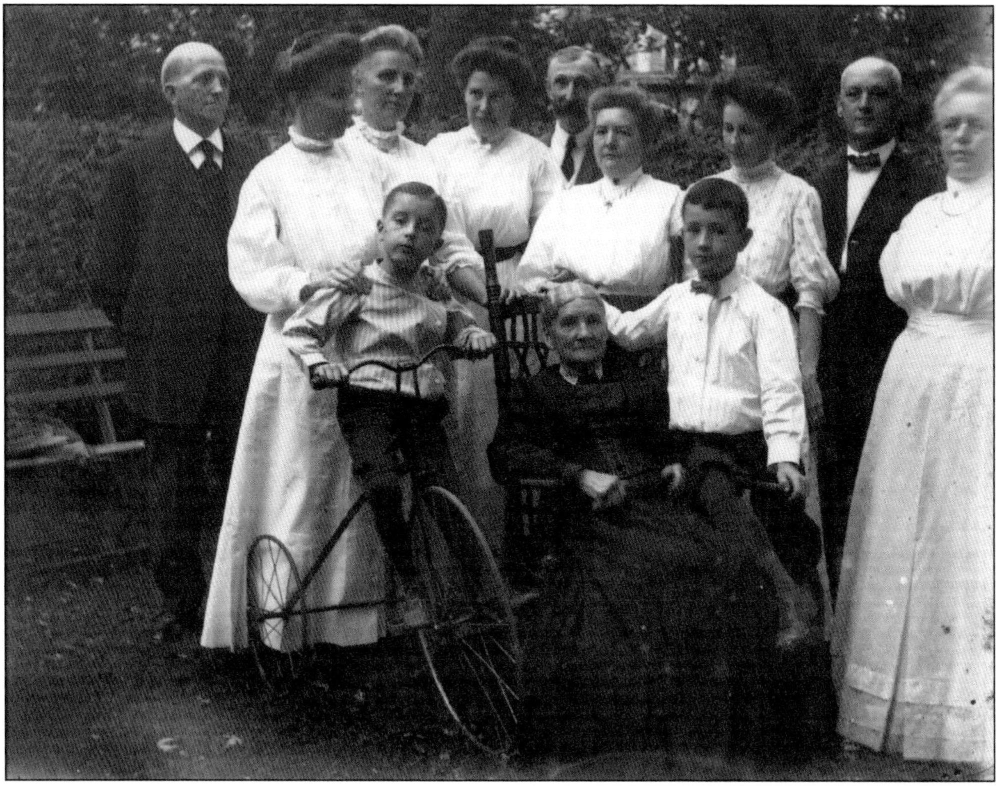

This photo depicts a multi-generational family group with the young boy at the left of the photograph on a tricycle.

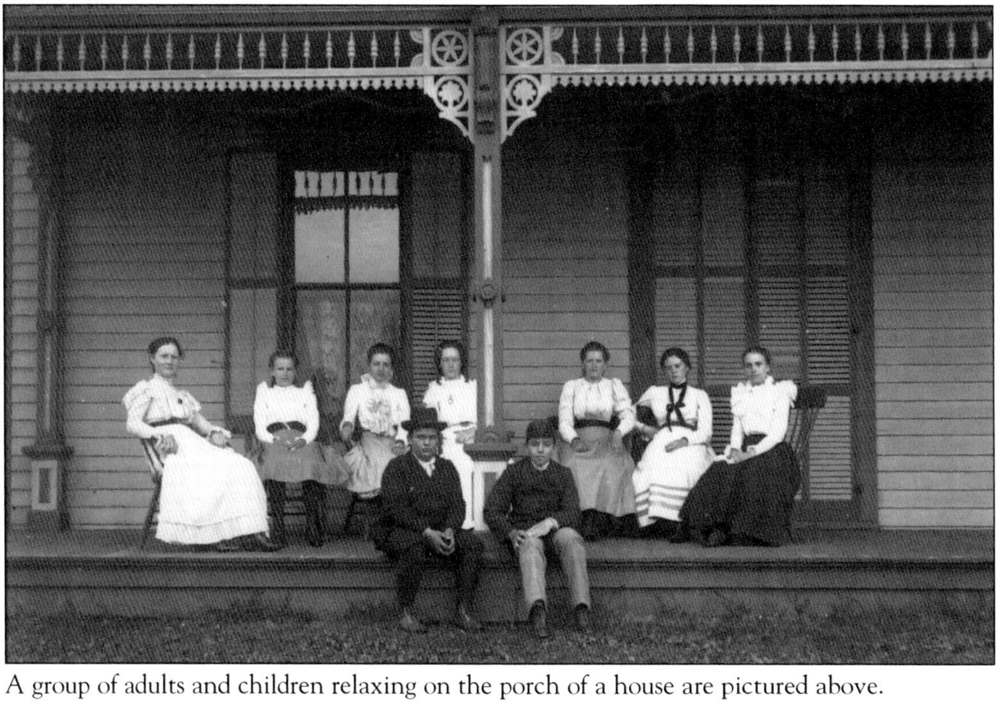

A group of adults and children relaxing on the porch of a house are pictured above.

Two young boys in their Sunday best are pictured outside of the new Primitive Methodist Church, which is now the United Church of Christ, at the crossroad of Maiden and Chestnut Streets.

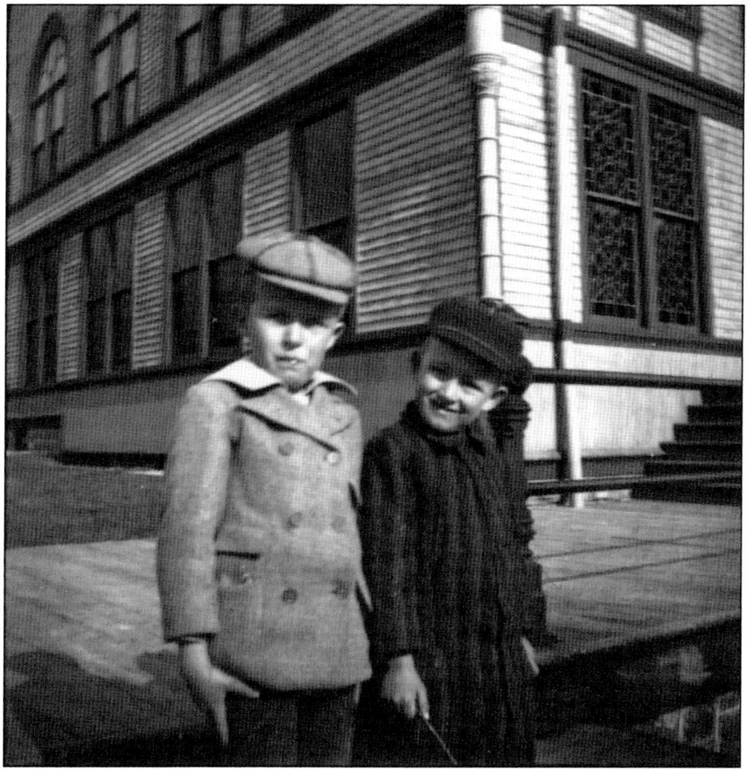

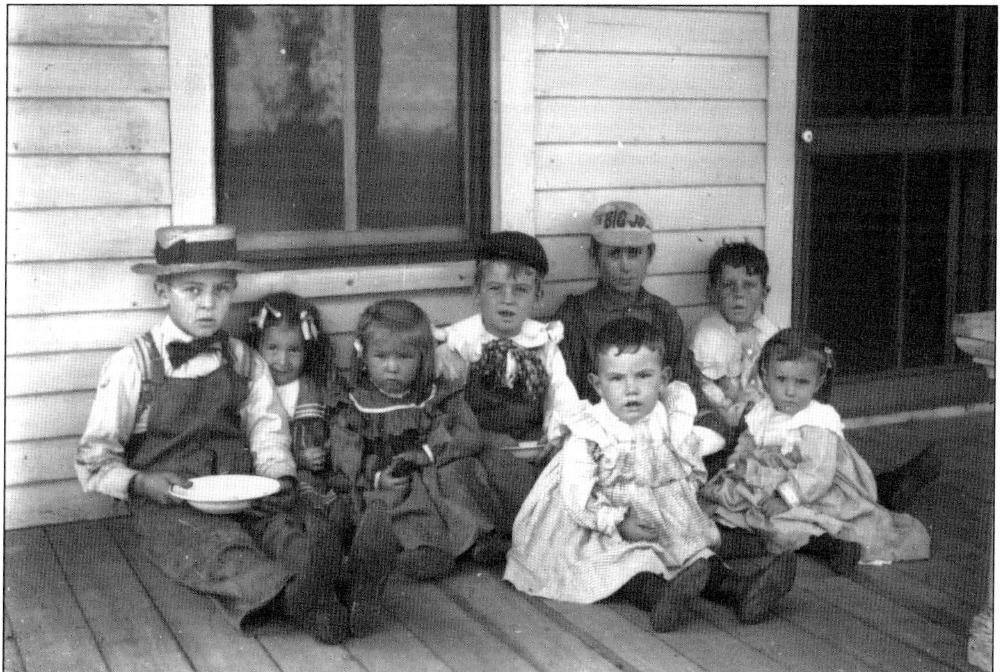

A group of children on a porch are pictured here. They have done a very good job of staying still for the photographer.

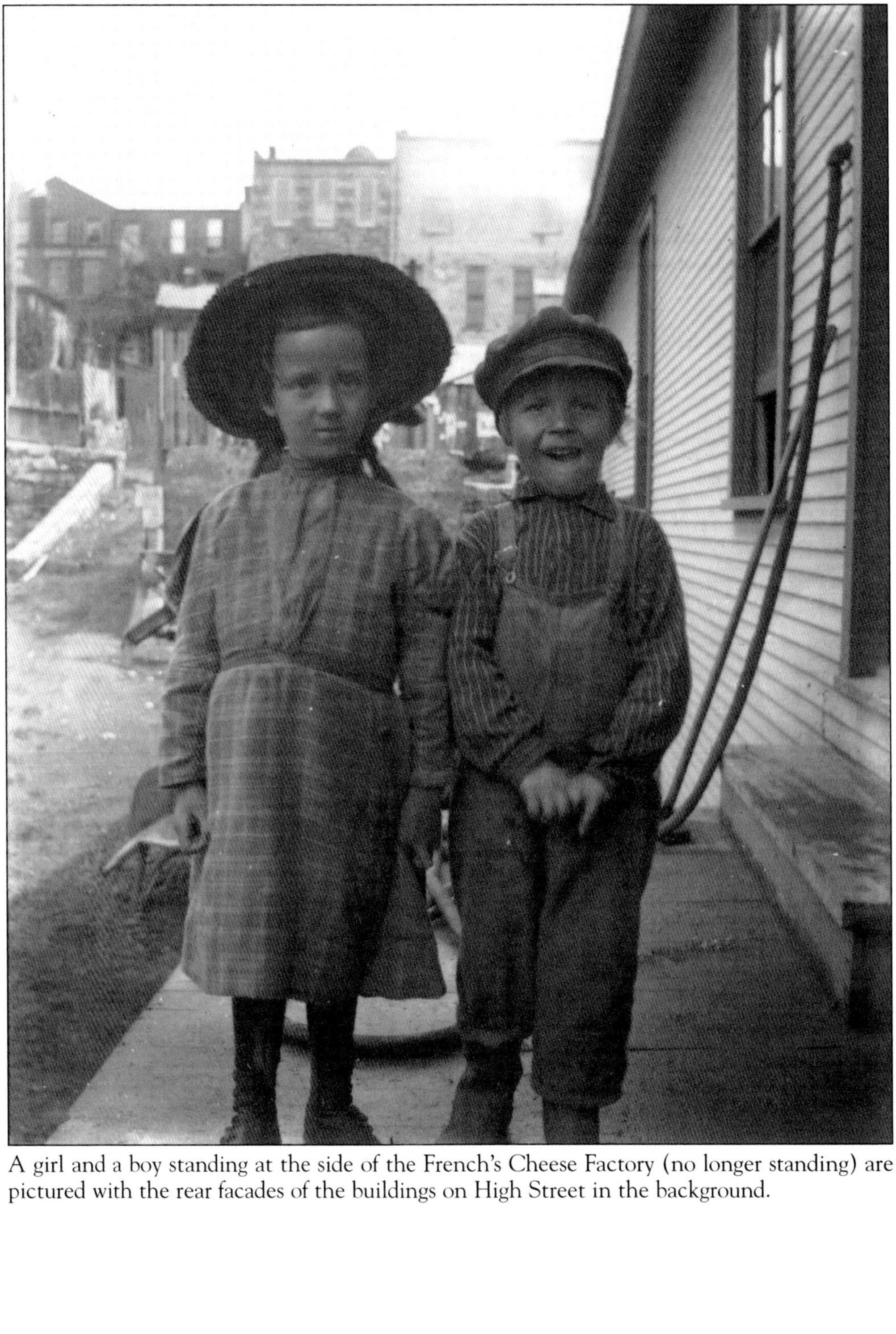

A girl and a boy standing at the side of the French's Cheese Factory (no longer standing) are pictured with the rear facades of the buildings on High Street in the background.

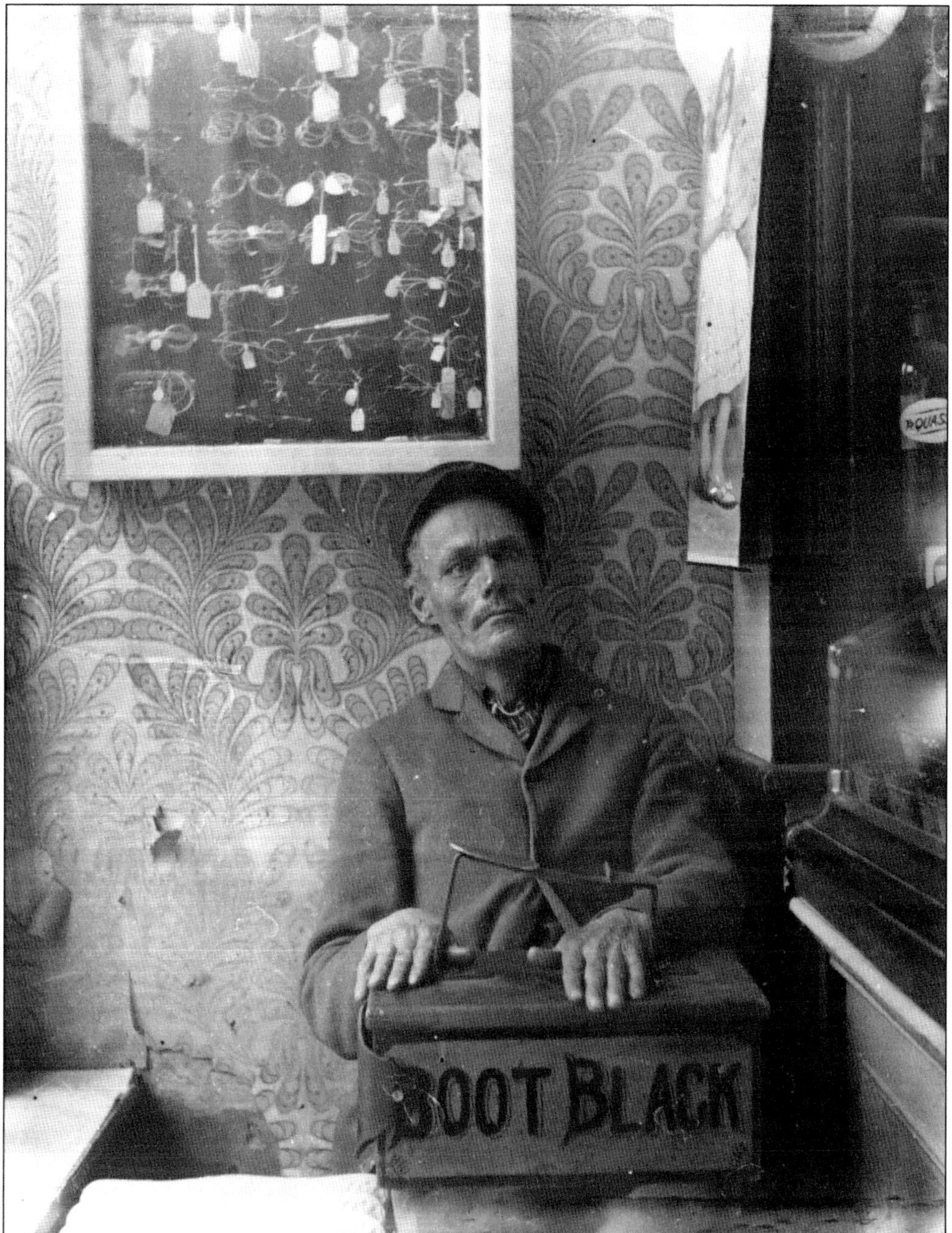

This is a picture of a bootblack, one who shined shoes for a living, taken in a drug store—likely the interior of Dr. Vivian's at 128 High Street. Behind him is a display of eyeglasses.

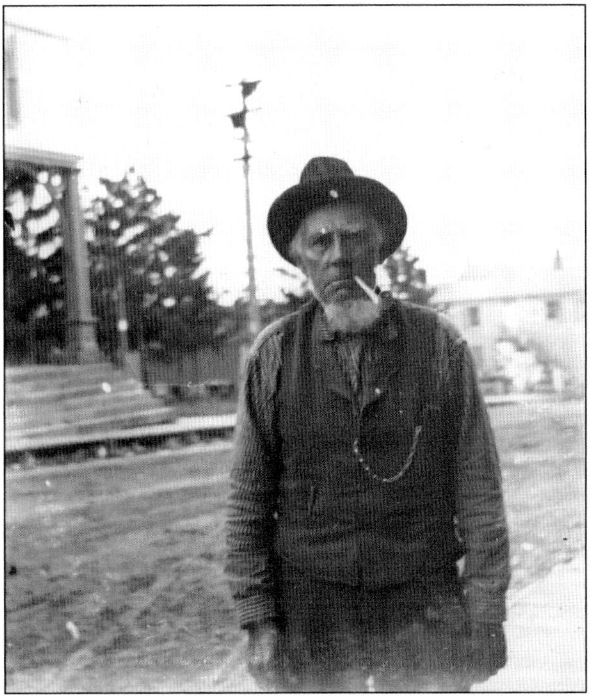

This is a portrait of a man smoking a pipe on High Street.

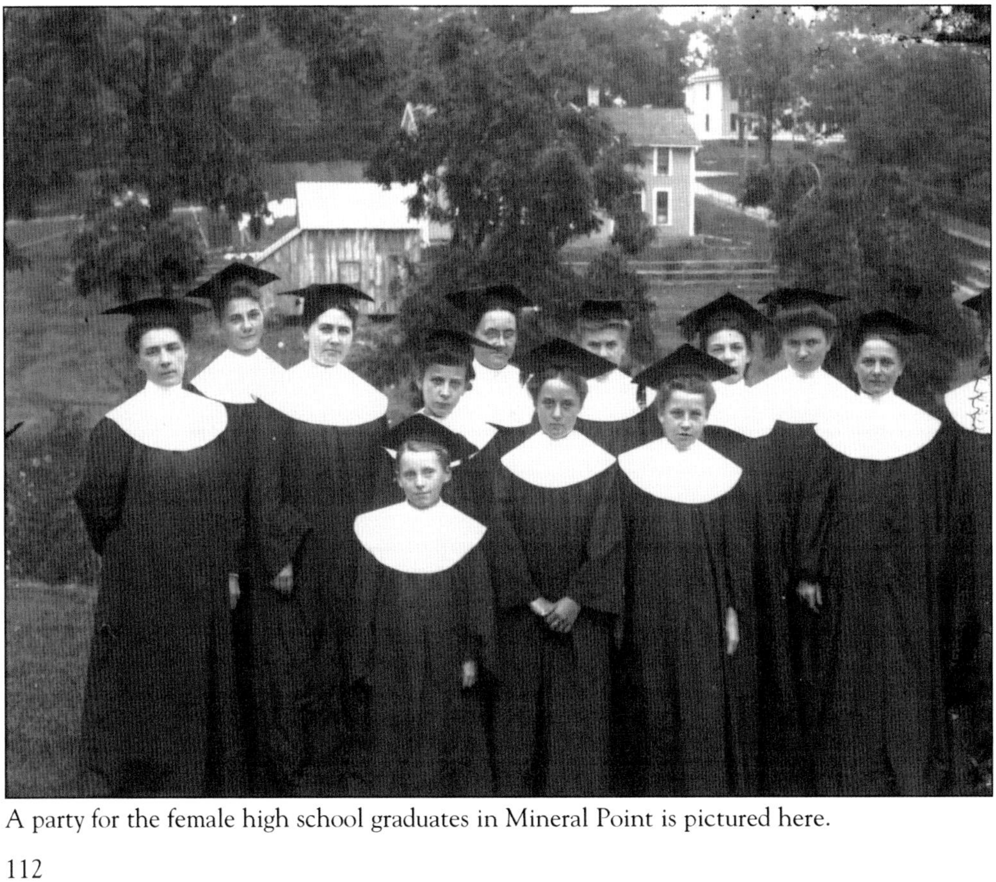

A party for the female high school graduates in Mineral Point is pictured here.

This is a woman on a bicycle in a shop. She wears an outfit suitable for riding a bicycle. For actual riding, her skirt would likely be cut to mid-calf length, and she would wear gaiters to protect her shoes and lower legs. Her jacket features huge "leg-o-mutton" sleeves made popular in the 1890s.

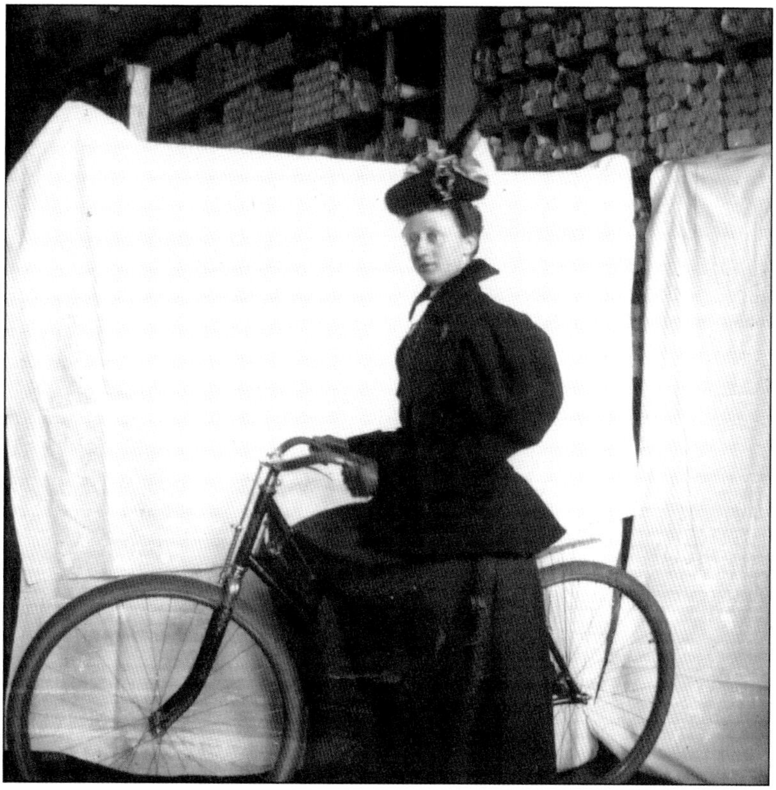

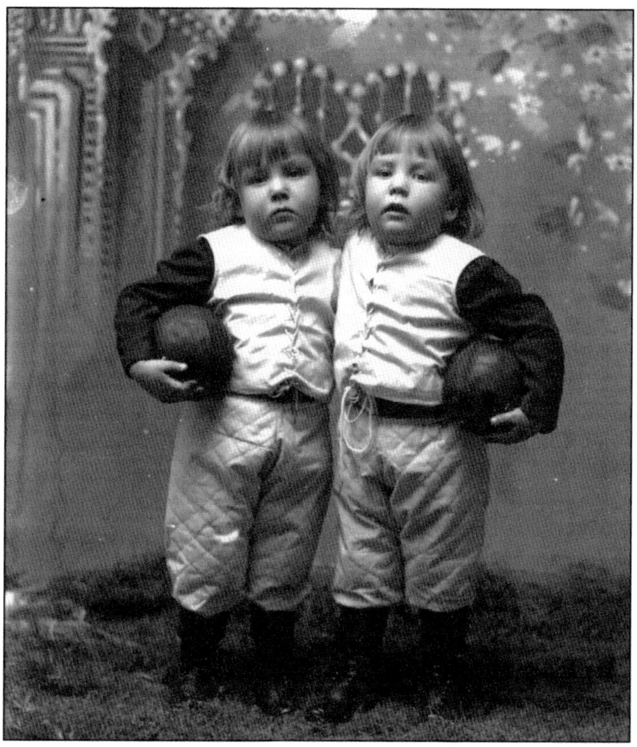

These twins are dressed for playing football. The padded trousers were standard equipment for football players at that time.

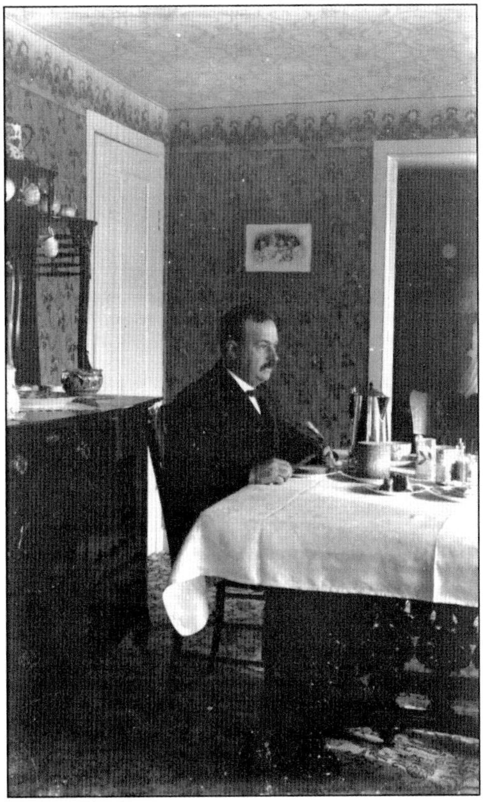

A gentleman at the dinner table is pictured here.

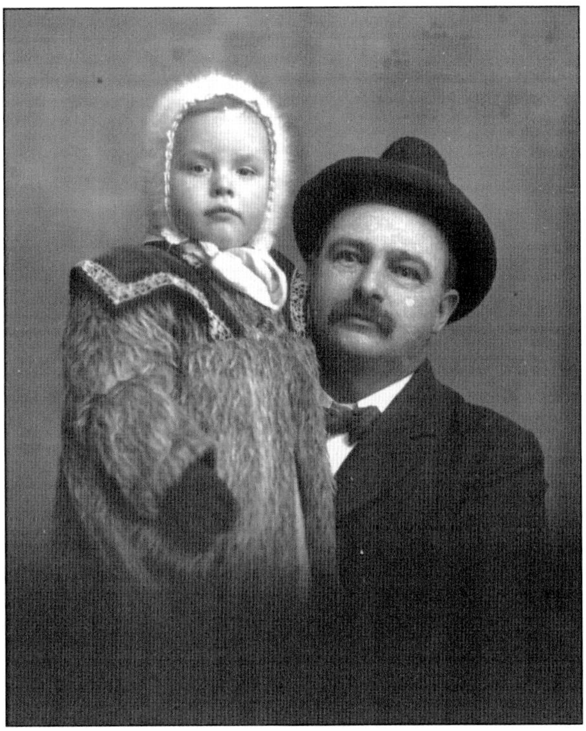

This is a fine portrait taken in a photographer's studio of a man and his daughter.

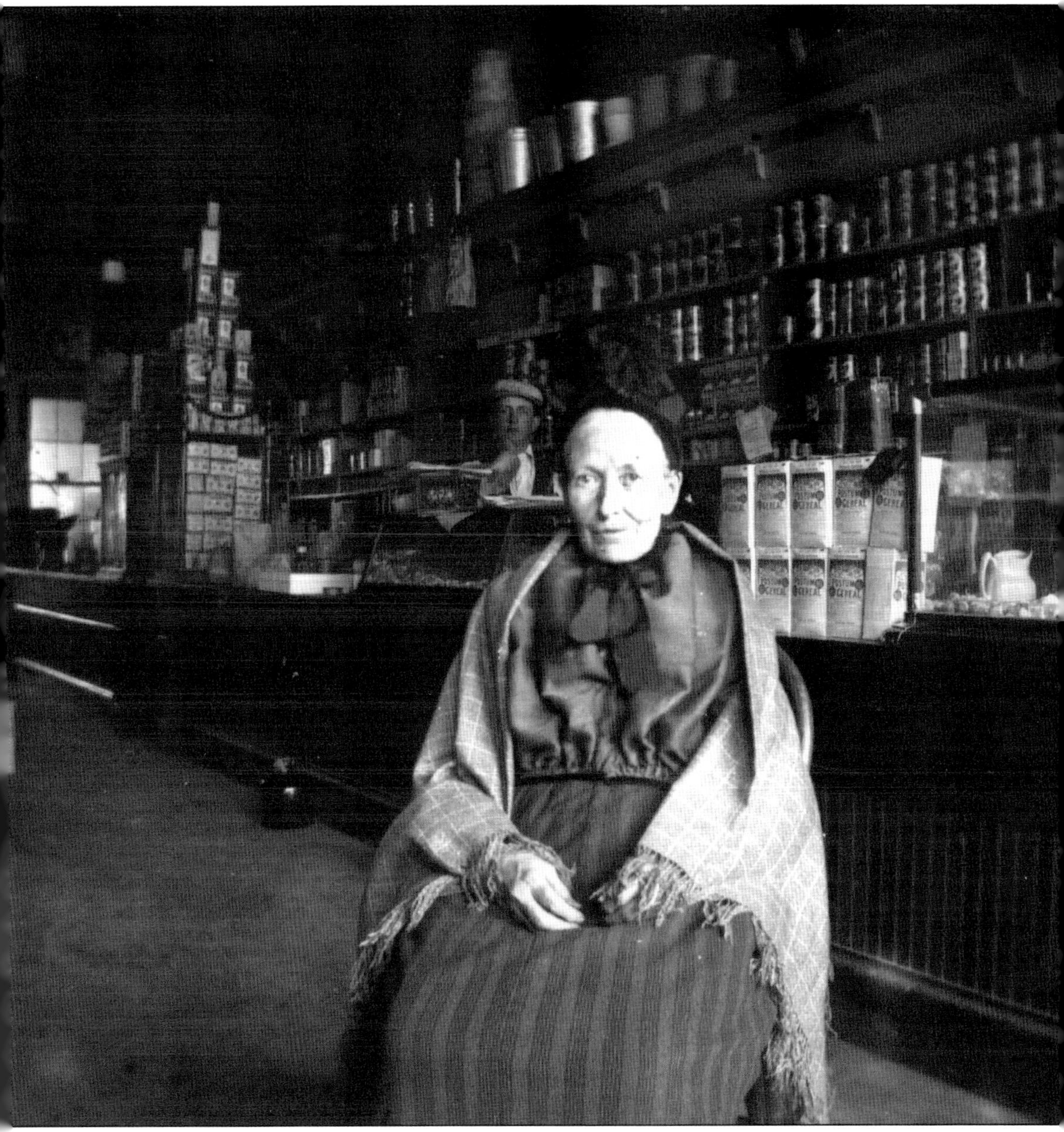

A woman is seated in a grocery store in this image. The clerk and his wares are visible behind the long counter.

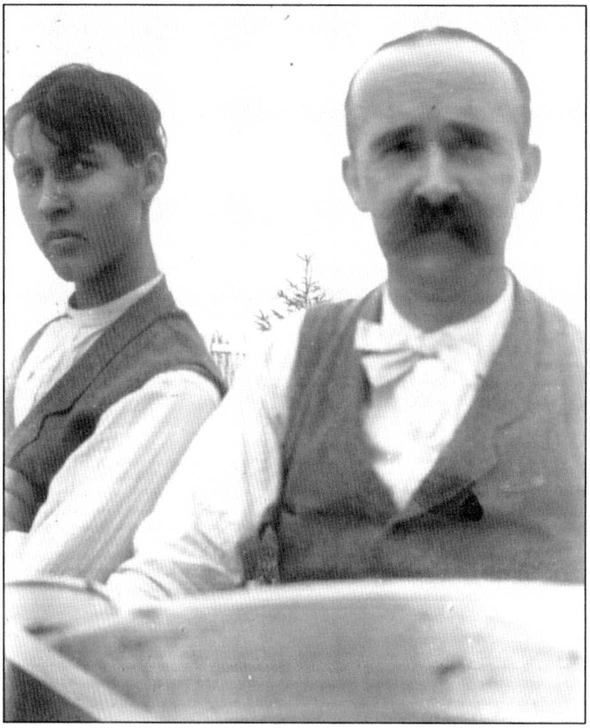

Italian immigrants to Mineral Point are pictured. The Italians came to work in the zinc mines and zinc plants mostly in the 1890s.

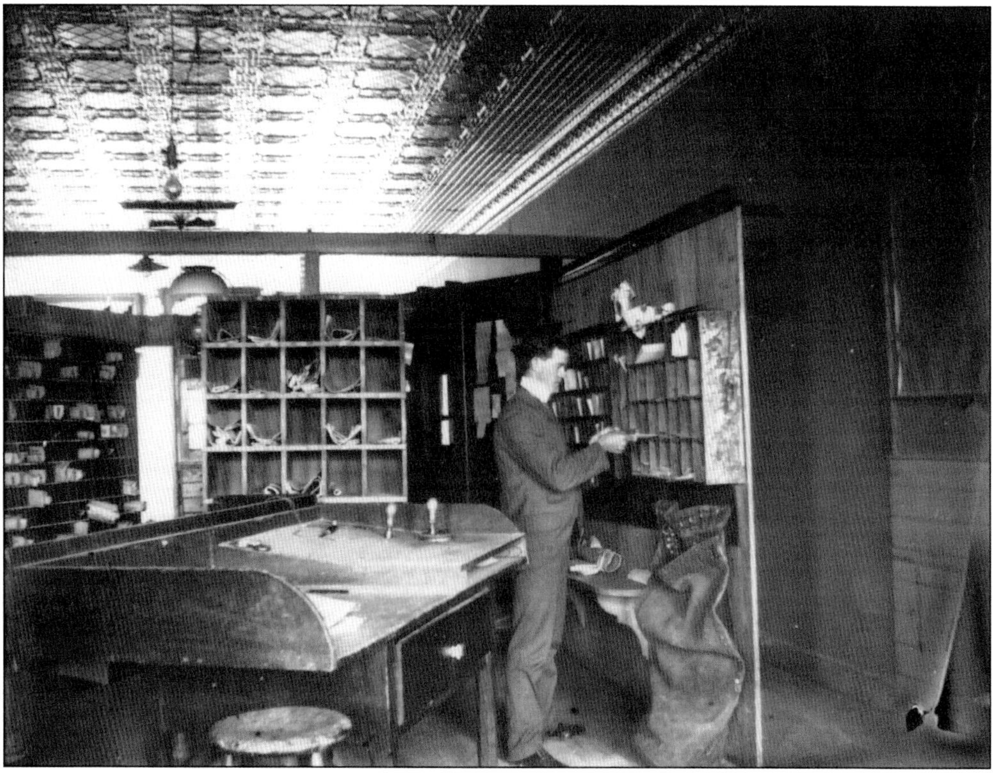

This image depicts the sorting of mail in the post office.

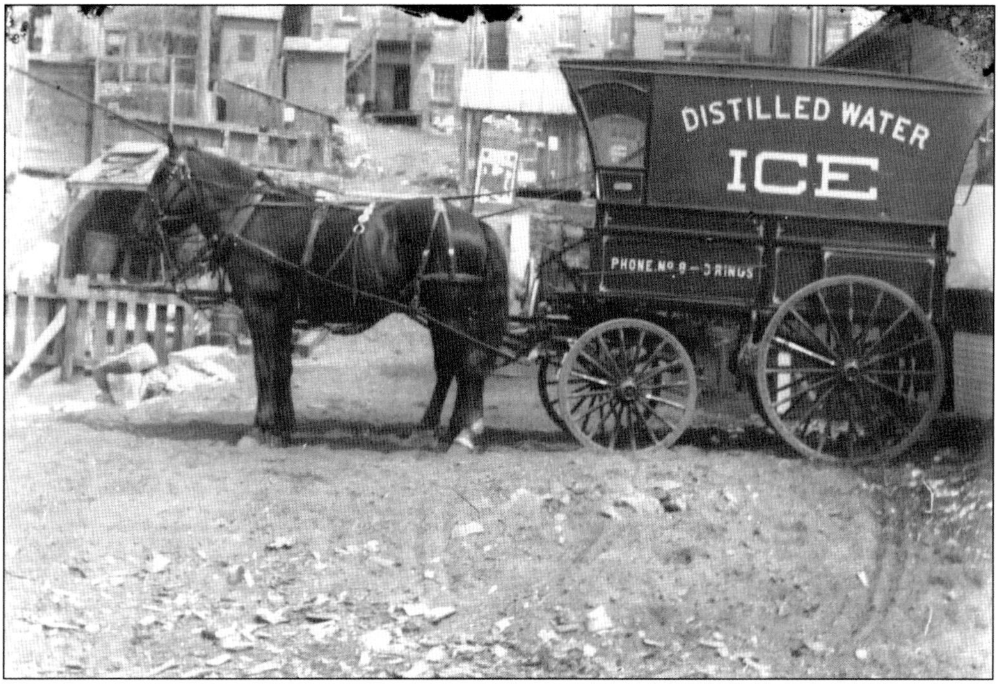

This ice wagon claimed to carry ice made from distilled water, which meant it would be safe to put in drinks, unlike ice cut from a pond in the winter. On the side of the wagon is the phone number—Phone No. 9—three rings.

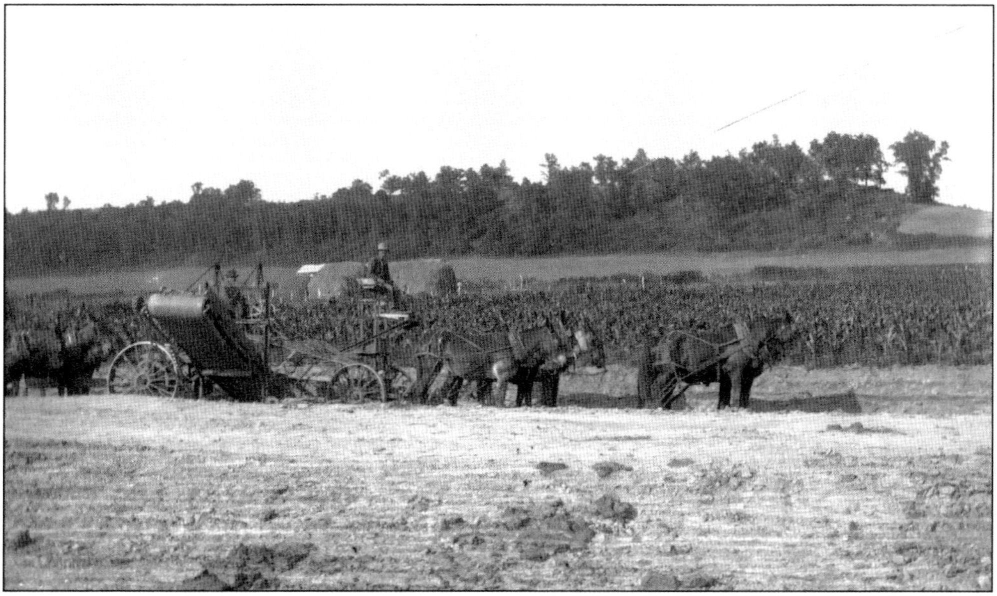

Grading a road using a team of six mules indicates that hauling the grader was heavy work. Roads were of critical importance to Mineral Point prior to the railroads and after. With no major navigable river adjacent to the town, roads were the lifeline to other communities and to eastern markets. In the 1820s, a route was established to Galena, Illinois. In 1837, a spur road—now known as Shake Rag Street in Mineral Point—was built to connect with the Military Road of 1835 and to other Wisconsin communities.

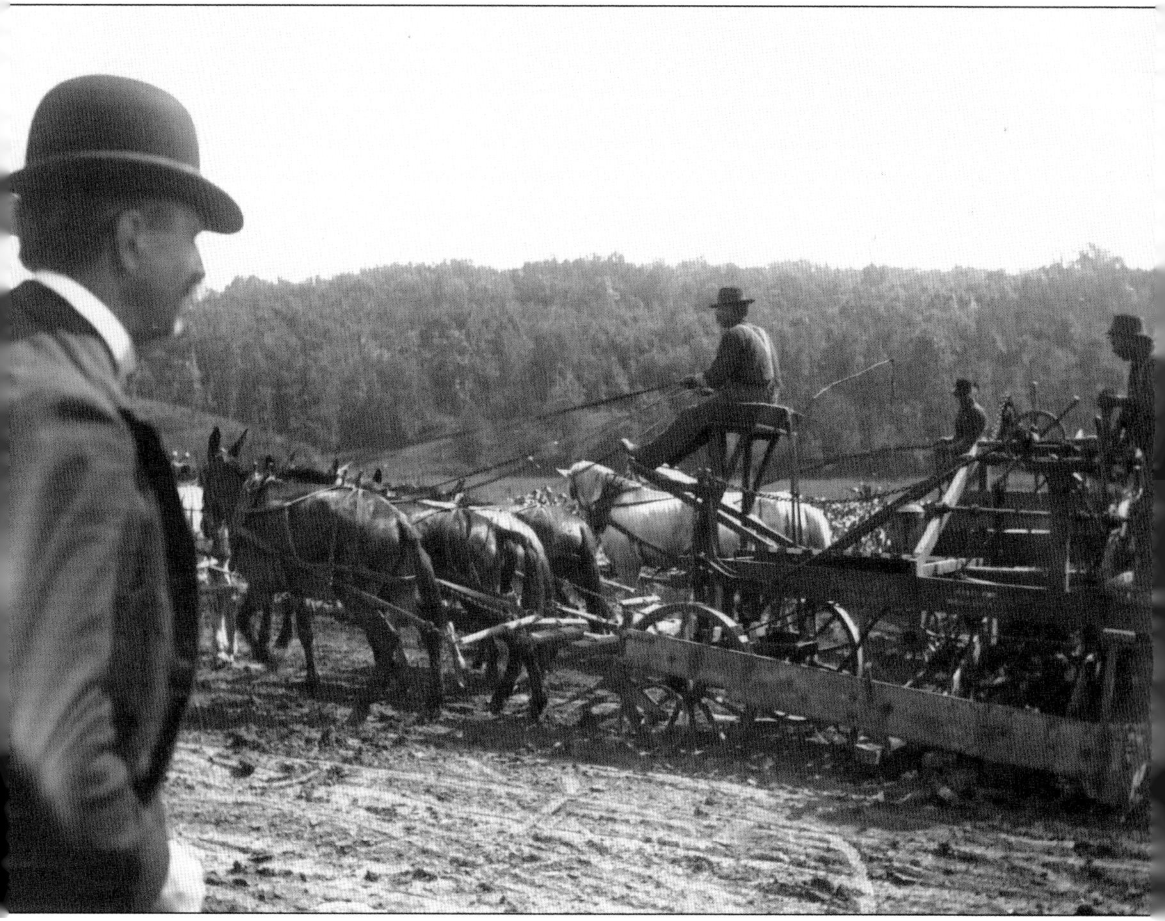

This is another photograph of road grading. The men on the grader are adjusting the height of the blades. The gentleman in the derby could be the foreman or simply an interested onlooker. This is a much more sophisticated method for grading roads than was used in the early part of the nineteenth century. Specifications for the 1835 Military Road stated it would be 35 feet wide, and all trees less than 12 inches in diameter should be cut to within 6 inches of the ground, making for an uneven surface and bumpy ride.

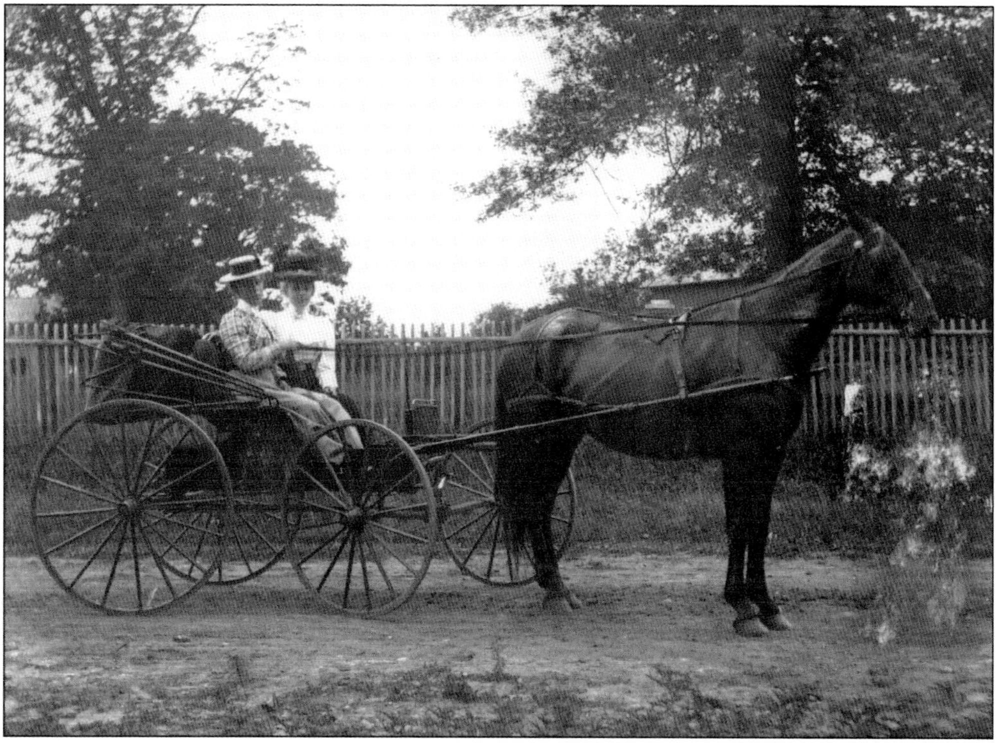

Two smartly dressed young women are out for a ride in their horse drawn carriage. Notice the fence behind the carriage. Most of the houses had fences such as this one to keep out livestock.

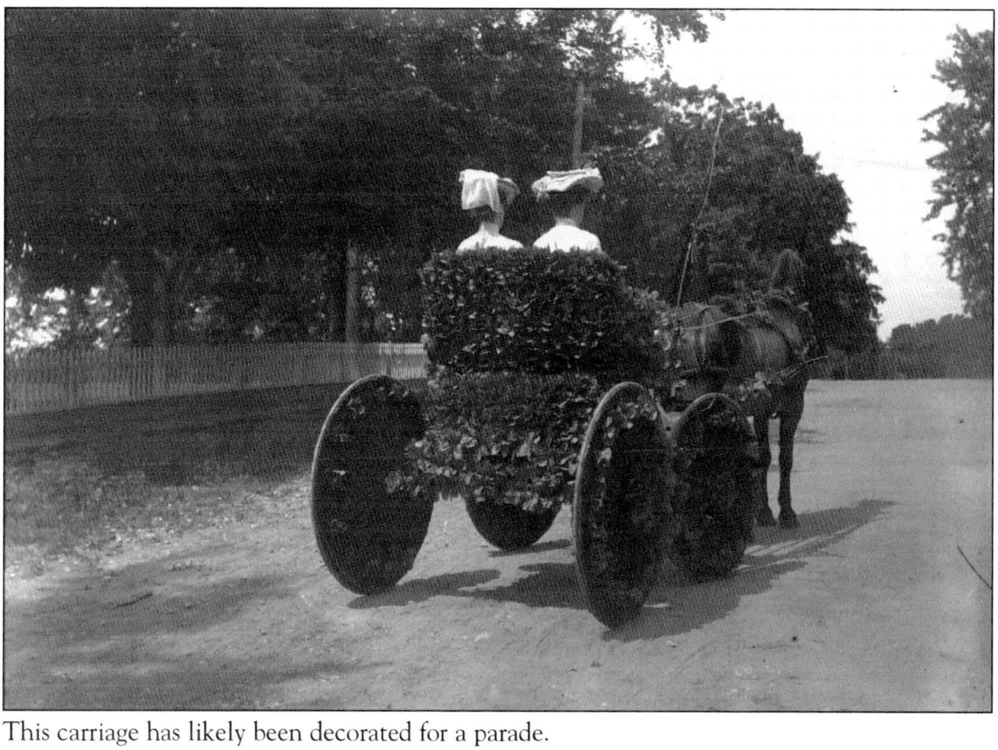

This carriage has likely been decorated for a parade.

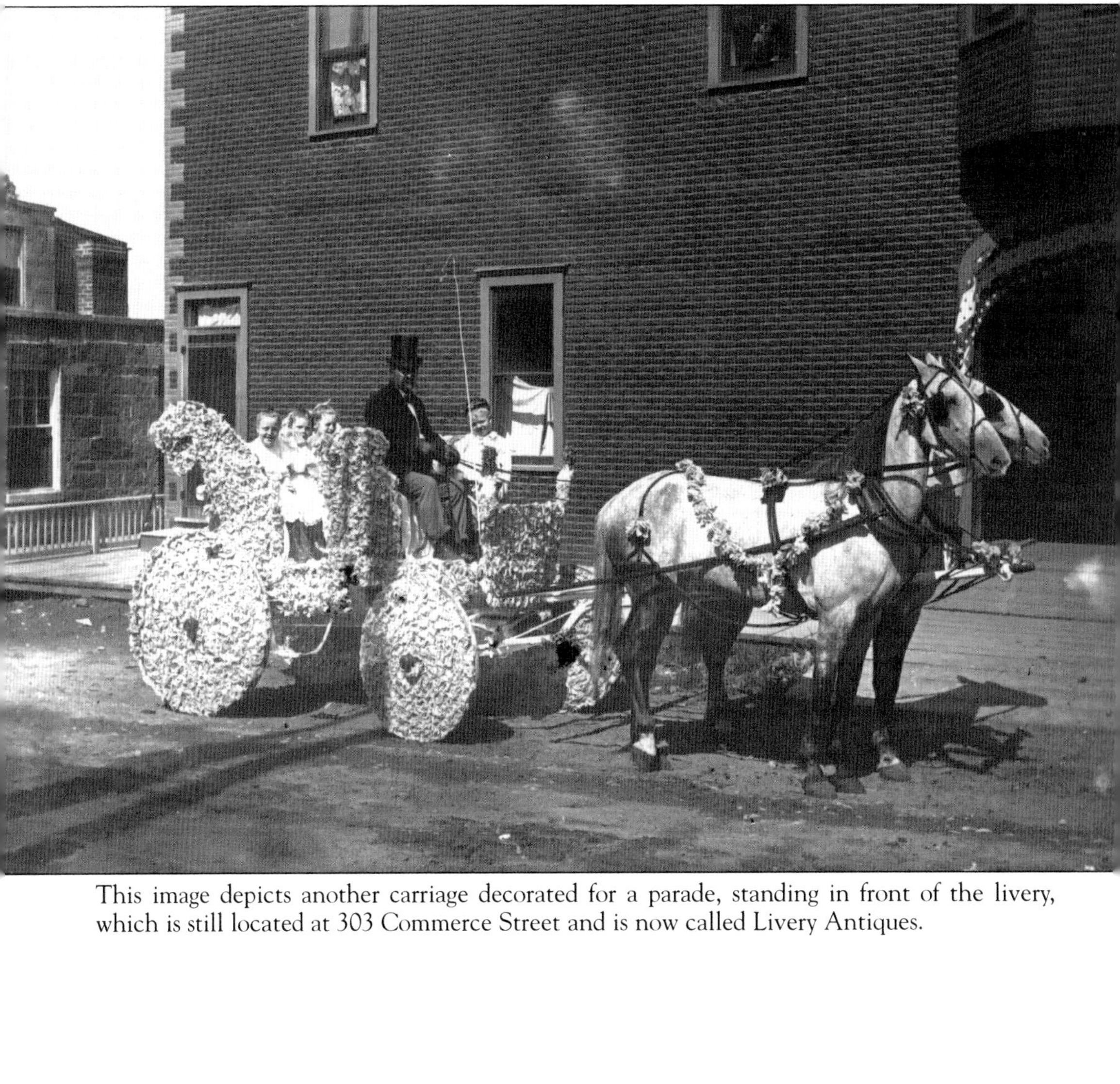

This image depicts another carriage decorated for a parade, standing in front of the livery, which is still located at 303 Commerce Street and is now called Livery Antiques.

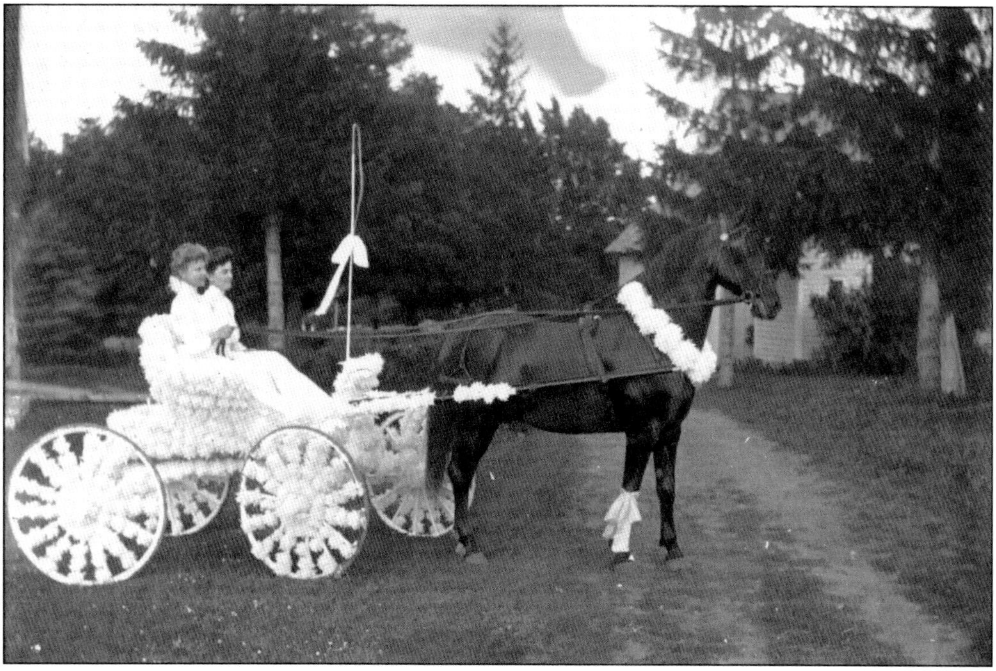

Yet another competition for a decorated carriage is pictured with decorations on the horse as well.

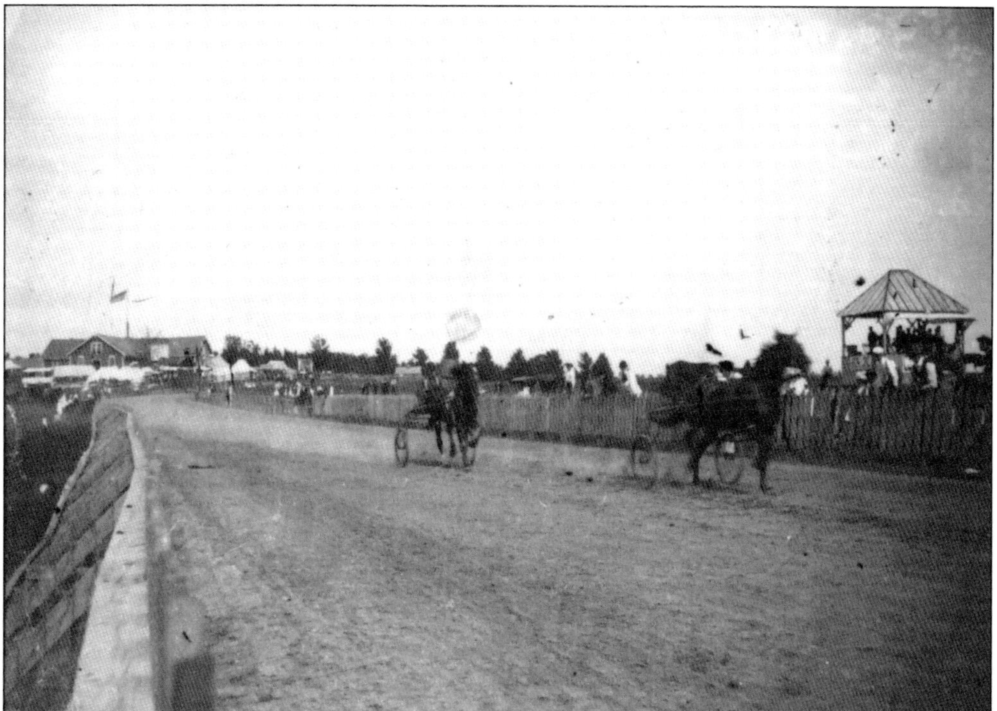

Harness racing has long been popular in Mineral Point. Today racing continues in the summer at the Iowa County Fairgrounds track on Fair Street and is a feature at the Iowa County Fair, which is still held there in September.

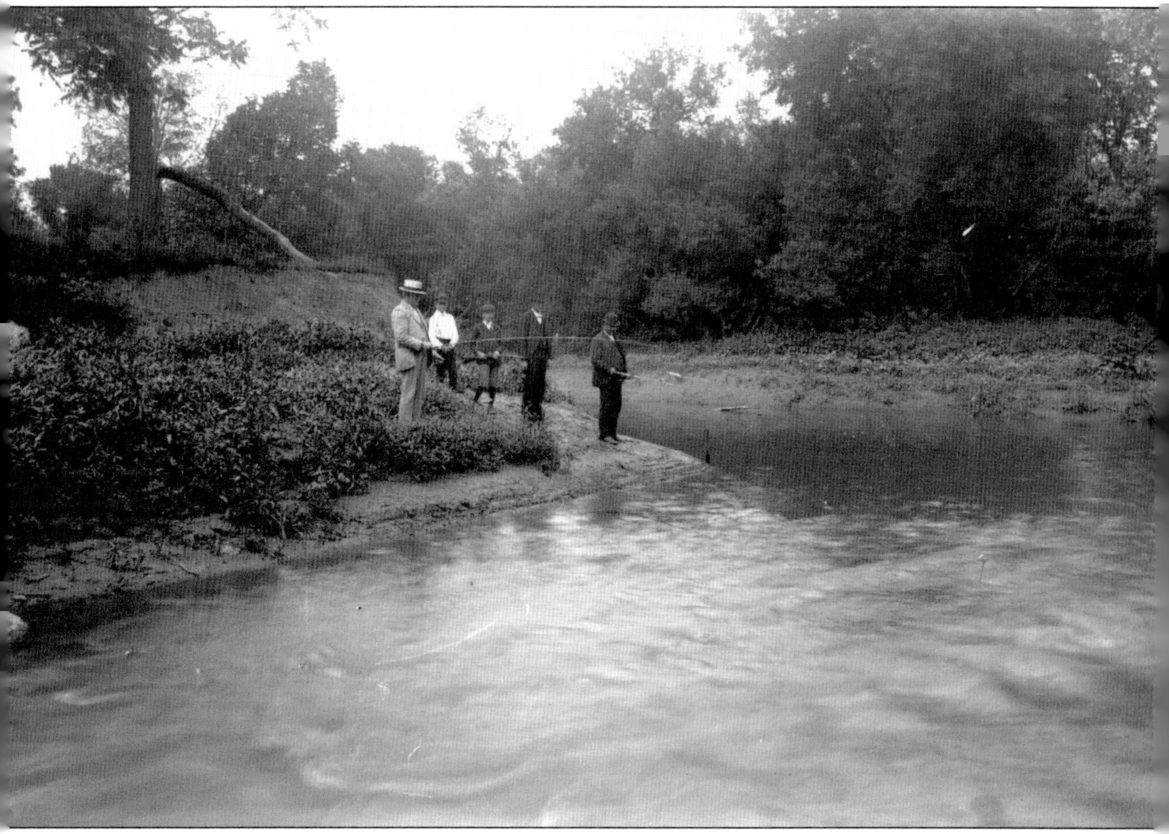

The long, thin rod held by the man standing closest indicates that fly fishing in the Pecatonica River was a popular pastime. The attire worn while fishing has certainly changed since this photograph was taken.

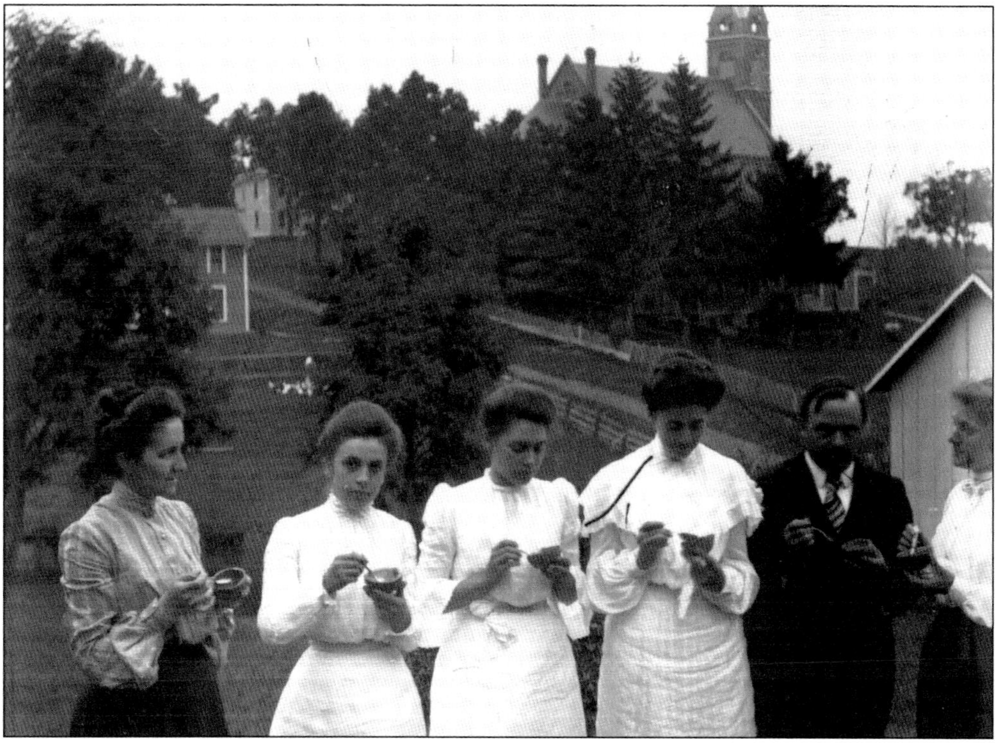

A family group enjoying ice cream is pictured here. The new St. Mary's church, built in 1901, is visible in the background.

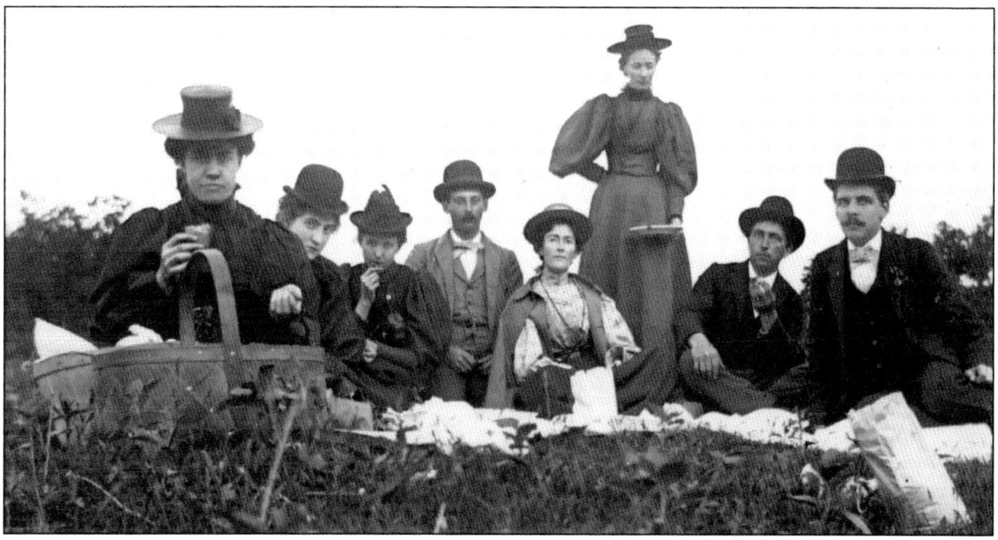

A group of women and men are pictured having a picnic. The woman standing wears a dress with "leg-o-mutton" sleeves made popular in the 1890s. Although Mineral Point was far from the centers of fashion, women could keep in touch with the latest styles by subscribing to popular fashion magazines such as *Godey's Lady's Book* or *Harper's Bazaar*. The man seated farthest to the right seems not to pay much attention to the latest in fashions. He appears to be wearing what was called a sack suit, comprised of three pieces—pants, jacket, and vest. These suits were worn for travelling and business from around 1878 on.

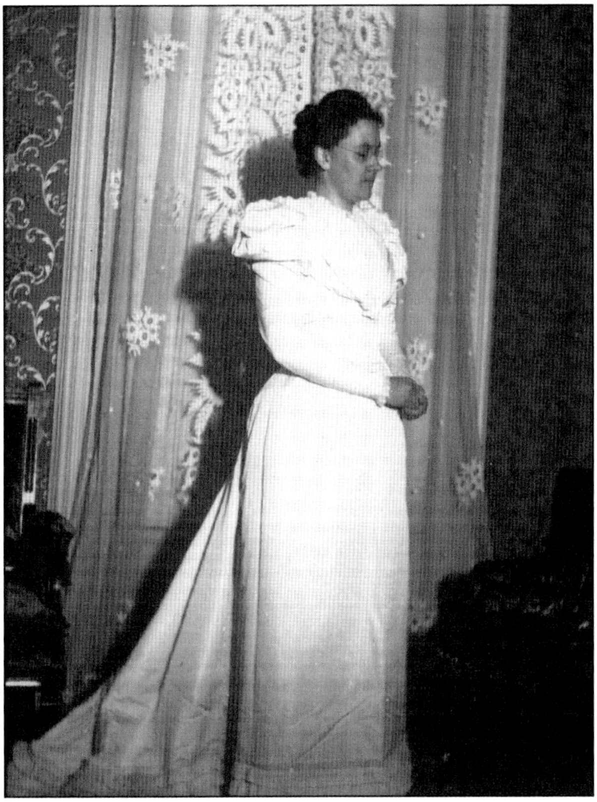

A woman in a wedding dress is pictured. This is likely from around the year 1900, due to features such as the "mousquetaire" sleeves gathered along the seam line with sleeve caps to emphasize the breadth of the shoulders, a V-shaped waist, and a gored skirt *en traine*.

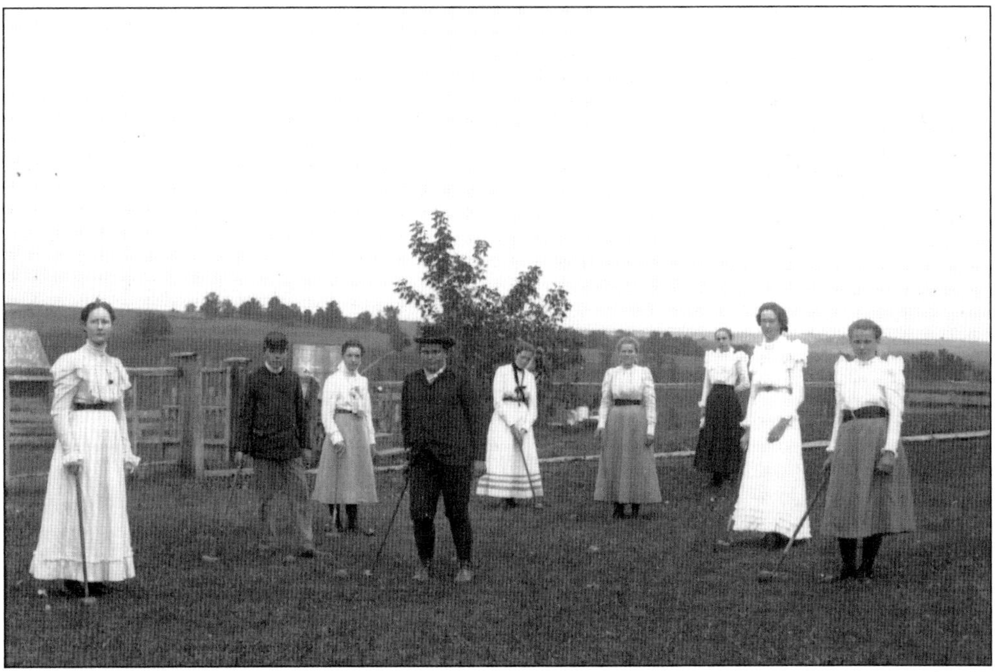

This image depicts a croquet party on the lawn. Several of the women are wearing mid-calf-length skirts, which were appropriate for outdoor activities.

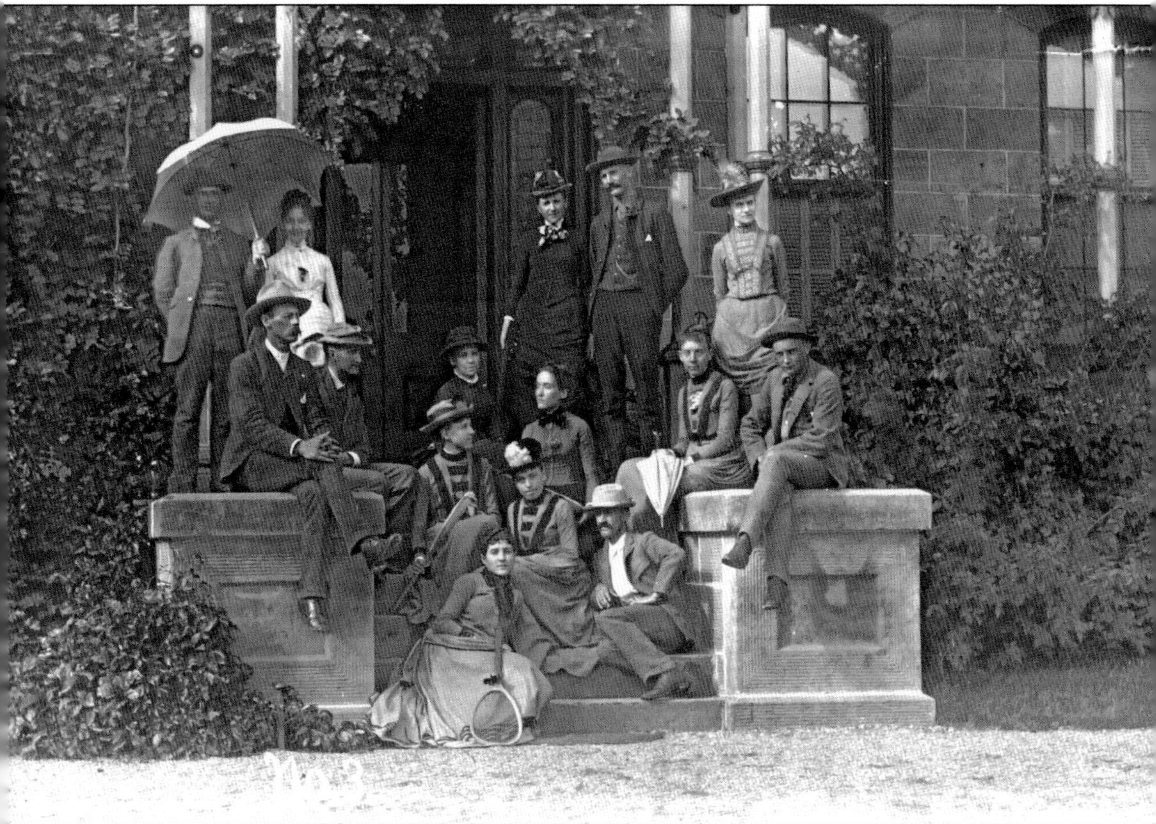

This photo was taken on the steps of the original Italianate-style porch of the Gundry House at 234 Madison Street. It was the home of Joseph Gundry from Cornwall who partnered in the Gundry and Gray store on High Street. Built in 1868 in an elaborate Italianate style, his family members continued to live there until 1936. In 1939, the family signed it over to the Mineral Point Historical Society, which had quickly formed to save the home from a wrecker's ball. Here we see a group of young men and women gathered. The woman seated on the bottom porch step holds a tennis racket likely used for lawn tennis. This photograph was taken prior to 1898, when the Italianate-style porch was replaced by one in the Neoclassical style, which is currently on the house.

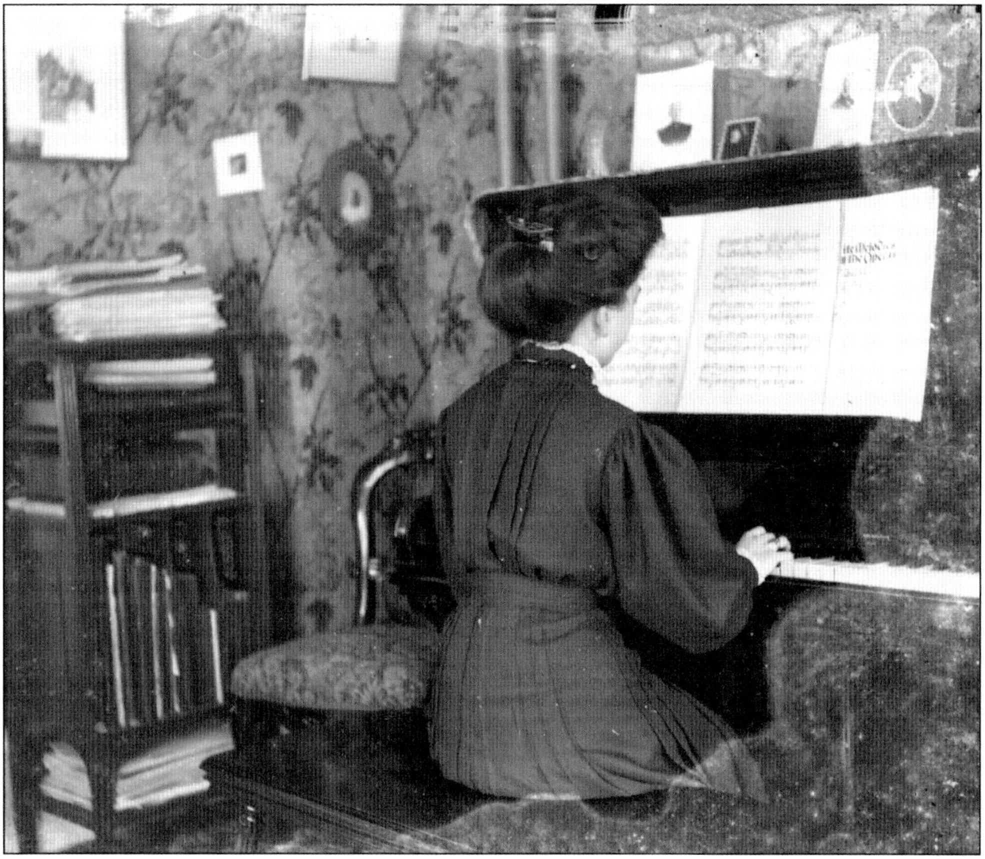

This is a photograph of a woman playing a piano—a popular pastime prior to the days of radio, television, tapes, and compact discs.

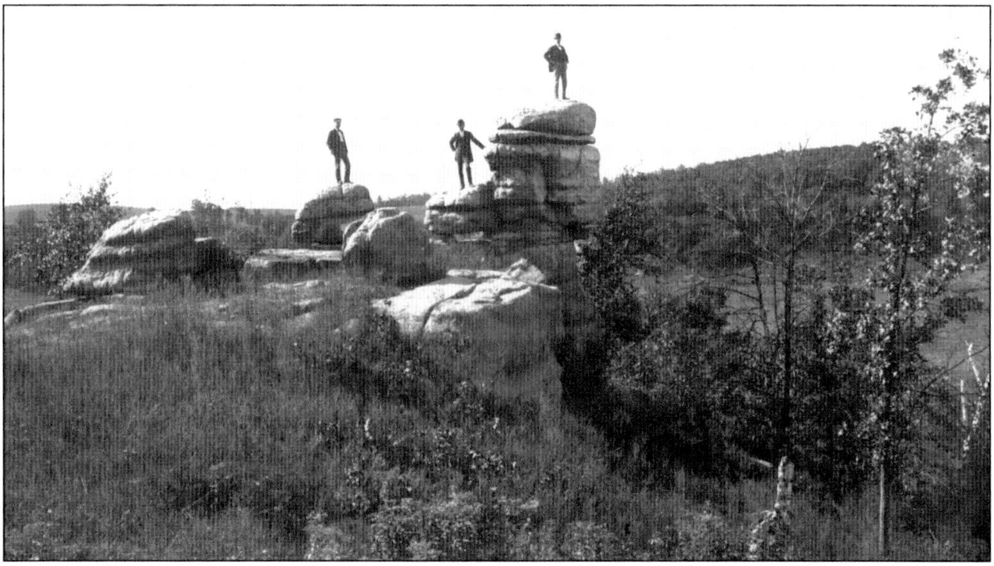

Castle Rock is a scenic spot located just to the west of Mineral Point. It was a favorite place for picnics and relaxation. Here three men are posing on the rock.

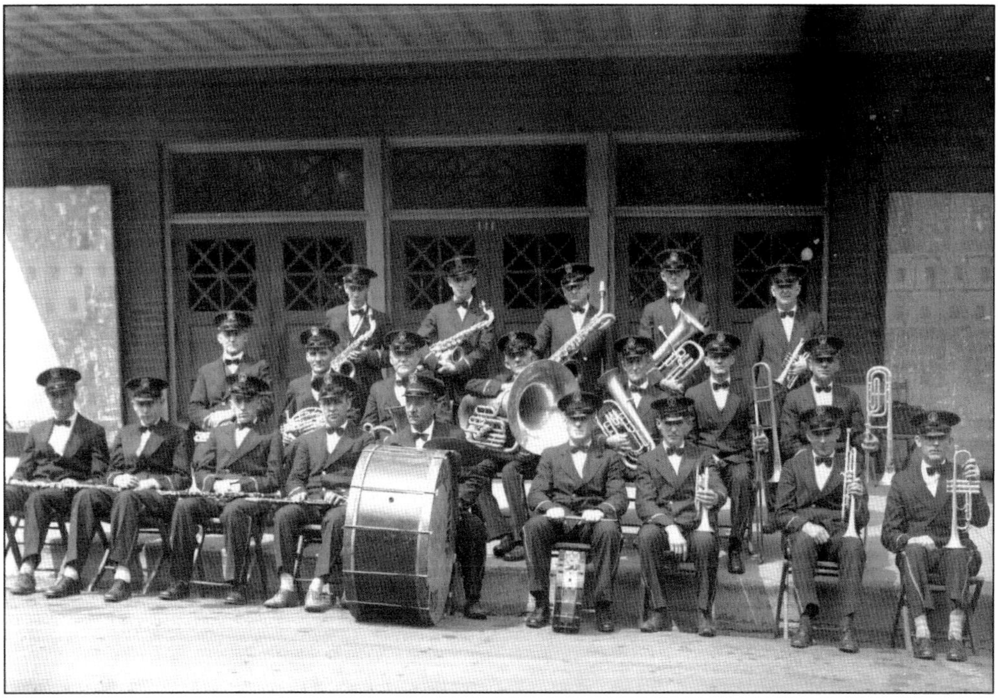

This photo of the Mineral Point Band was taken in front of the Municipal Theatre, which is now called the Mineral Point Opera House, at 139 High Street. This band is still active, giving several concerts every summer and is a featured attraction during Mineral Point's Fourth of July celebration. The band has a long history, and when the Mineral Point Miners' Guard returned home from the Civil War on July 2, 1864, the Mineral Point Band met them at the railroad station and escorted them to the United States Hotel. There Alexander Wilson, who came to Mineral Point from New York State in 1855, greeted and addressed them in his role as attorney general of the State of Wisconsin.

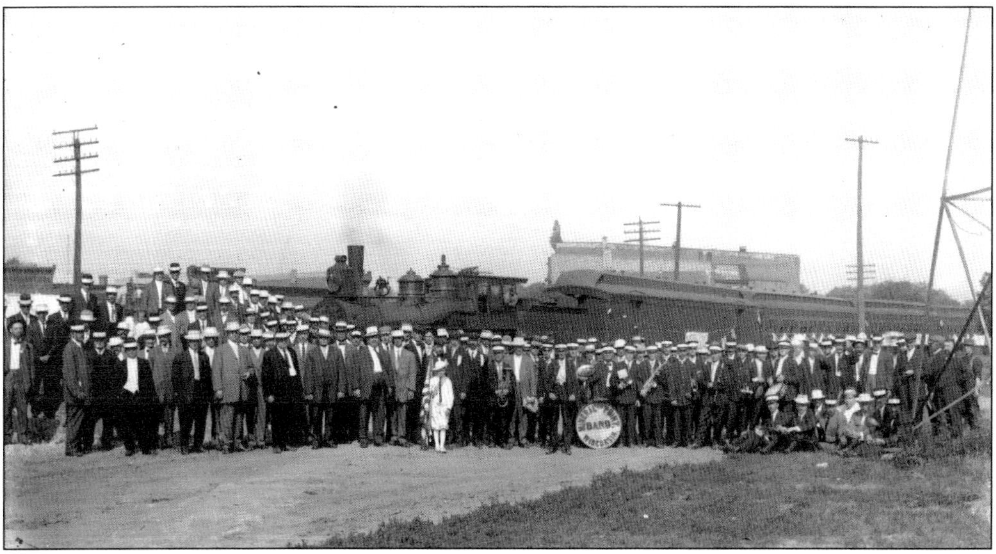

The Mineral Point Band is pictured meeting the train on the Chicago, Milwaukee and St. Paul Railroad.

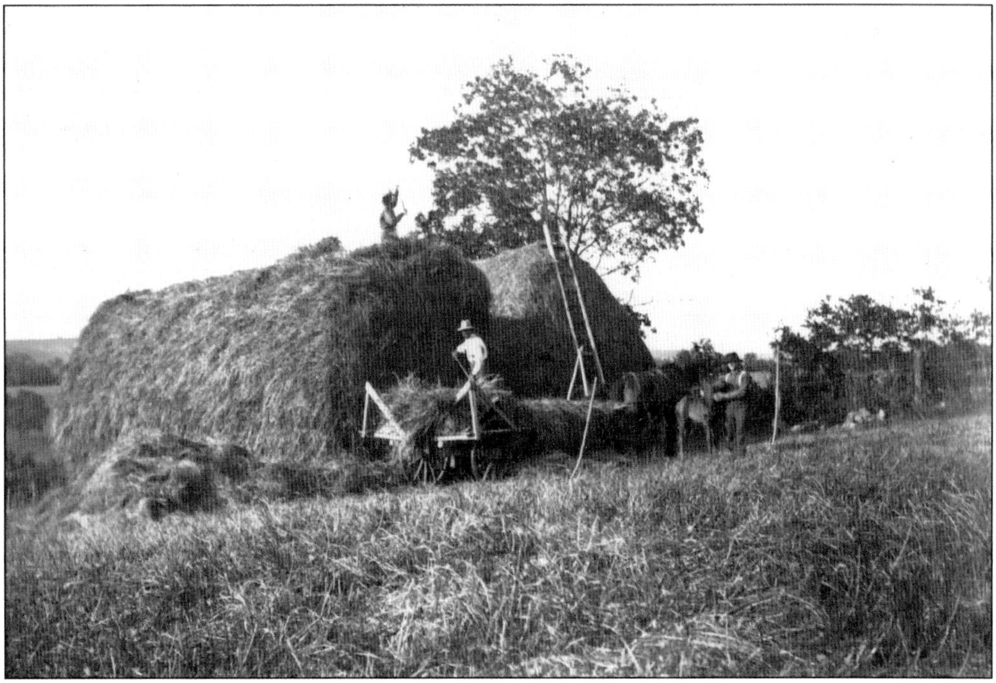

Mineral Point was unusual in making a successful transition from a mining town to an agricultural center when the mining was abandoned. Here farm hands are piling hay on the Spensley farm.

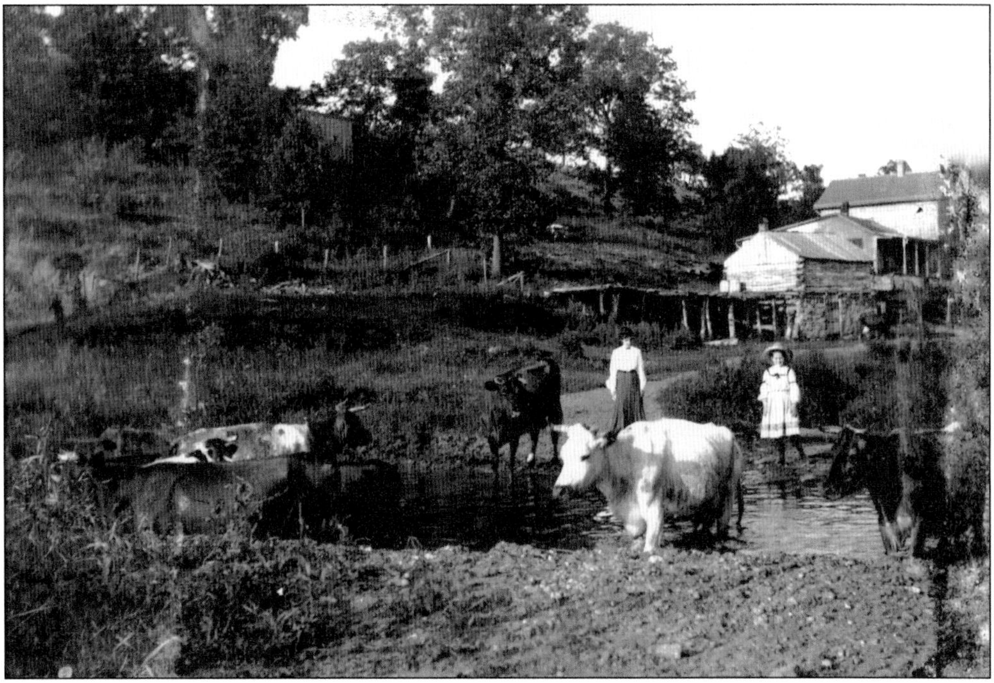

This is another farm scene with a woman and child posing near the water's edge with cows. Cattle were raised in the area for milk and for meat and continue to be an important source of income.